March 95

# WILLIAM AUGUSTUS
# DUKE OF CUMBERLAND

by the same author:

Field-Marshal Earl Ligonier
The Grenadier Guards
Gunner at Large

# WILLIAM AUGUSTUS
## Duke of Cumberland
## A Life

by
Rex Whitworth

**LEO COOPER**

London

# FOR MY WIFE

First published in Great Britain in 1992 by
LEO COOPER
an imprint of
Pen & Sword Books Ltd,
47 Church Street, Barnsley, South Yorkshire S70 2AS

Typeset by Yorkshire Web, Barnsley, South Yorkshire
in Plantin 10 point

Printed by
Redwood Press,
Melksham, Wiltshire

# CONTENTS

# ACKNOWLEDGEMENTS

I have to acknowledge, with grateful thanks, the permission graciously accorded me to work on the Cumberland Papers in the Royal Archives at Windsor, and also to study the great collection of the Cumberland maps in the Royal Library. I have also enjoyed permission to look at the many military and topographical drawings in the Print Room which undoubtedly owe their origin to the Duke of Cumberland. For help over many years I would like to express my great gratitude to Miss Jane Langton, former Keeper of the Archives and to the Hon. Mrs Hugh Roberts, Curator of the Print Room. I owe specific thanks to Mrs Donald Hodson for her expert knowledge of the maps. Dealing with the large iconography of Cumberland I have to thank both Sir Oliver Millar and Mr Christopher Lloyd, Surveyors of the Queen's Pictures, for their interest and advice.

I also acknowledge gracious permission granted to me to quote from documents in the Royal Netherlands House Archives at The Hague. I am beholden to Mr L. Van Dorp for information concerning Cumberland's relationship with his sister Princess Anne and Prince William IV, her husband.

From Germany I have received help from Dr Walter, Keeper of the Archives of Lower Saxony at Hanover, and from Professor Dr Franz, Director of the Staats Archive at Darmastadt (Hesse).

As regards American collections, I would like to thank Mary Robertson, Assistant Curator at the Huntingdon Library for help with the Loudoun and Calcraft papers. Miss Irene Moran of the Bancroft Library in Berkeley supplied information from the Chesterfield Papers.

Miss Alex Ward did a tremendous task for me in sifting the vast Newcastle and Hardwicke Collections in the British Library. Her skilful panning filtered out some real gold.

I must record the help and interest shown me by the late Earl of Albemarle over the Keppel Papers and the late Earl Spencer with the Poyntz Papers at Althorp. The late Viscount Barrington allowed me access to the Military Papers of the 2nd Viscount, the Secretary at War. Most of these MSS are now in County Record Offices.

Thanks to the kindness of the late Mr T.S. Wragg and his successor Mr Peter Day I was able to turn up substantial new material in the Chatsworth Archives. Catherine Armet supplied some interesting items form the Mount Stuart Collection, (Bute Papers).

The late Sir James Fergusson started me on the hunt in Scotland. I am grateful to the staffs of the Scottish Register of Archives, the Scottish Record

Office, the National Library of Scotland and the District Council of Edinburgh. Cumberland's great activities on the Turf are well reflected in the Rooms of the Jockey Club at Newmarket where many early racing records are preserved. I am grateful for permission to quote from the Match Books.

I must single out the staffs of particular County Record offices for most willing assistance, namely: Kent, West Sussex, East Suffolk and Ipswich, Derbyshire, Nottinghamshire, Bedfordshire, Buckinghamshire, Dorset, Northamptonshire and Northumberland. Lancaster Museum turned up for me the Order Books of Studholme Hodgson. The Royal Artillery Institution Library, the Royal Engineers Library at Brampton, the Regimental Archives of the Grenadier and Coldstream Guards, all produced items of value and I am particularly grateful to Dr Alan Guy at the National Army Museum for help with the Townshend, Dury and Aldercron MSS located there.

Finally I must pay a tribute to the staffs of the British Library MS Reading room and the P.R.O. for aiding me over a long period of research: also the library staffs at Nottingham University, Leeds, (Sheepscar) and Sheffield City Library, as well as the Guildhall Library in London. They all dealt most patiently with many queries I put to them in running items to earth.

I would like to record my gratitude to Mr Conrad Swan and Mr Patric Dickinson of the College of Arms for their efforts in trying to clarify for me the unsupported evidence in the Complete Peerage suggesting that the Duke had three natural daughters.

I must thank two close friends: Mr Rohan Butler of All Souls, a great 18th century man (though on the wrong side of the Channel), for his great encouragement and helpful comments, and Mr George Ward for reading the proofs so expertly.

Last of all I owe thanks to Judith Hayter for her great application in supplying a discipline worthy of Cumberland to my rather idle text and to Mrs Sue Cox for typing the early drafts.

## ILLUSTRATIONS

I am very grateful to Miss Sarah Wimbush at the Courtauld Institute of Art and Mrs Judy Egerton at the Tate Gallery for help in locating pictures of Cumberland and his activities in various Collections, and particularly the work of Sawrey Gilpin and Stubbs.

I acknowledge the gracious permission of Her Majesty the Queen to reproduce copyright material of pictures and drawings in the Royal Collection, nos 12 and 16, as well as the sketch map of Hastenbeck, which is based on three battle plans by Du Plat, Cumberland's Hanoverian draughtsman, in the Cumberland Maps.

I would also like to acknowledge permission to reproduce copyright material as follows:

No. 1 The National Trust.

No. 2 Private Collection. Photograph by Courtauld Institute of Art.

Nos. 3, 9, 10, 13, 14 and 15 The Trustees of the British Museum.

No. 4 Government Art Collection.

Nos. 5, 19, 20, 21 and 22 The National Portrait Gallery.

No. 6 From the Collection of the Marquess of Linlithgow on public display at Hopetoun House.

No.7 The British Library.

No. 8 The Director of the National Army Museum.

No. 11 From *Horace Walpole*, by W.S. Lewis, (Hart Davis).

No. 17 His Grace the Duke of Norfolk. Photograph by the Courtauld Institute of Art.

No. 18 Messrs Sothebys.

No. 23 The Trustees of the Chatsworth Settlement.

No. 24 Private Collection.

The picture of Cumberland as Ranger of Windsor Park on the book jacket - Peter Nahum Gallery, London.

Rex Whitworth

# THE DESCENDANTS OF KING GEORGE I

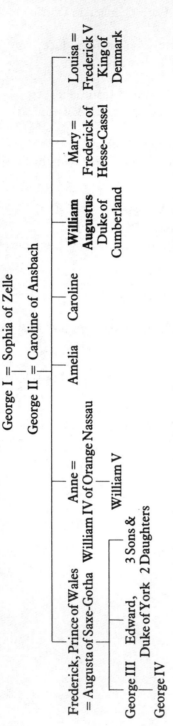

# THE DESCENT OF KING GEORGE I AND THE YOUNG PRETENDER FROM KING JAMES I

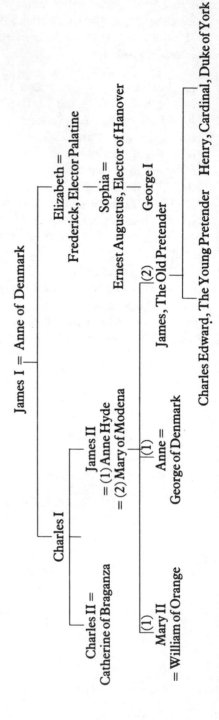

# MAPS

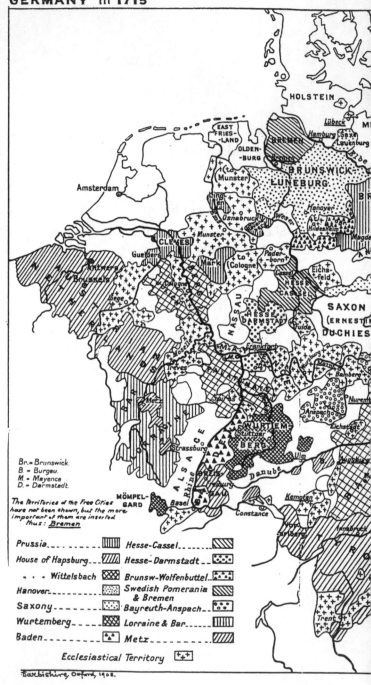

## GERMANY in 1715

Br.= Brunswick.
B. = Burgau.
M.= Mayence.
D.= Darmstadt.

The Territories of the Free Cities
have not been shown, but the more
important of them are inserted
Thus: _Bremen_

Prussia............ ▥  Hesse-Cassel........... ▨
House of Hapsburg... ▨  Hesse-Darmstadt.. ⠿
─ ─ ─ Wittelsbach ▧  Brunsw-Wolfenbuttel ⠿
Hanover........... ⠿  Swedish Pomerania ▨
Saxony........... ⠿  & Bremen
Wurtemberg...... ▨  Bayreuth-Anspach.. ⠿
Baden.......... ⠿  Lorraine & Bar...... ▥
Metz........... ▨

Ecclesiastical Territory ⊞

Barbishire, Oxford, 1908.

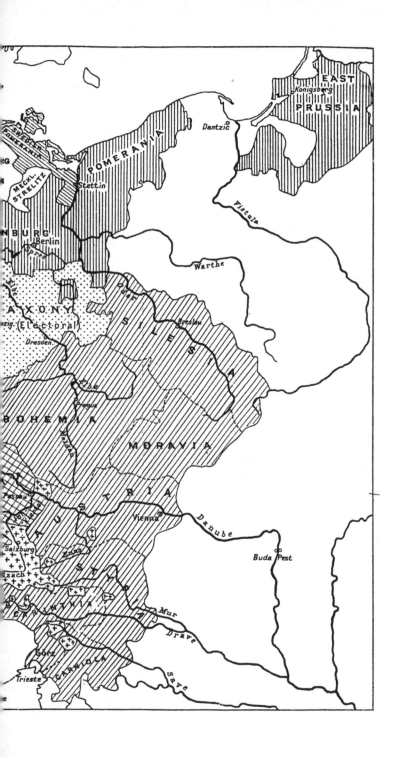

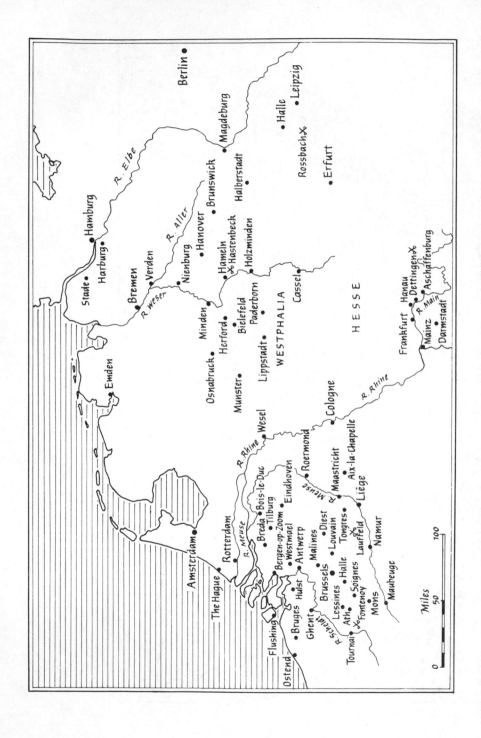

# A note about the calendar

THE JULIAN CALENDAR was used in Britain until 1752 when the Gregorian one used in continental Europe was introduced. The difference of eleven days ('lost' as 3-13 September, 1752) can be confusing. In this book, when events are taking place in Britain the date can be assumed to be Old Style (OS), unless otherwise indicated as New Style (NS); until, of course, September, 1752.

I have ignored the additional complication that the first day of the year used to be not 1 January but Lady Day, 25 March. Thus, when the text says 'the last day of the year' it means 31 December.

# Introduction

A MAN MALIGNED by his contemporaries may respond in either of two
ways: refute their lies publicly or maintain a contemptuous silence. But a
man maligned by posterity has no such choice; his reputation rests, for good
or ill, in the hands of future historians and biographers. William Augustus,
the Duke of Cumberland, suffered the slings and arrows of his own day with
dignity and public silence — but history has never done him the service of
a full assessment. By posterity he is remembered chiefly as 'the Butcher of
Culloden', his name thus linked to the image of a capricious sadist. Nothing
could be more unfair.

William, Duke of Cumberland was the second and favourite son of George
II. He was the first truly British member of the Hanoverian royal dynasty
and the last Captain-General of British land forces. He was a loyal son who
incurred the King's wrath; a brave soldier who reformed the British army;
an honourable man treated with dishonour; a plain-dealing man with no
interest in politics who in later life became embroiled in political intrigue; a
bachelor who in private life divided his energies between horse-breeding,
hunting and racing. In person and personality, he was larger than life. When
he died, at the age of just forty-four, he left an immense gap in the lives of
those around him. More than that: it can be argued that his early death
deprived the nation of one of the wisest and most steadying influences in the
restive years of the later eighteenth century.

And yet the reality has been outweighed by the myth. Almost without
exception, historians and other writers have concentrated on just six months
of the Duke's life: the Battle of Culloden in April, 1746, and subsequent
efforts to root out Jacobites and other supporters of Charles Edward, the
Young Pretender, in Scotland. Only Evan Charteris, a Scottish lawyer and
historian, has sought to cover a wider span of the Duke's career, in two thick
volumes published twenty years apart, in 1913 and 1934; and even Charteris
reached no further than the year 1757. It is significant that the only serious

attempt to present the Duke's life and work in a wider perspective should have been made by a Scot; much of the ignominy heaped on the Duke's head has derived from his supposed abuse of Charteris's fellow countrymen.

Most of the lies can be traced to the Jacobites. Let it be repeated that the Duke of Cumberland and his army trounced the Young Pretender's men at Culloden, that it was a fair battle, and that subsequent treatment of the Scots – admittedly harsh – resulted at least in part from England's suspicion of her new partner in the Union. But the Jacobites, whether imprisoned, in hiding or in exile, now had time on their hands: time to weave elaborate lies, embroidered with half-truths and delusions. 'Bonnie Prince Charlie' was never so much the hero as when he was on the run from the Duke of Cumberland's troops, but the glamour and the romance of the Young Pretender's sojourn in the Highlands belongs to the realm of fantasy. Nevertheless, a pretty story is worth retelling; when the Jacobite threat to the Hanoverian throne had faded, even the English started to repeat the tales.

Culloden was important in that it reasserted the supremacy of the Protestant Hanoverian claim to the British Crown; but in the life of the Duke of Cumberland it was just one milestone, not even the most significant. In one sense it can be seen as a distraction from his continental campaign against the French, which eleven years later resulted in defeat and humiliation. Here again the Duke's enemies found opportunity to indulge their malice, heaping recrimination on his head when responsibility for the disaster lay principally back in London. As Captain-General, an army reformer and a leader of men, the Duke of Cumberland deserved more praise than censure. He also deserved recognition for his valiant attempts to combine the military career which he himself had sought with the diplomatic tasks thrust upon him: coalescing the allied armies into an effective fighting force or negotiating at Kloster Zeven. It was Kloster Zeven that saw his downfall, and yet even as the spiteful gained a fleeting pleasure from his wretchedness, the Duke was already entering the greatest stage of his career, that of elder statesmen.

A friend and confidant to politicians like Henry Fox and the Duke of Newcastle, the Duke of Cumberland reluctantly accepted yet more responsibility on his nephew's accession to the throne. As well as retaining an unparalleled authority in military affairs he now found himself drawn into affairs of state. Yet still the vicious pens scribbled against him, misinterpreting, disparaging, libelling.

However, the Duke of Cumberland himself is partly to blame for the way his memory has remained at best indistinct, at worst abased. Not only did he fail to quash the libel and slander, he also deliberately and regularly burnt his personal and political correspondence. His precise reasons can only be guessed at, but no sinister motive need be inferred; he was a prudent and practical man with an innate reluctance to commit himself to paper — and a certain impatience with those who sought to cover their tracks with a trail of paperwork.

Lack of evidence may be no hindrance to story-tellers, but it does complicate life for the historian. Any biographer of the Duke of Cumberland is forced, willy-nilly, to widen his researches. But, by combing the Royal Archives at Windsor Castle and the papers of his friends and colleagues, it has been possible to trace the quite numerous remaining letters written in his own hand. Together with other contemporary sources, these have allowed me to fill in substantial areas of empty canvas in this first full-length word portrait of the Duke. If the picture that emerges does not show a man of admirable energy and common sense and formidable integrity, the fault is mine.

# 1

# The Early Years

A LITTLE AFTER SEVEN O'CLOCK in the evening of 15 April, 1721, Prince William Augustus was born at Leicester House, London, in the presence of his father, the Prince of Wales; the Duchesses of Dorset and Shrewsbury; the Countesses of Pembroke, Grantham, Cowper and Bristol; various Ladies of the Bedchamber and one Woman of the Bedchamber; Sir David Hamilton, the physician, and Mrs Crane, the midwife. A month later the baby was strong enough for Mrs Crane to depart to her native Suffolk.

William's parents were George Augustus, the future George II, and Caroline of Ansbach. His grandfather was on the throne, the first of the Hanoverians, having acceded to the Crown upon the death of Queen Anne in 1714. George I's chief virtue was, perhaps, that he was not Anne's half-brother James, the Pretender, a Roman Catholic and thus barred from the British throne. The new King of the United Kingdom of England, Scotland and Ireland was also the Elector of Hanover, and Hanover was where he had left his heart. He never quite became British. He spoke poor English, surrounded himself with German courtiers and displayed scant regard for British sensibilities — at one stage even suggesting that St James's Park be dug up and planted with turnips. What is worse is that he can be held responsible for the founding of a deplorable new tradition: outright hostility between the Hanoverian kings and their heirs.

When George Augustus arrived in England with his father, the two men were already estranged. The chief reason was the son's bitter resentment at the treatment of his mother, Sophia Dorothea — divorced as an adulteress and forbidden to see her children. But George Augustus was no better in his treatment of Prince Frederick, who as a boy of just seven, was left behind in Germany when the rest of the family moved to London. This enmity between fathers and sons was not merely a family matter; it was exploited by politicians and others pursuing their own ends. Indeed, by the time of Prince William's birth, his home — Leicester House, an unpretentious mansion facing south across what is now Leicester Square — had become a focus for the attentions of all out-of-favour politicians, hoping to create the nucleus of a new administration when the existing one collapsed.

The days before the christening of Prince William must have been an anxious time for his parents, though the baby was not the focus of their concern. At the last christening, in November, 1717 (of a puny princeling who later died), there had been a terrible quarrel. The Prince of Wales had invited the King to be one of the baby's godparents and the King had agreed; at the last moment, however, the King objected to his son's choice of a second godfather and nominated his own: Thomas Pelham-Holles, Duke of Newcastle. The Prince of Wales vented his fury at this paternal interference on the unfortunate Newcastle, who ran off to complain to the King. The King's reaction was to order his son and daughter-in-law to be evicted from St James's Palace: it was now that the Prince of Wales established his independence and bought Leicester House. The King, however, had retained custody of his grandchildren, three little girls and the infant boy, and, possibly as a result of the cruel separation, the infant died. Naturally, this tragedy only widened the breach between King and Prince of Wales. Not until the spring of 1720 were they reconciled and the parents reunited with their children, though the reconciliation was a flimsy affair and the mutual antipathy of the King and his heir continued to simmer.

However, on 2 May, 1721, Prince William Augustus was christened, and the day was happily unmarred by feuds. His godparents included the King and Queen of Prussia (she was his aunt) and Ernest Augustus, Duke of York, who was his grandfather's brother.

While his parents conducted what amounted to a rival court at Leicester House, the young prince grew up in Savile House, the nursery annexe, doted upon as an only son while his elder brother Frederick still languished in Hanover. In addition to his three elder sisters, Anne, Amelia and Caroline, he soon acquired two younger ones, Mary and Louisa. He was no doubt fussed over and spoilt as the only boy in the nursery, and among his admirers he could count his grandfather who, when William was just two, expressed a wish that his portrait be painted. Michael Dahl, the Swedish-born painter, was approached but he objected that he had not yet been asked to paint the Prince and Princess of Wales. Furious at the man's impudence, the King retaliated by giving Dahl no further commissions and at once made Charles Jervas the new court painter in his place. It was nearly four years, however, before Jervas executed the first state portrait of William.

At the age of four William was given a number of well sounding titles: Marquess of Berkhamsted, Earl of Kennington, Viscount Trematon, and Baron of the Isle of Alderney. He was also the first royal prince to be made a Companion Knight of the Bath at the re-establishment of this order by

George I in 1725. William was spared the rigours of the ceremonial bath that preceded installation, though the ageing King and the maturer knights dutifully took the plunge. William's tutor, Sir Andrew Fountaine, was installed as proxy, and a diminutive child-sized sword was laid on the altar in an act of dedication to the service of God and King. When Jervas finally painted his portrait — just the first of innumerable official portraits — William was depicted in the robes of the Order of the Bath. As an honour, the Red Ribbon of the Bath was second only to the Blue Ribbon of the Garter and this honour, too, was bestowed on William in May, 1730.

In July, 1726, William was created a royal duke and given the title Duke of Cumberland. Though held before him by Prince Rupert of the Rhine, the soldier prince whose greatest achievement was his support for Hudson's Bay Company, the title is perhaps also associated with later and lesser personages: Henry Frederick, brother of George III, and Henry's son Ernest. Neither man was deserving of respect and, sadly, they may be said to have tarnished the title and by association demeaned the memory of William Augustus.

William's father, born in 1683, had been educated in the usual manner of German princes, with a good grounding in languages, the classics and history. It was, however, the military life that held the greatest attraction for him and military affairs that most animated him. He had indeed proved himself in battle, at Oudenarde, and earned from the playwright Congreve the title 'Young Hanover Brave'. Denied command by his father, he contented himself with hunting and horse races. He was a good dancer too, and spoke English well, though apparently with a heavy accent, and clearly relished the lively social life revolving around himself and the Princess of Wales. While not unperceptive, his intellectual prowess was limited, his appreciation of fine arts even more so; but both fields he could safely leave to the Princess of Wales.

Caroline was a strong personality, a crucial influence on her husband in particular and her family in general, yet had the sense to exert her powers discreetly. Daughter of the Margrave of Ansbach, she was orphaned at the age of thirteen and brought up by the King and Queen of Prussia. Blessed with an enquiring mind and encouraged to exercise it, widely read and able to think for herself, poised and accomplished in the social graces, with a confident taste in art and design, she was surprisingly well matched with her sensual, choleric, soldier husband.

It was natural that Caroline, with her enthusiasm for the intellectual pleasures, should guide the education not only of her daughters but of her beloved son William. The choice of Sir Andrew Fountaine as tutor was very probably hers; he was widely travelled and a brilliant linguist, with a broad range of interests from collecting antiquities to contemporary literature (Swift was a particular friend). In the early years, William was mainly taught

7

with his two younger sisters, Mary and Louisa, at Savile House. Caroline knew that education was something much broader than lessons in a schoolroom, however, and encouraged her children to learn the pleasures of stimulating company — which they could find within the walls of their own home. Chiefly thanks to her, Leicester House was a hub of intellectual activity, visited by philosophers and poets, scientists and theologians, scholars and artists of every kind: men like Sir Isaac Newton and Edmund Halley, George Berkeley, the Irish philosopher, Joseph Butler, who later became Bishop of Durham, and Jonathan Swift whose *Gulliver's Travels* was published to immediate acclaim in 1726. Another regular visitor was John Gay, the poet and playwright, best remembered today for *The Beggar's Opera*; in the late 1720s he published his *Fables*, dedicated to the young Prince William.

It must have been somewhat daunting for the children to have such an energetic and accomplished mother, but William for one adored her. Her sudden enthusiasms could sometimes lead her astray, as when she removed some third-rate paintings and substituted a glorious Van Dyck commissioned by Charles I; her husband was furious and obliged her to have the Van Dyck taken down and the mediocre portraits rehung — he belonged to the school that knows what it likes and likes what it knows — but occasional errors were forgivable in one so much beloved.

In summer, when the King's household moved to Hampton Court, the gaiety and gossip at Leicester House was similarly transferred to Richmond Lodge, set in the Old Park beside the river, where additional delights such as hunting were shared by the children. While William and his sisters played in the innocent earnestness of childhood, political intrigues were deepening around them. The focus was usually Robert Walpole, who since April, 1721, had been Chancellor of the Exchequer and First Lord of the Treasury: in effect Prime Minister, the first in Britain. Walpole was a man of enormous ability with ambition to match. His skill at manipulating others towards his own ends was unparalleled; he was the chief architect, for instance, of the 1720 reconciliation between King and Prince of Wales. Moreover, while most ministers were seen as the King's men and thus unwelcome in the court of the Prince of Wales, Walpole managed to stay on good terms with the Queen, through whom he hoped to reach the heir to the throne.

The King still hankered after Hanover. In fact, he could not resist making frequent return visits, mostly of several months' duration. In the King's absence, the Prince of Wales was technically guardian of the realm but so hedged in with restrictions that this in itself exacerbated his hostility towards his father. In Hanover the King felt at home; among the biddable folk of his Electorate, he could forget the tedious and disputatious British. He even took an interest in his grandson, Frederick, still living in semi-seclusion in the Electoral capital. Without family, surrounded mainly by courtiers, it is perfectly credible that Frederick consoled himself with a mistress, as several sources have suggested, at the age of just seventeen. At any rate, the King and his daughter, Sophia Dorothea, Queen of Prussia, together hatched a plan to marry Frederick to her daughter Wilhelmina. Frederick seemed willing and the marriage was arranged for 1727, though the King did not see fit to discuss the matter with the Prince of Wales.

In May, 1727, the King once again set off for Hanover. This would be his seventh visit. It was also his last. Delayed en route in Holland, he finally resumed his journey on 10 June, and suffered a stroke while travelling. His coach took him to the castle of Osnabrück, the very place where he had been born. But he was dead.

The news was broken to George Augustus by Walpole. King George II, as he now was, showed no emotion. Indeed, the old King was so little mourned in Britain that he was very soon forgotten.

At the age of six, William was too young to understand the full significance of all the changes taking place around him, although in the usual childish process of osmosis he certainly absorbed what was happening. He attended the coronation, a muddled and tedious affair lasting all day, and afterwards found himself guest of honour at an evening of flattering speeches by the boys of Westminster School. The headmaster, Dr Freind, was keen to win royal favour for his school.

Dr Freind's brother, a doctor of medicine rather than letters, had been court physician to the Queen for some years and had attended William during minor illnesses. His appointment was remarkable in that he had in 1722 been imprisoned in the Tower of London as a known Jacobite sympathizer, a close friend of Bishop Atterbury who had plotted in the cause of the Old Pretender. Caroline obviously trusted him, though, at least in medical matters, for she authorized him to inoculate her younger children against smallpox – admittedly after consulting Sir Hans Sloane, who had tested the new procedure on selected criminals and charity children (the criminals were released as a reward). Thanks to this immunization, William escaped the scourge that swept the nation in the coming year. He did fall ill, however, soon after his mother became Queen, possibly with influenza; despite her heavy burden of duties, she sat up with him all night and exchanged anxious notes with Mrs Clayton. The former midwife was now a Lady of the Bedchamber (later Lady Sundon), with special responsibility for the younger children's welfare. But on the whole William was a healthy child.

One momentous event for the family in late 1728 was the arrival, at long last, of poor Frederick from Hanover. George Augustus could no longer keep his son and heir at arm's length, though he did nothing to make the young man welcome. Aged twenty-one, Frederick was about to meet his brother and sisters for the first time.

It is hard to understand why Frederick was so detested by his parents; his mother disliked him even more than his father. Suggestions that he was illegitimate or a substitute for a stillborn infant are entirely without foundation, and George Augustus never made any attempt to disown him. The subject remains mysterious; but, whatever his faults, the boy was not to blame. Though he seems to have arrived in London with every indication of wishing to make peace with his parents, their hostility was implacable. Naturally their antagonism would have brushed off on their other children. Educated, thanks to their mother, towards openness of mind, it may be surmised that they would eventually have grown to judge Frederick for themselves. Yet loyalty to their parents and the long years of separation had created an almost unbridgeable gulf; Frederick's brothers and sisters would never feel entirely at ease with him nor he with them.

It was a terrible ordeal for Frederick, treated as an intruder in the intimate family circle, excluded from those shared memories and little jokes, laughed at for his foreign ways and subjected to petty humiliation by his parents. Moreover, it was not just the family who regarded him with disdain; courtiers, ministers, everyone who heard George Augustus fulminate against 'my half-witted coxcomb' naturally supposed that Frederick was everything his father said and worse. Formally, the King acted quite correctly; he created Frederick Prince of Wales, gave him a seat at his right hand on the Privy Council, and granted him an annual allowance. But the allowance was small, like the apartments and staff he was given. And, of course, the King had forbidden the planned marriage between Frederick and Princess Wilhelmina of Prussia. George II had no reason to dislike his niece or offend his sister, but he loathed his brother-in-law the Corporal, as he referred to King Frederick William I of Prussia, and, even more importantly, he wanted to impose his own will on his son. Thus were the scales loaded against Frederick, and it was natural that he should become the catspaw of out-of-office politicians and, just as his father had been, the focus of opposition to the King's lawful ministry.

William, more than fourteen years younger, was given all the love and care that Frederick had missed, and this included the best education available. In 1730 William started to attend Westminster School (Dr Freind's endeavour had paid off) for daily instruction in the classics, and there became acquainted with the sons of some of the most important families in the land. One contemporary of his at Westminster was George Keppel, the future third Earl of Albemarle, who would become his ADC, secretary and close confidant. These lessons were in addition to the schoolroom routine at St James's Palace, where the royal children were taught by an impressive galaxy of private tutors, and were augmented by Queen Caroline's continued efforts to encourage them to broaden their interests by visits to the theatre and attendance at formal levees.

It was in July, 1731, that the Treasury officially approved William's first separate establishment. The King gave him his own personal suite of rooms in each of the royal palaces — St James's, Kensington and Hampton Court — together with a household staff to run the apartments and an allowance of £6,000 per year. The staff included two grooms of the bedchamber, four footmen, four pages, a huntsman (Mr Philip Goldman, with 'horse and eight dogs' according to the household accounts[1]) and huntsman's boy, not counting all the coachmen and stable staff. To supervise the household a governor was appointed, Stephen Poyntz, aided by a sub-governor, Mr Windham. Sir Andrew Fountaine returned to his collection of antiquities at Narford Hall, his home in Norfolk, while Poyntz managed not only the household staff but the personal tutors. Poyntz was a diplomat in his mid-forties, a former scholar at Eton College where he sometimes took his young charge; on one occasion the school's annual ram hunt was taking place and William was privileged to strike the first blow at the wretched animal; another time William presented the newly elected King's Scholars with green blankets for their beds.

William's tutors were a distinguished company. Apart from Dr Phillips, a classical grammarian, and Monsieur Palairet, a Huguenot refugee who taught French, they included Dr Robert Smith, a professor of astronomy at Cambridge who had been recommended by Sir Isaac Newton and whose job was to teach the boy mathematics. There were two tutors for history: Nicholas Harding taught William the laws and constitutional history of England, while Philip Zollman taught him the history of the burgeoning empire, along with modern history and geography and, for good measure, the German language.

Further lessons deemed essential for the royal student included instruction in the principles of ballistics and gunnery, by a Mr Hawksbee who taught at Woolwich Academy, and in fortress design and field engineering by an aged engineer officer, Captain Thomas, who had planned the walls of Londonderry. William also learnt the principles of shipbuilding from, among others, Sir Jacob Acworth, Surveyor to the Navy. Architectural drawing and design was another important subject at that time when British architecture was acquiring a new and glorious self-confidence and grace; again William had the best of tutors, Henry Flitcroft, Clerk of Works to the royal palaces. More social graces were passed on by Mr Weidman, the German music teacher, the younger Bernard Lens, who taught drawing and painting, and a French dancing master by the name of Dunoyer who seems to have been somewhat exasperated by William's clumsiness. In this respect, at least, he did not take after his parents.

By all accounts William was a good scholar. According to Peter Wentworth, his Groom of the Bedchamber, when two hussars presented William with a petition in Latin, at the age of fourteen William was able to respond in fluent conversational Latin. But he was not as studious as his eldest sister Anne, a serious young woman with a talent for music – she had been an excellent pupil of Handel's – and a fair hand with the paintbox. In temperament he was more like Amelia, herself more than ten years his senior, whose enthusiasm for horses and hunting was considered shockingly unladylike. All the children followed the hunt, in an open carriage with the Queen if they were unable to ride, and their zeal caused much comment. Amelia had several falls, and William too; but he relished the chase and impatiently refused to be cosseted even when badly cut and bruised. One day when he was sixteen he went out hunting during a storm, afterwards swimming his horse across the river to Hampton Court, changed his clothes and rode off to a party in Vauxhall Gardens – this at a time when he was ill with measles. He paid for his recklessness, though, when he fell ill with a serious fever; the King's fondness for his son was apparent to all in the great anxiety he showed during the critical days that followed.

Always self-assured, even cheeky (the King and Queen more than once had to confine him to his room, and they were not above physical chastisement), William was nevertheless the apple of his parents' eye. He had developed an interest in military affairs, which no doubt endeared him to his father, partly through letters from Peter Wentworth's son George, who described the soldier's life with enthusiasm and humour. He pleased his mother by showing interest in the arts and sciences. Although sometimes indulging in boyish high spirits, he could conduct himself with princely decorum when required.

In fact, the contrast between William and Frederick could not have been more marked, particularly in these early years when the Duke of Cumberland was still a boy. Even in physical appearance they differed: Frederick's sallow complexion against William's high colour, Frederick's lean build against William's chubbiness. Frederick enjoyed music and playing cricket. William adored thrashing through the forests on horseback. But most of all, William was loved by his parents while Frederick was not. It is not surprising that stories were told of rivalry between the brothers, contrasting the well-educated young English boy with the German import, but the rivalry was more supposed than real. Admittedly William was the first truly British member of his family; although his father and brother both spoke good English, neither had been born and bred in Britain. And loving attention was lavished on William whereas Frederick was neglected and despised.

Frederick might well have felt resentful, but there is no evidence of any scenes of confrontation, even when William was older.

In 1734 Anne was married off to William IV of Orange-Nassau. George II had personally chosen his daughter's bridegroom, but the family all expressed dismay at the Prince's appearance: 'a baboon' Anne called him; a monster, according to the Queen; 'a dwarf' wrote Lord Hervey, Caroline's witty but malicious friend. But Anne resigned herself to her fate and the marriage took place in London, followed by the usual public bedding ceremony. When the Prince and Princess of Orange finally betook themselves to The Hague, George turned his mind to a bride for Frederick.

Frederick had long had a mistress, a Miss Vane, one of his mother's ladies-in-waiting who also bestowed her favours upon Lord Hervey. When the mutual deception was uncovered the two men rather naturally took umbrage, but Frederick agreed to pay the lady off with £1,500 soon after her sickly baby was born. The affair was public knowledge, and when both the lady and her child died the blame was somehow laid at Frederick's door. It was time the Prince of Wales had a wife.

George II himself, with Caroline's acquiescence, had a longstanding mistress, Henrietta Howard, Countess of Suffolk, but was growing tired of her. Now that he was king he had resumed his Hanoverian connections with enthusiasm and would make increasingly frequent visits. It was during one such visit, in early 1735, that he found himself a new mistress, Madame Amalie Wallmoden, and also found a bride for Frederick. She was Augusta, daughter of the late Duke of Saxe-Gotha, seventeen years old, shy and unable to speak any English; but she was ideally suited, in the King's eyes, for Frederick because there were no important political or dynastic considerations to upset the German balance.

Augusta arrived in London the following April and the marriage took place immediately. It was a mean and hasty affair, particularly in comparison with Anne's recent wedding. William, newly turned fifteen, led her up the aisle of the chapel in St James's and that night helped his brother to don his nightshirt. The King overcame his repugnance sufficiently to attend the bedding ceremony, while the Queen cast a critical eye over her daughter-in-law's underclothes.

Shortly after the marriage, the King doubled his son's annual allowance to £50,000: a less than generous gesture when the Civil List included the sum of £100,000 intended for the Prince of Wales. Unwisely the King then returned to the arms of Madame Wallmoden in Hanover, while the Prince was left behind to nurse his grievances, encouraged by a growing band of supporters.

Although happy enough with his new bride, Frederick felt insulted by the fact that in the King's absence the Queen, advised by Walpole, was appointed guardian of the realm rather than himself. He returned to his former dissolute ways, gambling and running up heavy debts as he bought first Carlton House in London and then a house at Cliveden overlooking the Thames, constantly surrounded by a sycophantic retinue of dilettantes and out-of-favour politicians. Ill advised by the latter, in February, 1737, he allowed some of his friends to raise in Parliament the question of his allowance, attempting to force the King's hand; but the motion was dismissed. He was not unpopular with the public, however, who considered that the King treated him unfairly.

In fact the King was the target of some sharp criticism for his extended trips abroad, and for taking a German mistress. In the previous year the Queen herself was hurt at her husband's prolonged absence and wrote suggesting he bring his new mistress back to England. But he was still in Hanover that autumn when the Gin Act was passed by Parliament, provoking riots in the streets: 'No gin, no king!' the mobs shouted at the Queen as she drove through London.

Reluctantly George II returned, without Madame Wallmoden, in January, 1737. All seemed well for a time, but the dispute over Frederick's allowance and his own poor health – he had piles – made George increasingly bad-tempered; his habit of turning his back on anyone who displeased him caused a 'Rumpsteak Club' to be formed by those so treated. But worse was to follow.

The Princess of Wales was pregnant. Both she and Frederick were vague about when the child was to be born but they were all at Hampton Court for the summer when, one evening at the end of July, Augusta went into labour. Frederick had decided that no child of his would arrive under the same roof as the King; he secretly called for a coach, bundled Augusta into it and drove with his screaming passenger to St James's Palace. They arrived just in time. A tiny princess was born, without the customary gathering of family witnesses.

The Queen, hastening to visit her daughter-in-law, was as reassuring and comforting as any grandparent could be. Not so the King. He had been defied and insulted, and constitutional precedent had been ignored. Frederick had risked the lives of his own wife and daughter. After consulting Walpole and his cabinet, the King took his revenge – but carefully. As the Earl of Hardwicke, recently appointed Lord Chancellor, explained to the young Duke of Cumberland during a special briefing, too harsh a sentence on the Prince of Wales would give ammunition to the opposition politicians. The blame was to be cast upon the Prince's political cronies; so long as he continued to listen to them, the Prince would not be allowed to live at St James's. Six weeks later the Prince's entire household had moved to Kew. The King and Queen expressed themselves relieved to be rid of their son.

But for all the care he had taken, the King had simply recreated the conditions that had pertained at Leicester House: conditions ideal for the nurture of opposition.

This crisis, which undoubtedly affected William, albeit to a lesser degree than others of the family, was as nothing to what followed. In November, 1737, Queen Caroline died. With immense physical courage she had borne an illness for years, its exact nature unclear but possibly related to gynaecological complications following the birth of her last child, Louisa. At the end she was unable to conceal her sufferings any longer, and endured an agonizing ten days surrounded by frantic surgeons and physicians, and, of course, her family, excepting only the Prince of Wales.

The death of Caroline, as described by the devoted Lord Hervey, is one of the great domestic dramas in the history of the British monarchy. The King was half out of his mind with despair. William and his sisters were constantly at the Queen's bedside, trying to control their grief while she calmly took her leave of them. According to Hervey, Caroline spoke to William most lovingly, calling him her 'chief hope' and telling him to

be a support to your father and double your attention to make up for the disappointment and resentment he must receive from your profligate and worthless brother. It is in you only I hope for keeping up the credit of our family when your father shall be no more. Attempt nothing ever against your brother and endeavour to mortify him no way but by showing superior merit.[2]

The young Duke of Cumberland was so overcome by his beloved mother's death that her last words to him are likely to have remained a vivid memory for the rest of his life.

# 2

# By Land and Sea

WILLIAM WAS SIXTEEN when his mother died. She left a huge gap in his life. As he wrote sadly to his sister Anne in The Hague, Caroline had been 'the best of mothers and the dearest of friends'. However, he was a young man with his own life to lead and he soon recovered his equilibrium. He was also beginning to acquire a wider understanding of the world. He had met all the senior ministers of the day, and many other figures of national and international standing. Walpole was a particularly familiar figure, having wielded power since well before William was born. Philip Yorke, Earl of Hardwicke, was a relative newcomer who had been Lord Chancellor only since February, 1737, but another notable whom William certainly knew was Thomas Pelham-Holles, Duke of Newcastle, the same man who had once fled to George I with tales about William's father. Newcastle was a ubiquitous character, fussy and seemingly weak-minded but possessed of impressive staying power; he would become a regular feature in William's life. At this time he was Secretary of State, Southern Department (responsible broadly for Ireland, the colonies and southern Europe), while his opposite number in the Northern Department (responsible for relations with northern Europe) was the Earl of Harrington.

Walpole's position now was in some doubt, and not merely because the Queen was dead and he no longer had her as a conduit to the King. His problem was that he lacked credentials in the dimension of foreign affairs, and the relative peace of the past two decades was starting to crack. The King, for all that Walpole despised him, had a better appreciation of, for instance, the threat posed to European stability by France. But first it was an Anglo-Spanish dispute that Walpole had to worry about.

Ever since the Treaty of Utrecht in 1713, ending the War of the Spanish Succession, Spain had been nursing a grudge towards Britain; in particular she wanted to overturn the *Asiento*, the agreement by which Britain had a monopoly of the slave trade in the Caribbean. The British, in turn, were furious at interference, amounting to piracy, by the Spanish *guarda-costas*, whose supposed role was to prevent smuggling. When a merchant captain by the name of Jenkins claimed that his entire cargo had been seized and his ear had been severed during one encounter with *guarda-costas*, the British erupted with righteous rage. Now, while Walpole vainly tried to prolong the peace, the opposition, orchestrated by friends of the Prince of Wales, 'the Patriot Boys' as Walpole mockingly called them, urged war with Spain.

For once Frederick and his father were in agreement. The King was all for war. He began to recover his spirits, and, though he genuinely mourned the loss of his Queen, went to Hanover to fetch his mistress. In this he was following Walpole's advice, and he no doubt felt encouraged by the memory of Caroline's acquiescence. Indeed, the Queen on her deathbed had advised him to marry again; sobbing, the King had told her: 'No, I'll have mistresses.' Madame Wallmoden was therefore brought to London and installed in society, ennobled as Lady Yarmouth. Fat, ill-featured but by no means unintelligent, she became a useful sounding board for those who preferred not to tackle the King directly; she thus, to some degree, inherited the political influence wielded by Caroline herself.

What William and his sisters felt at this move, and how they regarded the usurper, can only be guessed at, but the sudden arrival of the Hanoverian favourite was not welcomed by the British public. Already unpopular for his treatment of the Prince of Wales and for his growing preference for Germany and all things German, George II now became the target of abusive broadsheets and scurrilous comment. One day a cruel verse was posted outside Kensington Palace:

Here lives a man of fifty-four
Whose royal father's will he tore
And thrust his children out of door
Then killed his wife and took a whore.[1]

By referring to the 'royal father's will' the anonymous writer showed that he had a good memory, for the affair of George I's testament had long been settled, to the new King's satisfaction at least. When his father died and the will was shown to George II, he not only suppressed it but displayed hitherto unknown resources in persuading others that the will was invalid. Above all George II objected to the scheme laid down by his father for Britain and Hanover to be separated after Frederick's death, one to be inherited by Frederick's first-born son, the other by his second son (neither of whom yet existed). George II had his own scheme for separating Britain and Hanover, a scheme discussed with Caroline and, naturally, favouring William. If his parents had had their way, the Duke of Cumberland would in due course have inherited the English throne while Frederick got Hanover.[2] But in the event, constitutional difficulties prevented the separation of Crown and Electorate.

As it happens, the Prince of Wales now acquired a son and heir: in June, 1738, Augusta gave birth to the future George III. The nation was delighted and the court of the Prince of Wales became correspondingly more popular, though the news was received coolly by the King and the rest of the family. His sisters found it impossible to forget Frederick's scandalous behaviour on the birth of his first child and still treated him as an outcast. William, on the other hand, whatever he thought of his brother, showed him nothing but civility. On one occasion William escorted Amelia and Caroline to the theatre and found the royal box occupied by Frederick and Augusta; it was a blunder, but, given the intention, they could have squeezed in together. Unfortunately, watched of course by an eager audience, Amelia made the situation worse by refusing to curtsy to the Prince and Princess of Wales, and was loudly hissed by the onlookers, whereupon Caroline fainted. William bundled his sisters off home but returned minutes later and, after exchanging formal bows as required, took his seat in the box with every appearance of composure.

While diplomats bustled back and forth between Britain and Spain, attempting to secure peace for Walpole, the warmongers' cries grew louder: loudest of all were those from merchants and citizens of the seaports, whose livelihood was threatened by these Spanish practices. Their fears were increased by French attempts to gain a share of the lucrative Atlantic trade. In 1733 France and Spain had signed a Family Compact, the first of a series of agreements with ominous implications for Britain. French policy had long been conducted by Cardinal Fleury, the aged tutor of Louis XV; this wily old man was regarded by Walpole as a friend and a restraint on French aggression, but his influence was slipping. War between Britain and Spain, if it broke out, would almost certainly be to the advantage of France.

William was no doubt following the arguments with closest interest; instinctively loyal to his father, he would have regarded Walpole's fears as weakness. As for himself, he had reached the age when a young man considers his future employment, and he was vaguely considering a life at sea. In broad terms his upbringing would have emphasized the importance of the navy to a maritime trading nation like Britain, especially with the growth of the colonies; besides, though there is no evidence to prove it, the King and his advisers no doubt suggested a naval career as one among several possibilities. Politically it would have been a shrewd move, countering suggestions that the Hanoverians had the mentality of landlocked Europeans. As a boy William had shown particular interest in the navy, encouraged by Sir Jacob Acworth, who took him to launchings and impressed him with stories of great sea battles and making landfall in exotic places. Now, in 1739, with war brewing, the young Duke of Cumberland had a decision to make.

Life at court was tedious without Queen Caroline and her animated friends. Baron Bielfeld, one of the King of Prussia's secretaries, describes St James's Palace at about this time as 'smoking and dirty and quite sufficient of itself to inspire melancholy ideas':

> Since the death of the Queen, the King has never kept a public table. H.M. dines and sups alone in his own apartment. The Prince and Princess of Wales neither lodge or come to court. The Duke of Cumberland and the Princesses Amelia, Caroline and Louisa eat also in private and admit none whatever to their table or even to be spectators of it. This life of perpetual retirement renders the court to the last degree spiritless.[3]

The King's children obviously found time on their hands. William, emerging from adolescence, could not have failed to notice the warm feelings that Amelia nursed for the Duke of Newcastle or the flirtatious exchanges between her and the Duke of Grafton; but both men seem to have been deterred by her mannish devotion to field sports. Princess Caroline was suffering the pangs of unrequited love for Lord Hervey, and the younger sisters were not much company for William either. More and more he pursued his own ends.

By 1739 William's personal position had been enhanced by an increase in his allowance, to £12,000 a year. Not only did he now have his own little hunting lodge and parkland within Windsor Forest; in addition to his rooms in Hampton Court and Kensington Palaces he had a fine apartment in St James's Palace, formerly the one allotted to the Prince of Wales. Here he began to hold levées, formal receptions attended by ministers, diplomats, officers from the army and the navy, church dignitaries, and many other important men of the day. He renewed acquaintanceship with young men who had been at Westminster School or Eton, and the young friends began to lead him tentatively along the paths of sexual adventure.

At this stage rumours began to spread of William's amorous exploits, though there was, as often is the case, more gossip than action. Two of his mother's old cronies swapped scandal from Windsor: 'Our forest rings with the gallantries of H.R.H. the Duke,' wrote Lady Hartford to Lady Pomfret, 'and the kind assistance Lord Henry Beauclerk has lent him in managing an interview with the daughter of a yeoman.'[4] Beauclerk was the local Windsor MP, and it seems to have been his well accepted duty to procure feminine company for the Prince.

Lord Egmont, a supporter of the Prince of Wales who sought to reduce

Cumberland's standing, was an avid collector of tittle-tattle, as his diary frequently shows:

> This week Miss Williams, an actress, was complimented in the green room by her fellows of the honour done her by the Duke of Cumberland in taking her for a mistress.[5]

Then Egmont added piously: 'But 'tis to be hoped this is a scandal.' Nor could he refrain from recording an even more unlikely tale concerning Cumberland and a Miss Wilson, an orange-seller turned actress (shades of Nell Gwynn) – 'and a very pretty woman she is.' Apparently Cumberland gave her £400, less than the £600 offered her by Lord Clinton, yet when the latter visited the lady he was informed

> that the Duke of Cumberland was with her so he was asked to wait next door. The Duke of Cumberland then came in... and immediately recognized Lord Clinton and uttered a challenge for another place.

But again Egmont adds prudently: 'Some do not believe this story true and I have it not confirmed.'[6]

Thus early in his life it was Cumberland's fate to be linked with bawdy speculation, some good-natured but some inspired by malice. Such sallies into London's demi-monde characterized the life of all young men of fashion, and the Duke of Cumberland counted such men among his friends; it is not impossible that he ventured into murky waters himself. But there were many improbable tales that in some quarters gained a damaging currency. Certainly there is no evidence of him acting in the foolish way of his elder brother, who on one occasion had naively asked a guard in St James's Park to try and arrest a trollop of the town who had made off with his watch, a story which had set the worldly-wise and contemptuous Queen laughing her head off.

More probably the young Duke of Cumberland found pleasure in romantic dalliance at private supper parties given by his friends, at masquerades and balls or at those fashionable haunts, Vauxhall and Ranelagh. For, as Baron Bielfeld remarked, 'If the court be languid, the town in return is highly animated.'[7]

Whatever the truth of his early amours, hunting remained William's great passion. The stag was the usual royal quarry, foxes being deemed fair game only for lesser mortals. In the season, which ran from August to November, there were two or three meets a week, at Richmond Park, Epsom or Banstead Common, Hounslow Heath or Epping Forest – and if the royal hunt master considered it necessary he would bring a carted stag, or late in the season a hind, to ensure good sport. The royal buckhounds were kept at Windsor, and similarly transported when required. But the best fun was in Windsor Forest, where there was more chance of finding a wild stag, rather than one previously caught and then set loose by the master. On hunting days, generally Wednesdays and Saturdays, the royal party would set out from London well before dawn, driving down to Windsor with the Household Cavalry as an escort against highwaymen. On a good day the hunters might rouse two or three stags, and the chase might last till darkness fell. An injured stag or one that was obviously old and weak would be killed; a stag giving a really good run, however, generally had its life spared. On one occasion, in September, 1737, the last meet in which the Queen took part, a hind was roused at Hounslow, chased across the river almost to Guildford and on the return was caught trying to cross the Thames again near Staines; on the Queen's orders, the hind was allowed to live.

William had been given his first hunter at the age of eight, and by now had developed not merely a love of horses but a good eye in judging their qualities. His father had received a string of Arab horses soon after the Queen's death, and a Mr Hedges at Windsor owned an elderly brood mare descended from the great Godolphin Arab himself; very soon William was turning into an enthusiastic horse breeder. In 1739 he sent one horse for which he had high hopes to his brother-in-law, the Prince of Orange, but then, to his chagrin, had to apologize as the animal turned out less than satisfactory; his excuse was that a heavy round of duties had prevented him from ensuring that the animal was fully tried out and properly vetted.

As often as he could William would escape to his little lodge at Windsor; even out of season, he found plenty to occupy his time. He helped Mr Jenison, Master of the Royal Buckhounds, to design bigger and better kennels. He contributed to improvements within Windsor Forest, such as a bridge built over the millstream at Sunningwell and two new ridings constructed over the Great West Road between Basingstoke and Blackwater. He got to know every ditch and pathway of the royal forest between the castle and Ascot and Bagshot Heath and all along the river by Englefield Green and Egham. He also visited his governor, Stephen Poyntz, who had bought himself a pleasant country house at Midgham, near Newbury, and built a special suite of rooms for the Duke. From here William used to ride up to the nearby Berkshire downs to watch horse racing at East Ilsley, and was so taken with the sport that he later started a training stable for horses bred at his own stud at Windsor.

But in 1739 the country was preparing for war and for the young Duke of Cumberland the round of official duties was increasing. With his father or his brother he was frequently in attendance at formal ceremonies such as the launching of ships at Deptford or inspecting the defences and stores at Portsmouth. He was fully aware of the crisis facing the country, and of the widespread fear that Britain's coastline was vulnerable to foreign landings. After twenty-five years of peace, the country's defences had fallen into disrepair, and the standing army — such as it was, for the nation had objected to the cost of maintaining it during peacetime — was a shambles, ill-disciplined and ill-led, the officers mainly appointed and promoted by the system of purchase. The navy was in less desperate straits; the officers were more professional, most of them having spent years learning their job as midshipmen, and, although conditions were appalling on board ship, discipline was better. But with war approaching, the navy was bound to be in the front line, and preparations took on an added urgency throughout the summer of 1739.

In January, 1739, Walpole's negotiations with the Spanish had produced the Convention of El Pardo, by which Spain was to pay compensation for the *guarda-costas'* depredations. But the money was never paid. The Convention was widely condemned as settling nothing, and denounced by one man in the House of Commons as 'insecure, unsatisfactory and dishonourable' and 'a stipulation for national ignominy': the MP in question was William Pitt, a friend of the Prince of Wales and already a name to remember.

Walpole's influence was ebbing. In July Admiral Vernon was sent out to the West Indies with eight ships and orders to assail the *guarda-costas*. In October war was declared on Spain, and in November Vernon achieved a notable success by capturing Porto Bello (the modern Portobelo, Panama), a home port of the troublesome Spanish coastguards. The news was greeted in Britain with great celebrations, but it was hardly a decisive victory. At home, anxious plans were made to repel a possible Franco-Spanish invasion. Recruitment was stepped up and troops were deployed to coastal camps. Steps were taken to repair, equip and man the fleet. Six new regiments of marines were to be raised. Parliament discussed a proposal to launch a combined operation against the Spanish naval base of Cartagena.

Meanwhile the King's attention had turned to Hanover, now under threat from France; he feared that Denmark too would fall into the sticky embraces of the French, and signed a deal agreeing to pay Denmark for 6,000 troops. This, at a time when Britain was hard pressed to defend herself, caused some parliamentary discontent and the King began to seek other ways of securing Danish support. In time-honoured fashion he decided that a dynastic match might be the solution, and started lengthy negotiations to marry his youngest daughter, Louisa, apparently the prettiest and liveliest, to the King of Denmark. It was suggested, moreover, that the marriage might be a double one, with the Duke of Cumberland marrying the Danish Princess Louise. In the meantime another marriage was arranged, that of George II's fourth daughter, Mary, with Frederick, the Landgrave of Hesse-Cassel, a principality to the south of Hanover. The latter arrangement was concluded in May, 1740, with a hasty ceremony in the Chapel Royal, St James's Palace, at which William stood proxy for the absent Landgrave; the Danish negotiations, however, were to continue for another three years.

In the spring of 1740 the King set out again for Hanover. Before he left, however, he nominated his second son to the colonelcy of the 2nd or Coldstream Regiment of Foot Guards.

At nineteen, the Duke of Cumberland was relatively old to be receiving a first commission in the army; when James Wolfe joined his father that summer as a volunteer he was just thirteen. Up to now, most of Cumberland's military knowledge was theoretical and he was sensible of his lack of training; nevertheless, he was determined not to be an embarrassment to the Guards. The regiment had two battalions, one of them encamped at Hounslow in April, 1740, along with the rest of the Foot Guards and Horse Guards, and thither Cumberland went from Windsor.

Chiefly he took this opportunity to make himself known to the officers and gain the confidence of the NCOs and men, and at once started on a round of entertainment, charming all with his 'affability and good sense.'[8] But at the same time he launched a programme of improvements in training and discipline. Within a very short time he had raised both standards and morale and, in the words of Lady Hartford, rendered the Guards 'an ornament and a safeguard, instead of being what they had too often been before, a nuisance and terror to the places of royal residence.'[9]

Despite the apparent success of this, his first taste of army life, Cumberland still felt drawn to a career in the navy. He was no doubt frustrated at the lack of action during the summer of 1740, but he also felt dissatisfaction with the supervisory nature of his role; rather than adorn the encamped army as a Colonel of the Guards, he therefore applied to go to sea as a volunteer.

The King agreed. According to Lady Hartford, a friend of the late Queen, there was some thought of making Cumberland Lord High Admiral upon his return: 'I am glad of it,' she wrote, 'since I know it is what Queen Caroline always wanted for him, who dreaded seeing him as a *pilier d'antichambre*.'[10] And so, while the Prince of Wales applied in vain for an army appointment, his younger brother set off in August, 1740, to join the Home Fleet.

It was to be a short and less than glorious episode in the life of the Duke of Cumberland, although it began well enough. He was received with great ceremony at Portsmouth by the veteran Commander-in-Chief, Admiral Sir John Norris, aboard whose flagship, HMS *Victory*, he was to sail. Norris, seventy-nine years old, had served with distinction in the Mediterranean, the

North Atlantic and the Baltic, but all his experience was to avail him nothing during his forthcoming battle to make sense of changing and conflicting orders. One problem was that, with the King in Hanover, the country was effectively ruled by the Lords Justice, the regency council, which could not make up its collective mind over a strategy by which to fight the war. Another problem reflected the administrative weakness that characterized a nation unprepared for war: the ships were barely seaworthy, and, just as important, insufficient provisions had been arranged.

Norris' orders, broadly, were to intercept the Spanish fleet, and also to embark troops from the Isle of Wight for a combined operation against Ferrol in north-west Spain. In the middle of all the confusion, he had received, at two days' notice, information that the King's son was to sail with him. But he had taken it calmly, and greeted the Duke with every semblance of delight in this honour.

Cumberland's retinue at Portsmouth included Poyntz; his sub-governor, Windham; his equerry, Anthony La Melonnière; and two pages and three footmen − all except Poyntz being due to embark with the young volunteer. As luck would have it, the wind was foul and the whole party had to stay the night in the Dockyard. The following morning Cumberland and the others joined the Admiral in a pinnace waiting to take them out to *Victory*. In his diary Norris wrote:

> As we rowed out of the harbour by the Gun Wharf all the guns of Portsmouth saluted as we passed them by − the ships were all manned and cheered us as we passed. When HRH was on board I struck my flag and hoisted the standard, then according to my orders all the men-of-war saluted with 21 guns, beginning when Admiral Cavendish of the Blew should fire his gun. When that was over I asked H.R.H. if he could approve that we should answer with 21 guns, which was done.[11]

Cumberland would stay in Norris's cabin while he took the Captain's. *Victory*, though technically a rebuild of *Royal James*, was a first-rate warship of a hundred guns, displacing 1,920 tons. The crew prepared to sail.

Two days later *Victory* and the rest of the squadron were still at anchor. The westerly wind had turned into a gale and the Admiral was forced to wait. He took the Duke round to Cowes to review the troops waiting to embark. The troops were duly put through their paces by Brigadier-General Wentworth, marching past their royal visitor in grand divisions and demonstrating a certain skill in their platoon firing exercises.

The Duke then attended a reception in Newport at which the Mayor and corporation bestowed upon him the freedom of the borough, and he in turn held a dinner for the civic dignitaries, returning to *Victory* late that night. Shortly afterwards, the squadron sailed.

No sooner had the ships weighed anchor than they were forced to drop them again, sheltering in St Helens Bay from the fierce north-wester. Here they were joined by the other squadron of the fleet under Admiral Sir Chaloner Ogle, who told Norris that 621 of his men had fallen sick and he had only enough water for a month. Norris, conscientiously keeping the Duke informed of all his decisions, sent an urgent message to the Duke of Newcastle, explaining that Ogle would be held up until adequate provisions were forthcoming.

Finally, after nine days of waiting, Norris sailed his squadron — into near disaster. The ships were off Portland by night when the look-out warned of an unknown vessel bearing down on *Victory*. The helm was put hard over, but too late to prevent a collision. *Victory* was rammed in the bow, the stranger carrying away her cutwater. The Duke was woken, according to a letter Poyntz wrote to Newcastle, by 'a universal scream and outcry close under his cabin window from the ship who had done the damage and who thought themselves sinking.'[12] The Admiral, in his nightshirt, was on deck at the first hint of trouble, conducting operations through his speaking trumpet, but it was not until the new day dawned that the culprit's identity was revealed: HMS *Lion*. Both ships had been badly damaged and, according to the papers, twenty-eight men had been lost on *Lion*. The squadron returned to St Helens.

While the Admiral assessed the situation, news came in of another collision, between *Superb* and *Suffolk*. There were more urgent messages for London. Norris had decided to move his flag and stores to HMS *Boyne*, considerably smaller than *Victory*, and hasty reorganization eventually resulted in accommodation fit for the Duke and his retinue. Poyntz had meanwhile heard of the collision from Windham and arrived at Southampton in a state of high anxiety, insisting on being taken to see the Duke. But Cumberland was in perfect health, and, as Poyntz reported: 'The Admiral and all officers speak of his calmness and the propriety of his behaviour.'

Again the squadron set off. Again the ships ran into a gale, and again they were forced to seek shelter, this time in Torbay. Waiting for the winds to drop, the Admiral's flagship was visited by a deputation of city fathers from Plymouth, who rowed out to present the Duke with the freedom of the city in a gold box.

Now London decided that Norris should embark troops for a raid on the Spanish port of San Sebastian. The squadron was kept waiting in Torbay while General Handasyde's Regiment was marched from Newbury and embarked, one company to each of nine ships. Now there was another change of plan: it was heard that the Spanish squadron had left Ferrol. While messengers galloped urgently back and forth between Admiral and Admiralty, Cumberland grew impatient. He was not alone; he saw one wretched sailor dive overboard and attempt to swim ashore, only to be caught and sentenced to a hundred lashes. He learnt not about the thrill and satisfaction of controlling a great ship in the teeth of a storm, or the pleasure to be had on first glimpsing a foreign port, but about the misery and boredom and need for patience. He danced on deck with the sailors and watched the troops being disembarked. He wrote to his sisters Amelia and Caroline describing the tedium of life aboard ship, and Amelia told the Duke of Newcastle. At last, in mid-September, Newcastle told the young volunteer he could return to London.

Although plans were agreed for a combined operation in the West Indies, involving Lord Cathcart and General Wentworth, whose troops Cumberland had inspected at Cowes, and although he requested permission to join the operation, he never did. The King was delighted by his son's spirit but refused to let him risk his health in that notorious climate. It was just as well. Not only was the expedition a fiasco, but the men died in scores from yellow fever; the huge expenditure of manpower and material achieved not a thing.

The Duke of Cumberland's naval career was over.

# 3

# The Battle of Dettingen

IN THE WINTER OF 1740 there was a sudden international crisis. Charles VI, the Holy Roman Emperor, died in October, leaving his daughter Maria Theresa to inherit the Empire. Foreseeing trouble over a woman donning the imperial mantle, Charles had tried to strengthen her position with the Pragmatic Sanctions, a series of agreements by which Britain, Hanover, Prussia, France and Spain, among others, acknowledged Maria Theresa's right of succession. However, shortly before Charles's death, Frederick II had acceded to the Prussian throne and promptly invaded Silesia, one of the imperial dominions.

George II, who had only just returned from his summer in Hanover, was outraged at his nephew's behaviour. He urged that Britain should offer immediate assistance. But Britain was already embroiled in war with Spain, albeit a fumbling and half-hearted war, and Walpole was reluctant to risk another. While the King, as Elector of Hanover, made energetic efforts to secure aid for Maria Theresa, in Britain he first had to persuade Walpole and Parliament to follow his example. In the end it was the British public that persuaded Walpole; popular feeling was very much in Maria Theresa's favour, and the great Whig politician knew his power was waning. In April, 1741, he yielded to the inevitable and committed Britain to the support of the late Emperor's daughter.

The young Duke of Cumberland had meanwhile returned to his command of the Coldstream Guards. With his brief naval career already a fading memory, he had resolved to devote his future to the army, and specifically to army reform, starting with the Guards. He spent most of 1741 and '42 endeavouring to improve standards among the officers — he had at least one sacked for going absent from his detachment at Windsor — while keeping a constant eye on international events.

By the summer of 1741 King George had realized that his beloved Hanover was in the front line. France and Spain had reneged on their agreements to support Maria Theresa and the French in particular were threatening to seize territorial advantage in the relative vacuum of power. As the imperial dominions then comprised not only Austria, Hungary, Czechoslovakia and Lombardy but also most of modern-day Romania and Yugoslavia and all of Belgium, it seemed to power-hungry politicians like the Duc de Belleisle in France that land was theirs for the taking. But George II was determined to safeguard his Electorate and despatched Electoral emissaries to all the courts of Europe in an attempt to secure neutrality for Hanover. His efforts were successful, and timely, for French troops were already in Bohemia and Westphalia.

The King's concern for Hanover was not popular with his British subjects. Walpole, too, was in trouble, for he was unfairly held responsible for lack of progress in the war against Spain. News had arrived that summer of reverses on the Spanish Main: the combined military and naval attacks led by General Wentworth and Admiral Vernon had failed to make any further impression on the haunts of the *guarda-costas* and, though British trade had suffered, the Spanish merchant fleet was scarcely inconvenienced. Although Walpole had survived the spring 1741 election, the opposition had won ground: men like Lords Carteret and Pulteney were eagerly anticipating the great man's fall. It came in February, 1742. After twenty-one years in continuous power, Walpole resigned.

The King was dismayed. Walpole had been not only his prime minister but, despite disagreements over the conduct of the war, his friend. And it was as the King's friend that Walpole managed to influence the choice of men to follow him. Thus, while Walpole now took a seat in the Upper House as the first Earl of Orford, the new administration continued in much the same fashion as the old. Nonentities took over Walpole's ministerial positions and the only change of note was the replacement of Harrington by Carteret as Secretary of State (North).

Carteret was a brilliant diplomat with a flair for languages and a rare grasp of European affairs. The King liked him. In fact, Carteret's only problem was his haughty disregard for fellow politicians, most of whom detested him. Thus, lacking a power base in the Commons, he would not be able to maintain his position for long. Nevertheless he was not slow in making his mark on the European scene.

Carteret's first task was to persuade Maria Theresa to come to terms with Frederick of Prussia at least temporarily, by recognizing his conquest of Silesia; then she would concentrate her efforts against the French. He achieved his task by a subsidy of £500,000 and the promise of British troops, in addition to Hanoverian and Hessian mercenaries paid in British gold. By further financial inducements he inveigled the Austrian Netherlands into contributing troops to support the beleaguered Empress, and attempted to persuade the Dutch also to join the Pragmatic Army as it came to be called; but the Dutch were nervous of risking the direct hostility of France.

As yet Britain and France were not technically at war. Britain had 16,000 men in Flanders, commanded by an aggressive Scot, Lord Stair, who wanted to march on Paris. The French army, 50,000-strong under Marshal Noailles, claimed to be acting on behalf of the Elector of Bavaria, a contender for the imperial crown. The British, along with the other allied contingents, were acting as auxiliaries to Austria. But no one was deceived. The day was fast approaching when war would erupt.

Against this background of military and diplomatic manoeuvres, the Duke of Cumberland found himself playing a dual role: soldier and bachelor prince.

In February, 1742, Cumberland was promoted to the colonelcy of the 1st Guards, which, alone among British regiments, was capable of forming three separate battalions, and which was the senior regiment in terms of precedence within the infantry. Two months later he came of age and took his seat in the House of Lords and in mid-May he was sworn in as a privy councillor: all of which was a source of considerable pleasure to the Duke. Rather less to his taste was the role of pawn in dynastic match-making. Negotiations with the Danish royal family had been continuing for years, with George II proposing a double marriage: the Duke with Princess Louise of Denmark, and her brother the Crown Prince with the Duke's youngest sister, Louisa.

Cumberland was not enthusiastic about marriage to the Danish princess. Her appearance was not in her favour and Horace Walpole, youngest son of the former prime minister, described her as 'a bolus'. More to the point, Cumberland had scented his chance for military action; everything he heard was indicating war against the French, and he wanted an active part. Reluctant for once to submit to his father's will, he asked Walpole, now Lord Orford, what he should do, and the ever wily politician advised him to press for such a huge marriage settlement that Parliament would never approve it. This Cumberland did, and the ruse worked; Henry Pelham, brother of the Duke of Newcastle and by then First Lord of the Treasury, did not dare even to raise the subject in Parliament. The King blamed Parliament, and the Danes thereafter proved less amenable to George's requests for troops to join the Pragmatic Army. Louisa's marriage, however, was arranged for the following autumn.

Two other brides had also been proposed for Cumberland, both of them German. The Duke of Argyll was in Berlin during 1742, taking part in the talks to ease the Prussian threat to Hanover, and seems to have suggested a marriage between Cumberland and Wilhelmina of Prussia, the same princess who fifteen years earlier had been considered by George I as a bride for his grandson Frederick. Cumberland certainly knew of the scheme, for Egmont records that he had consented to his name being put forward in this way,[1] but if he expressed a personal opinion of the scheme it has not been preserved.

The other marriage proposal was put to George II by one of his Electoral ministers, Baron Münchhausen. The lady in question was Caroline Louise, nineteen years old and the daughter of Louis VIII of Hesse Darmstadt. It was a less important connection than that already made by Cumberland's sister Mary, now Princess of Hesse, but from the Hanoverian point of view it would reinforce dynastic loyalties. Moreover, Hesse Darmstadt lay in the bosom of Germany east of the Rhine, an area that might provide a suitable battleground on which to engage the French. The King resolved to inspect Caroline at the earliest opportunity.

At the end of 1742 the Duke of Cumberland was promoted to major-general. Even better, he knew now that he would soon be in action. Carteret had finally secured Dutch agreement to join the Pragmatic Army, and the King himself intended to lead the allied troops against the French, with his second son at his side. The Prince of Wales had asked to join the campaign but his repeated requests were and would continue to be turned down out of hand.

In April, 1743, Cumberland left England with his father. It was his first trip abroad; everything was novel and interesting. The King was keen to share his love of Hanover with his son, and found time not only to show him the family palace at Herrenhausen but also to teach him the art of boar-hunting. Cumberland with his fondness for hunting took to this variation with instant success. Carteret, the Secretary of State, who accompanied them to Hanover, reported afterwards to Newcastle that he had seen Cumberland spear four boars in succession in a single hunt. Carteret had decided that he approved of Cumberland. He wrote to Newcastle:

> The Duke's behaviour here is as good in all respects as is possible and I who am not easily caught with young men, tho' Princes, begin upon acquaintance to have a very good opinion of him. This journey has done and will do him a great deal of good.[2]

Lord Stair and the British and Dutch troops, leaving their winter quarters, had already set off across Europe towards the Rhine, where they would meet up with the Hanoverians and Hessians and then intercept the French. However, the King sent orders restraining Stair; with the French threat so close now to Hanover, he was anxious to avoid a confrontation that might spill over into his Electorate. Besides, the King wanted to lead the Pragmatic

Army himself. He ordered Stair to camp the troops along the River Main and wait.

In June, 1743, the King was ready. He set off from Hanover with a vast train of baggage, heading majestically south for the 250-mile journey. Cumberland set off separately, with a lesser entourage, and found time to break his journey at Cassel and spend two nights as the guest of his sister Mary. At last they joined Stair's troops, and the situation was far from favourable.

Marshal Noailles, commanding the French army, had quickly spotted the weakness of the allies' position, strung out along the right bank of the Main. The British and Dutch were based at Aschaffenburg, twenty miles from Hanau where the Hanoverians and Hessians were encamped; their supply and communication lines were thus dangerously stretched. Noailles planned to cross the river and cut those lines, then trap the allies in an ambush − a mouse-trap, as he called it.

Arriving at Aschaffenburg, the King saw the danger at once. He gave orders for the troops to move out, following the river towards Hanau. Noailles was one step ahead of him. A large detachment of the French army, led by Count Grammont, had crossed the Main via two pontoon bridges and occupied positions just outside the little village of Dettingen. The plan was to let the allies proceed as far as Dettingen, then launch a two-pronged attack: Grammont from the allies' front and Noailles himself from the rear. The allies would have nowhere to go; they would be caught on the narrow plain between forested hills on their right flank and the river on their left.

The King kept his head when the French artillery opened up from across the river, and even when his leading cavalry reported back about French positions to their front. He ordered his troops to redeploy in attack formation, to break through the French blockade ahead. It was a long, slow process: 40,000 men had to be manoeuvred on that narrow plain; the baggage train had to be got off the road and out of the way; the infantry and cavalry had to be given new orders. Although Cumberland's own Regiment of Guards was, much to their disgust, included with the rearguard, he found himself in a key position. Serving as a subordinate general officer, a deputy to General Clayton, he was required to help deploy the infantry in such a way as to let the cavalry to their rear pass through to the assault. While persistent artillery fire raked the lines of the allied advance, Cumberland was at the forefront, issuing orders to his ADCs, making sure the orders were carried out, keeping alert for new directions from his father. He was in his element.

The King, too, was exhilarated by the noise and action and danger. Suddenly there was a new swirl of movement ahead: the French had moved out of their prepared positions at Dettingen. After a four-hour wait while the allies redeployed, Grammont had lost patience. Thinking perhaps to take advantage of the seeming chaos on the plain, he advanced on the allied troops. True, the first charge of his cavalry frightened the British infantry into firing ineffectively and too soon, but King George brought up his artillery and sent the infantry forward with orders not to shoot until at point-blank range. Drawing his sword and advancing with the line, the King directed his men personally, and when his horse bolted he continued on foot with General Howard's Regiment, earning the infantry's cheers.

In a crescendo of cannonfire, with muskets flashing and bullets whizzing, it was hard to see what progress had been made, but the French were already falling back. The allied infantry had shown great discipline and courage, keeping close order and waiting to the last minute before firing. Suddenly a rain of spent bullets hit Cumberland and his horse. Pulling hard on the reins and sitting tight, he managed to regain control of his frightened charger and rode back to his proper station, only to be struck by a discharge of grapeshot. He had been hit in the calf of the leg, just below the knee. Much to his chagrin he was carried off the field before the action finished.

But by then the Battle of Dettingen was almost done. The cavalry took over where the infantry left off, and by sunset that June evening the Pragmatic Army under King George II had won a notable victory against the French. Noailles was pushed back across the Rhine, reeling from terrible losses and defeat. Allied losses, though heavy, were only half those of the French, but now the King's first concern was for his wounded son.

Cumberland's orderlies had taken him to where the surgeons were doing their best to help the wounded. His conduct was closely observed by all around him, and none found reason to criticize. On the contrary, he had sufficient self-control and courtesy to request that a French officer, the Comte de Fenelon, be attended first. Taken all round, he won much praise that day for his behaviour on the field. James Wolfe, now with Duroure's Regiment, called him 'very brisk' and noted that 'his presence encourages the troops and makes them ready to undertake anything.' He later commented:

> I had several times the honour of speaking with him just as the battle began and was afraid of his being dashed to pieces by the cannon balls. He gave his orders with a great deal of calmness and seemed quite unconcerned: the soldiers were in high delight to have him so near them.[3]

The Duke of Richmond, Master of the Horse, admired his 'generosity and compassion to the prisoners' and asserted that Cumberland's wound gave concern 'not only to the King but I really believe to every man in the whole army.'[4] The King, of course, was delighted with both his victory and his son's part in it. According to Colonel Russell of the 1st Guards, he said in everybody's hearing: 'William, I'm glad you behaved so well — you acted like my son. If you do well, I shall not be sorry for your wound.'[5] And he promoted Cumberland to lieutenant-general.

Not everyone was so free with praise, however. In fact Russell himself was disapproving of Cumberland, his own colonel, and remarked that he was too serious and too strict: a common criticism at a time when military zeal was regarded among army officers as unfashionable. George Townshend, who served as a volunteer and would later become the Duke's ADC, was so disgusted by the whole muddled affair that he left the army and went off to Switzerland.

Indeed, the King, although admired for his personal bravery, was already being criticized on several counts. Firstly he had worn throughout the battle the yellow sash of a Hanoverian general, which prompted scathing remarks among the British. More importantly, against the advice of experienced generals like Lord Stair, he had failed to press the advantage and pursue the French. He was also held responsible for the delay in meeting the French, and for the overstretched supply lines. But after all, he had led the motley collection of troops called the Pragmatic Army to victory over the considerably larger and more coherent French army.

Cumberland's wound, according to Ranby, the chief army surgeon, was a classic of its kind; the wound and Ranby's treatment of it featured largely in his textbook on the subject of gunshot injuries. Luckily no bones were smashed, but the tendons had been damaged and the hole made by the shot was 'as big as a hen's egg and the extremities of some of the muscle which it had torn asunder in its passage were drove quite out of the wound.'[6] Although Cumberland had already lost a good deal of blood when he reached the first aid tent, Ranby took a further twenty ounces of blood from his arm, then applied a light dressing. Cumberland was in considerable pain and quite unable to use the leg, so he was driven by coach to Hanau, some fifteen miles from the battlefield, to spend the night. Again he was bled and an 'emollient clyster' was put over the wound; meanwhile he was given four-hourly doses of Gascoigne's powders with nitre.

On the following day he seemed more comfortable and, after he was subjected to another bleeding, his whole leg was wrapped in a bread-and-milk poultice. But the attendants had difficulty in keeping their patient quiet: 'His spirits are so high and his tongue runs so fast that we are in eternal fears that he will talk himself into a fever.'[7] And that is exactly what occurred. Possibly from shock, possibly from an infection, Cumberland was seized by a terrible fever. For a few days his life seemed to be in danger. There being signs of mortification, Ranby seriously considered amputation.

But infusions of bark helped calm the fever and slowly the patient began to recover.

The King was so worried about his son that his own health suffered for a time, but, when Ranby suggested Cumberland be sent home to recuperate at Bath, neither he nor his father would hear of it. In a letter to his sister Amelia, Cumberland said he was determined to stay with the army despite the lameness that would preclude him from taking an active role. In another letter, this one to the Duke of Newcastle, he made light of both injury and his role in the battle: 'The little part I had in the success was cheaply bought at the expense of a little pain.'[8]

# 4

# Invasion Threat

The Duke of Cumberland had tasted action and he liked it. After the Battle of Dettingen, despite his injury, he was as eager as could be to return to active service. But the King and the physicians were agreed that first he must regain his health – no matter how long that took.

Historians have tended to underestimate the wound that Cumberland received at Dettingen, but it would continue to affect him for the rest of his life. He was confined to bed in Hanau for more than a month, and in August he still needed a crutch as well as a cane to support him. The enforced immobility no doubt contributed to his excessive weight gain: though always inclined, like his father, to stoutness, he was now obese. One of his physicians, a Mr Hay, told the Duke of Newcastle that Cumberland was 'not so prudent as he should be in his diet'[1], while Colonel Russell and others remarked that his grossness might hinder his recovery. But Russell was not alone in welcoming the absence from duty of the Guards' over-keen young colonel.

Certainly Cumberland was bitterly frustrated by his lameness, and fought to resume normal life. In mid-August, against Ranby's advice, he insisted on mounting a horse to review his troops. Day by day he managed to do more and more, hobbling around with his stick, but for the rest of his life he would always feel happier on horseback.

Even from his sickbed, however, Cumberland managed to make his contribution. He had one of his ADCs, Robert Napier, draw up a careful plan of the battlefield which became the basis of an engraving by John Pine of which he later gave copies to friends, including the Duke of Montagu, Master General of the Ordnance. It was the start of a life-long interest and the first item in a huge and valuable collection of such maps. He also made a determined effort to stay in touch with events in the aftermath of the battle. General Clayton, his immediate chief, had been among the 260 British killed at Dettingen, but the 1st Guards, under General Ilton, had hardly been engaged at all. The most interesting development was Lord Stair's resignation, whose tactical advice had been repeatedly ignored by the King. George II was now not merely the titular head of the Pragmatic Army but the de facto head as well.

With winter approaching, the King had decided not to seek another confrontation with the French, but he was not yet ready to return home. Before leaving Hanau he paid a visit to a nearby schloss where Caroline Louisa of Hesse Darmstadt was staying. He had not forgotten Baron Münchhausen's suggestion that this young princess might make a suitable bride for Cumberland.

Caroline made a most favourable impression on the King, who expressed himself delighted by her looks and bearing. At their interview he told her that she was to make her own choice, and kindly let it be known that his son was not seeking marriage on mercenary grounds alone. She received good reports of Cumberland from one of her father's ministers in Darmstadt, who described him as an agreeable looking young man, 'not tall, but courteous and considerate and of obvious integrity.'[3] News of the King's match-making visit got out and for a time raised considerable expectations in Hesse Darmstadt; Caroline herself was highly embarrassed one day, when riding past a column of allied soldiers near Hanau, to be cheered and saluted as the future Duchess of Cumberland. But the couple never met. He was still confined to bed with his injury, and she preferred another suitor. She eventually married the Margrave of Baden Durlach and died in 1783.

In late September, 1743, the King and Cumberland made preparations to return to England. The campaign season was over and so the Pragmatic Army found itself winter quarters around Oppenheim on the Rhine. Cumberland left his regiment with them, hoping the 1st Guards would set a more professional example that the rest could follow. This added to Colonel Russell's sense of grievance, for the Duke made it clear that only officers who were sick or Members of Parliament would be granted home leave. Russell was so determined to go home that he appealed to his sister Fanny, one of Princess Amelia's ladies of the bedchamber, to put in a word for him, not only with Amelia but with General Folliott, Lieutenant-Colonel of the 1st Guards, and with Sir William Yonge, the Secretary of War. Either this indirect approach or his own toadying to General Honeywood, left in command in Germany, eventually proved successful. Russell returned to England very shortly after his Colonel, telling his sister and all who would listen that Cumberland's attitude was 'outrageously and shockingly military.'[3]

The King returned to England on 26 November, arriving at Gravesend and proceeding to London amid welcoming cheers for his success over the French. Horace Walpole wrote:

> It was incredible how well his reception was: beyond what it had ever been before; in short, you would have thought it had not been a week after the victory of Dettingen. They almost carried him into the palace on their shoulders.[4]

Cumberland, at his father's side, was similarly hailed as a hero, and the distinct limp, noticed by all who saw him dismount from the coach, only served to enhance his image of a brave young prince returning from the wars. He was lauded in broadsheets and extolled in the streets, and the Prince of Wales — refused permission to join the campaign — was generous enough to have Wootton paint his brother's portrait to commemorate his part at Dettingen.

The political situation in London was less welcoming for Carteret, who had spent much of the past few months in tricky diplomatic confrontations. Apart from pacifying Frederick of Prussia in order to protect Hanover, Carteret had been trying to isolate the French and to bolster Maria Theresa, offering subsidies to the Bavarian Elector, Charles VII, and to anyone else who was tempted to join the French camp. But his efforts were not appreciated in London where they were seen as attempts to drag Britain ever deeper into the continental backwoods. Newcastle and his brother Henry Pelham, now in charge at the Treasury, together with their friend Hardwicke, condemned Carteret's efforts as expensive and risky, and not even in Britain's best interests. Long resentful at his high-handed methods, they now found a way to retaliate: they refused to pay the moneys Carteret had promised to Charles VII and to Maria Theresa.

The King was furious. Carteret was his friend and trusted adviser, someone who understood his feeling for Hanover. Furthermore, the King realized that many of the attacks on Carteret were really aimed at him — most obviously, those made by William Pitt. In January, 1744, in a debate in the House of Commons, Pitt overstepped the mark, implying not only that Hanoverians were cowards but that the King was one too. The King never forgave him.

But now there arose an even more pressing problem: there was a strong possibility that the French were about to invade.

This time the threat was a real one. Old Cardinal Fleury had died and his place as adviser to Louis XV had gone to the ambitious Duc de Belleisle, whose first great project was to defeat the Habsburgs and raise the Bourbons in their stead. But the interfering English had wrecked Belleisle's plans. Now other men had taken his place, men like Tencin, Maurepas and Amelot de

Chaillon, who determined to tackle the English on their own ground – in a word, to invade. They had reason to suppose that an invasion would win widespread support among the English, whose anti-Hanoverian sentiments were well known; moreover, the bulk of Britain's standing army was dispersed across the Continent, so London itself would be virtually undefended.

The expeditionary force, comprising fifteen regiments of infantry and one of dragoons, led by General Maurice de Saxe, the redoubtable German soldier of fortune, would be embarked at Dunkirk and shipped up to Maldon in Essex. The French fleet, based at Brest in Brittany, would keep the Royal Navy busy in the Channel while a battle squadron sailed with the invasion force and then positioned itself as a blockade across the Thames estuary. According to information received, once it became known that the French had landed there would be a great surge of support from the English: horses, tents and supplies would be eagerly volunteered.

The Duke of Newcastle in London had a much more efficient network of agents. As he told the Privy Council, of which of course Cumberland was a member, there had been an ominous concentration of troops in northern France, and the French fleet was manoeuvring suspiciously: an assault was to be expected very soon. The Privy Council took immediate action. On 12 February, 1744, orders were issued to concentrate such troops as were available round London. The forts at Tilbury and Sheerness were alerted. The Dutch were asked to send 6,000 troops. In the Channel Cumberland's old chief, Sir John Norris, was ordered to sea to intercept the French fleet. Cumberland himself was required to prepare the troops in London.

But the Admiral, now almost eighty-four, considered his orders ill-judged. With the French troops massing at Dunkirk and the invasion expected in Kent or Essex, he knew that the Royal Navy would be much more use up-channel. He therefore sailed his battle squadron for the Kent coast and waited for the French to arrive.

The French had made last-minute changes to their plans, most notable of which was the new landing point – no longer Essex, but up the Thames estuary. Saxe grew nervous; he was apprehensive about the amphibious element in any case. But in the first week of March he received word that the fleet had left Brest and was on its way. He ordered the embarkation at Dunkirk to begin.

The French battle fleet passed the Isle of Wight and, seeing nothing at St Helens, assumed that Norris's ships were riding innocently at anchor in the Solent. Within hours, however, they discovered their mistake. Norris was lying in wait, between them and the embarked troops. While the French were still considering this development, a powerful north-easter blew up. In mid-Channel the French fleet was blown off station and at Dunkirk the troop transports were driven ashore, some capsizing and many men being drowned. Only Norris, close to the shelter of the North Downs, was able to keep some semblance of cohesion, though many ships broke away and others dragged their anchors.

The gales lasted for two or three days, by which time the French fleet was totally dispersed and beginning to creep back towards Brest. Saxe was told to postpone the expedition *sine die*. With considerably more zeal for the task, he turned to plans for a new land campaign.

If Saxe was relieved to see the invasion plans abandoned, there was one man in France who felt bitterly disappointed. He stood dejectedly on the French cliffs at Gravelines and stared across the Channel towards England. He was the Young Pretender, Charles Edward Stuart.

It was Charles Edward who had originally urged the French to invade. His father James, the Pretender, aided by France and Spain, had hoped to take the English throne in 1715; then the Atterbury Plot had been discovered and the Jacobite rising thwarted. The Treaty of Utrecht had included a clause forcing the French and Spanish to acknowledge the Hanoverian supremacy and also requiring them to expel James. He had found refuge in Rome, and it was there, in December, 1720, that Charles Edward was born, the first of two sons for James and his wife, a Polish-born princess.

James had rather lost enthusiasm, but his elder son was now taking up the cause. It was his supporters who had exaggerated the anti-Hanoverian feeling among the English, and Charles Edward's readiness to believe them that had encouraged the French to plan their invasion. But the Young Pretender had been less of a help, more of an irritant to Saxe in his preparations; pilots, for instance, promised by the English Jacobites, had not turned up in Dunkirk, and those who did Saxe judged untrustworthy. And now, even when the whole project had been cancelled, Charles Edward was reluctant to accept the fact. Saxe was glad to be rid of him.

But the Young Pretender had not given up all hope. Surrounded as always by a fawning ring of Jacobites exiled with his father from Britain, he began to make new plans. Within eighteen months he would be on his way to an encounter with the Duke of Cumberland.

# 5

# Captain-General

THE FRENCH INVASION had been checked, but there were few in London who thought that France would not try again. Saxe was thought to be already planning a new campaign, and the French fleet had returned more or less intact to Brest. When news came of a naval battle off the French port of Toulon, it at first appeared that Britain's Mediterranean fleet, under Admiral Mathews, had scored a useful victory over both the French and the Spanish fleets, but later reports showed this to be illusory. The new French arrogance remained undented. No one was surprised, therefore, when Louis XV of France declared war on Britain and on Maria Theresa in the early spring of 1744.

In London, Cumberland and the troops had been stood down once the immediate threat of invasion receded. It had been an anxious but frustrating time for the keen young soldier, and, had he but known it, would later be seen as typical of this year of setbacks for his military aspirations. Nevertheless, it was a time when he learnt many a useful lesson in the political arts and in the limitations of a constitutional monarchy. Although instinctively loyal to his father, and thus no doubt appreciative of the loyalty Carteret showed to the King, he now saw that a politician required much more than royal backing – that Carteret was beginning to pay the price for neglecting his political friends. The King, though he grumbled, was shrewd enough to realize this too, and would eventually accept the inevitable.

Thus, while his thoughts turned towards the next campaign against the French, Cumberland was forced to remain a spectator at the political ringside. Carteret's most vociferous opponent was William Pitt, but there were many others in both Houses. Carteret was attacked for his extravagance, for handing out subsidies without being able to produce results, but most of all for keeping his parliamentary colleagues in the dark. He would have to go.

Eventually, of course, the King gave in. In November, 1744, Carteret was dismissed – or the Earl of Granville as he had become, having inherited the title in October. Lord Harrington took over as Secretary of State (North). But that was not the only change in the administration, for Newcastle and his brother used this opportunity to strengthen their position further: they found places in the government for miscellaneous friends and allies such as Lord Chesterfield, the Duke of Bedford and George Bubb Dodington. Justifiably called the 'Broad Bottom Administration' it even included a few Tories. Only Pitt, the dangerous one, was excluded. Reluctantly, the King agreed to all the changes.

Cumberland was horrified at the way his father was outmanoeuvred and humiliated by his ministers; he told Lord Orford that he deplored their attitude and 'hoped never to see such practice again.'[1] It was a vain hope.

Just as frustrating was the news coming from the Low Countries, where the weakening of Saxe's army offered an opportunity to exploit trouble. Like the King himself, Cumberland wanted to confront the French again. But the King was dissuaded from going by his ministers; and, perhaps out of pique, perhaps out of concern that his son had not yet fully recovered his health, he refused to let Cumberland go. In the Low Countries the British troops, with a few additions, had been put under the command of Field-Marshal Wade. The old soldier was gouty and worn out; the Dutch were reluctant to share their duties in the Pragmatic Army but he was unequal to the task of persuading them. His contingents spent the summer manoeuvring to little purpose, and at the end of 1744 he resigned.

Exasperated by the political intriguing and by his exclusion from active military service, Cumberland had continued to busy himself with matters pertaining to his colonelcy of the Foot Guards. His personal experience of battle had demonstrated the vital importance of discipline, and he was determined that this should begin at the top. Ignoring the resistance of his officers, he turned much of his attention to improving their professional standards.

But he also began to extend his social life. While continuing as often as he could to slip away to his little lodge at Windsor, to hunt and shoot, he regularly joined Amelia and her friends for cards and lively gaming sessions. He visited the Prince of Wales at Cliveden, Carlton House and Kew, and accompanied his brother to one of the earliest of cricket matches, when Kent played All England at the Artillery Ground. And, possibly, he enjoyed a summer romance with Ann Montagu.

The lady in question was some six years older than Cumberland, a daughter of Lord Halifax. According to Horace Walpole, they met while taking the waters at Cheltenham, and soon became the subject of speculation. She was reported to have claimed she was expecting his child. Lady Townshend, a pretty unreliable old gossip at best, embroidered the story by hinting that Ann suffered a miscarriage. Some writers suggested that she was already choosing her ladies-in-waiting; if so, she was soon disappointed. By the end of August the affair was said to be over. Ann subsequently made an unexceptionable but not very brilliant marriage to Mr Joseph Jekyll of Dallington, a Northamptonshire neighbour.

There was a happier conclusion that summer to an equally scandalous romance between one of Cumberland's childhood friends, Lady Caroline Lennox, and Henry Fox, whose future lay closely entwined with that of the Duke. Caroline was a great-granddaughter of Charles II, and her father was the Duke of Richmond; Fox was a politician, eighteen years her senior, with a reputation as something of a wastrel. The couple were married secretly, against her parents' wishes, but it was to prove a lasting and felicitous match.

Suddenly, early in 1745, the situation in Europe changed. The Bavarian Elector Charles VII died − the man whom the French had supported as Holy Roman Emperor. Now the Habsburg cause would certainly prevail, in the person of Maria Theresa's husband, Francis of Lorraine; but the French remained to be convinced.

Meeting in January, 1745, one of the first tasks facing the Broad Bottom ministry was to agree on a policy for Europe. It proved to be virtually unchanged from the one pursued by Carteret, and was rapidly approved by Parliament: Britain would continue to back Maria Theresa, directly with subsidies and indirectly with troops. Even Pitt now supported a continuation of the war against the French in Flanders. The Hanoverians would still be involved, but their troops would now be paid by Maria Theresa, aided by an increased subsidy from Britain. There was still, however, the problem of who should lead the allied troops against the French.

The King suggested Lord Stair. Maria Theresa suggested Marshal Königsegg. But the Dutch did not favour the septuagenarian Marshal. The Earl of Chesterfield was sent to The Hague for urgent negotiations. His prime task was to ensure Dutch commitment to the war; fearful of French aggression spilling over the border, they showed alarming signs of wanting to back out of their obligations. His talks were successful; not only did the Dutch agree to contribute troops, they agreed that the allied army should be commanded by the Duke of Cumberland.

Cumberland had not yet reached his twenty-fourth birthday. Although he had shown courage and a cool head under fire at Dettingen, he was undeniably lacking in experience; he would, however, be able to rely for advice on Königsegg who, for diplomatic reasons, was named commander *ad latus* or on a level with Cumberland. On 6 March, 1745, the King approved Cumberland's appointment as 'Captain-General of all His Majesty's land forces which are or shall be employed abroad in conjunction with the forces which are or shall be employed abroad in conjunction with the troops of His Majesty's allies.' One month later he would be on his way to Europe.

The office of Captain-General had last been held by Marlborough, who died the year after Cumberland's birth. A prestigious and high-sounding title, it was in fact more honorific than executive: there were no clearly defined responsibilities, no established powers or subordinate staff. Since the King was the constitutional head of his armed forces, Cumberland was merely Commander-in-Chief in the field; but he also carried the duties of chief of staff, responsible for tendering advice to the King.

In financial matters the Captain-General had no powers whatsoever: all payments were authorized by the Treasury, ultimately by Parliament. The supply of guns and ammunition to both army and navy was overseen by the Master General of the Ordnance, a largely political post held in 1745 by the Duke of Montagu. Nor did the Captain-General have any overall control of appointments, though as we shall see Cumberland would make his influence felt here as elsewhere. About forty army officers were MPs, and many other posts within the army were subject to the political spoils system: in effect, sinecures awarded for favours received. The King himself jealously guarded his prerogative of giving commissions, approving promotions and making appointments, allocating the regimental colonelcies and the many military governorships of fortresses and garrisons at home and abroad. More and more, however, he would learn to rely on his son for advice. Cumberland, in short, would make the office of Captain-General very much his own.

As Captain-General Cumberland earned no extra pay, but as Commander-in-Chief in the field he did receive £10 a day, together with the unprecedented sum of £5,000 to cover the necessary expenses of acquiring and supporting a military household (his civil household was separately financed). He also continued to receive about £1,000 a year as Colonel of the 1st Foot Guards.

For a young man it was a huge challenge, and Cumberland would have been less than human if he did not feel twinges of doubt at what lay ahead of him. But his old friend and governor, Stephen Poyntz, who knew him as well as anybody alive, was certain that he could meet the challenge; he told Lord Trevor, Minister at The Hague, that he was 'thoroughly and heartily convinced of the Duke's prudence.'[2] Besides, there was too little time for Cumberland to dwell on doubts; the Captain-General's presence was urgently required in Flanders. The campaigning season was about to start, and he had yet to meet not only the British troops but also his fellow Commander-in-Chief, Königsegg, and Prince Waldeck, commander of the Dutch field force. A German-born professional soldier of forty-two, Waldeck had seen considerable service, but a number of very elderly Dutch generals were bitterly resentful of his appointment and disinclined to acknowledge him as their legitimate leader.

By contrast with this hotch-potch array of military leaders, none of them likely to offer disinterested advice, he had already assembled a group of men on whom he could rely and who in most cases proved worthy of his trust. One of the key figures in his life at this time was Sir Everard Fawkener. A man of affairs, a former ambassador to Constantinople and friend to Voltaire, Fawkener possessed not only a considerable European reputation but a practical knowledge of state affairs. Cultured and cosmopolitan, there was no one better to handle the new Captain-General's voluminous correspondence with secretaries of state, foreign rulers and diplomats. Cumberland's military correspondence, on the other hand, was dealt with by Major Robert Napier, formerly with Lord Stair's staff; he was an experienced, level-headed man, a glutton for work and totally loyal. He was the channel for all Cumberland's dealings with the Secretary at War. In the field he issued operational orders and it was he who, for the first time, codified administrative, disciplinary and tactical practice. He also seems to have had the duty of co-ordinating the work of Cumberland's numerous aides-de-camp, who on the whole were distinguished more for their social and political weight than for their professional military merit − men like George Townshend and Henry Seymour Conway, most of whom came from prominent Whig families and had commissions in the Guards.

The army of which Cumberland now took command was about 45,000 strong, including 16,000 British troops (out of a total home establishment of 28,000), and the rest mainly Dutch and Hanoverian. Although Austria possessed a huge army, Maria Theresa had that winter recalled the main part of her force in Flanders to meet other threats to her realms; old Königsegg had been left with just eight squadrons of cavalry and two companies of Frei Corps. Against them was ranged the mighty French force under Marshal Saxe, estimated in April, 1745, to be 80,000, already assembling with menacing intent for the encounter in Flanders.

It was high time the new Captain-General took up the challenge.

# 6

# Fontenoy

IN A GLARE OF PUBLICITY Cumberland prepared to leave England. On 12 April, 1745, he received the sacrament at a public service at St Martin-in-the-Fields. He sent off an advance party to prepare lodgings for him in Brussels and to pick up six horses en route for 'purveyors, cooks, confectioners and other servants whose business requires more diligence than wheel carriages can make.'[1] With £1000 a month table money, Cumberland planned to offer considerably more lavish hospitality than his predecessor, Wade, whose meanness in 1744 had been noted by the ever critical Colonel Russell of the 1st Foot Guards. Five days later, early in the morning of the 17th, Cumberland himself left London with an impressive retinue: thirteen coaches, a hundred horses, including his iron-grey charger called The Lizard, and twenty-eight pack animals with a total weight of 140 tons baggage, all to be shipped from Harwich to Hellevoetsluis, a small port south of The Hague, at a cost of £400.

What Cumberland was thinking, as his coach rattled along behind the team of six horses, with Sir Everard Fawkener at his side, can never be known; but it is probably fair to suggest that his feelings were a compound of pride, excitement, apprehension and sheer thankfulness that the moment of departure had come at last. Perhaps he reviewed his objectives as Captain-General, to fight the land campaign in Europe and defend the home base, and looked forward to discussing tactics with the allied generals.

His first destination was The Hague, where he visited his sister Anne, Princess of Orange, with one small daughter to show for eleven years of marriage. But the visit was not entirely a personal one. Cumberland was assessing the Dutch resolve to fight, and what he learnt was not encouraging. The Dutch government, the States General, had led Chesterfield to expect an army of 44,000, instead of the 22,000 placed under Waldeck. Besides, most of the Dutch troops were on garrison duty in border fortresses like Mons, Tournai, Ostend and Ath, and they could not be redeployed by

Waldeck without the authority of the States General. The Prince of Orange, though amicable enough towards his brother-in-law, was similarly constrained by constitutional requirements, as well as by the prevailing Dutch ambivalence towards war with France.

Cumberland reached Brussels a few days later and was immediately plunged into critical discussions. Königsegg had received intelligence of enemy manoeuvres around Mons, only forty miles south-west of Brussels. The Captain-General agreed with Königsegg that the allies should concentrate in front of Brussels. While the orders were still being formulated, however, there came further reports, confusing and sometimes contradictory, of enemy troops withdrawing from Mons, encamped near Leuze, approaching Tournai. By 29 April it was clear that Tournai was most threatened, the great fortress on the River Scheldt. Cumberland called a council of war in his lodgings in Brussels.

The assembled council included Königsegg, Waldeck and General de Wendt, commanding the Hanoverians, as well as Sir John Ligonier, the very experienced general of the British infantry, and Sir James Campbell, general of the British cavalry. They agreed that Saxe's aim was to besiege Tournai, although no French troops had yet encamped or unloaded stores; that his main source of supply was at Maubeuge, some fifty miles away; and that the best chance of success lay in cutting his communication with Maubeuge and then moving against Tournai from the south-east. The orders went out to the allied troops: on the following day, 30 April, they were to start the march south from Brussels.

Cumberland and Waldeck accompanied the troops as they moved out along the main road towards Halle, but progress was slow and Waldeck returned that night to Brussels. Cumberland and the troops continued southwards on the road to Soignies. It was a frustrating business, hampered by constant rain that turned the dirt roads into quagmires. Despite parties of pioneers at the head of each column, to make the necessary ouvertures for wagons and limbers, the long chaotic snake of cavalry, infantry, artillery and baggage was repeatedly halted and literally bogged down. Meanwhile reports continued to reach Cumberland that Saxe was preparing to lay siege to Tournai. The Captain-General turned his column westwards. Although following minor roads, progress here was faster as the column found room to divide into three, moving roughly parallel. Advance parties found a French detachment at Leuze and quickly sent the enemy packing. Now, however, the allied supplies were lost; in the muddle there was an uneven distribution of rations, and discipline, already shaky, began to break. Men left the line to forage for food, and officers took to shooting game.

On 8 May, Cumberland wrote to Newcastle, 'I cannot bring myself to believe the enemy will wait for us.'[2] But the eager young soldier would not

1.  "Caroline was a strong personality". Queen Caroline and her beloved
William aged 10. (*W. Aikman, Hardwick Hall*)

2. "A good scholar" with "a naval career" ahead. Cumberland as a teenager. (*Amigoni, Private Collection*)

3.  Dettingen, 1743: "The Prince of Wales was generous enough to have his brother's portrait painted" and hung in Leicester House. The painter is probably showing Cumberland's Regiment, The First Guards, on the right, though they saw little action and complained of the King's neglect.

4. King George II, Elector of Hanover. "George II had complete faith in Cumberland." (*John Shackleton*)

be deprived of a battle. Saxe was lying in wait — literally lying, carried on a litter, for he was ill with 'the stone'.

While the French King Louis XV and the Dauphin arrived at Lille to watch the coming battle from the sidelines, Saxe had drawn up a plan to meet the allies east of Tournai and north of the River Scheldt. Although considerably hampered by the royal presence, as well as his own indisposition, Saxe deployed his troops with care. Having decided to hold a line six miles long, he ordered earth redoubts to be dug, some revetted and fortified, for his artillery. His infantry he disposed in hamlets and woods along the line, with gun batteries in a salient projecting towards the village of Fontenoy. Between Fontenoy and a wood some 800 yards to the west, the Barri wood, Saxe lined up more infantry in a sunken lane below the crest of a slight ridge, and the crack Regiment D'Eu he placed in a special redoubt hidden behind the tip of the wood. The French artillery would be supported by heavy siege guns, firing from across the river, and reserves of both men and *matériel* were already in the area for the attempt to take Tournai. It was this formidable defensive position that the allies planned to attack from the front.

On 9 May Cumberland and his generals had decided to make a three-pronged attack, with himself and the British taking the right (western) flank, the Hanoverians to their left, and the Dutch taking the easternmost flank. They quickly ran into the French outposts. After another pouring wet night these frontline positions were captured; the enemy survivors withdrew to their main positions beyond Fontenoy and behind the low ridge. Pending the results of overnight reconnaissance on the 10th/11th, the allies agreed to continue the attack as before, with Cumberland's wing on the right. His flank would thus take the brunt of Saxe's counterattack.

That night Cumberland's patrols reported the presence of gun batteries in Fontenoy, and further reconnoitring uncovered the existence of the Redoubt D'Eu, beyond the tip of Barri wood. Cumberland realized that both batteries and redoubt would have to be taken before he could unleash his assault column on the main French encampment below the ridge. He detailed a senior officer from his own regiment, Brigadier Ingoldsby, with four battalions of infantry, to advance at first light and capture the redoubt.

Early on the morning of 11 May Cumberland was on the battlefield, eager for news from Ingoldsby. But Ingoldsby had found the edge of the wood held by Saxe's irregular infantry and was hesitant about making an attack. The Captain-General sent his ADCs with encouraging messages — to no avail. Ingoldsby sent the aides back with requests for artillery. Eventually Cumberland could wait no longer. Over to his left it seemed the Dutch had begun to penetrate the village of Fontenoy, and they needed immediate support. He ordered two of Ingoldsby's battalions into the village with the

Dutch and sent Ligonier with the bulk of the infantry into a frontal attack on the lines. Cumberland himself encouraged the men not only with words but with his very presence: wherever the action was thickest, he was there in person. The British held their fire until the range had closed; despite the enemy guns, their discipline was good. The French lines were pulverized. The British broke through the enemy positions, but then met attacks from front and flank by the French cavalry.

This, Ligonier later said, was the critical moment. He thought the battle was won. The French troops were crumbling; whole regiments were breaking and running pell-mell past their sovereign. A serried mass of scarlet had invaded the French encampment. The British had rallied once more and fought off the enemy cavalry. But the Dutch advance had stalled and still the French cannon pounded the oncoming allies. Worse was yet to come.

Saxe's gunners were running very short of ammunition and within an ace of being taken from the rear; but to the west there now came support from General Lowendal, a tough Danish mercenary who now brought some of the fourteen reserve battalions to Saxe's rescue.

Cumberland was forced to withdraw. He had lost his cavalry commander, General Campbell, and was unable to manoeuvre his cavalry either through or round the village of Fontenoy; his hireling artillery drivers had decamped under fire. Now his right flank was in contact with Lowendal's fresh battalions. The British infantry were taking mounting casualties; without support from the Dutch or from the cavalry or artillery, they faced annihilation. Coolly the young Captain-General sent off a force of two regiments of infantry and a regiment of cavalry to hold a defile to their rear, then gave the order to retire.

It had been a costly battle for both sides. The French had lost 7,500; the British and Hanoverians combined had lost 5,600 killed or wounded, and the Dutch about 1,500. And for Cumberland the battle had ended in defeat.

The moment was bitter. As he watched his weary troops retreating towards Ath, supporting their wounded friends, it is said that he broke down. One of his aides, Joseph Yorke, a son of Lord Hardwicke, reported later that his master's eyes were 'bountiful of tears as he lamented the fate of so many of his countrymen.'[3] His concern was no mere sentiment; he did all he could for the wounded lying still on the battlefield, ordering as many as possible to be taken to the nearby Château de Briffeil, where he sent the regimental surgeons to tend to them, along with wagonloads of food and other necessaries.

However, to Cumberland's fury, the surgeons and their mates were taken prisoner, their instruments and medical chests stolen, the rations plundered by the French. As soon as he heard, he made the strongest representations to Saxe about his men's behaviour. Cumberland had also been enraged to learn that many of the wounded had been hit by irregular bullets and shell fillings. He collected some of the pieces of metal, stone and glass that the surgeons had removed from wounds and placed them in a wooden case, bound it in leather, then sealed it with the seals of the allied commanders and sent it to Saxe in the care of Joseph Yorke. Yorke also carried a personal and sharply worded note from his master in which Cumberland accused the French of deliberate breaches of the 1743 agreement, signed by Marshal Noailles, which had sought to improve treatment of the injured and any prisoners in enemy hands. Appealing to the humanity of Louis XV, Cumberland signed the note 'your affectionate friend'.

Saxe retorted equally sharply. The agreement had been broken by the British first. The French Maréchal Belleisle had been taken prisoner the previous winter, when he mistakenly entered Hanover, and had been removed in custody to Windsor. As to the actions of his troops, Saxe could not be held responsible. But the French King gave Cumberland a softer response, assuring Joseph Yorke that the wounded and prisoners would be looked after well. And, from then on, for the most part they were. In fact, one Benedictine priest at Douai was so assiduous in his care of English prisoners that Cumberland promised him special protection if he should ever come to England. Father Alban was to use this indulgence.

In the battle's immediate aftermath, Cumberland was apt to lay much of the blame on Ingoldsby who, by failing to obey orders, had contributed to the initial delays and confusion. He had the brigadier court-martialled for disobedience, but Ingoldsby was found guilty on a lesser charge, error of judgement, and was suspended from duty for three months; it was, however, the effective end of his career.

When his fury over Ingoldsby had cooled, and his ADCs and generals had all made their reports, Cumberland eventually came to the conclusion that the blame for defeat at Fontenoy lay rather with the Dutch. Waldeck had been a most lethargic commander; although making the attack on Fontenoy as agreed, he had failed to press it home, thus leaving Cumberland vulnerable on his left flank and blocking the way for the allied cavalry and artillery. According to old Königsegg, who was so exhausted after the battle that Cumberland lent him his carriage, only one Dutch battalion had made any progress under fire, and when they took cover in a ditch the whole Dutch advance had stalled. As for the Dutch cavalry, some had bolted when the French artillery opened up and the civil contractor hauling the British artillery had likewise fled. Königsegg did not blame Cumberland for defeat. In his despatch to Maria Theresa, he commended the allied attack plan as sound and the measures taken as appropriate; the failure in execution he blamed roundly on the Dutch.

Cumberland felt 'great uneasiness' he admitted to his sister, the Princess of Orange, about how his father would react to this defeat at French hands. But the King was in happy mood when the official despatch arrived in London, as he was just leaving for his beloved Hanover, and he took the news calmly. He was further reassured by the numerous and enthusiastic reports of his son's conduct as Captain-General.

Undoubtedly Cumberland had shown a dazzling display of personal courage. His horse was hit three times during the battle, and he was struck by a spent bullet on the elbow. One of his supernumerary ADCs, Richard Lyttelton, wrote:

> The Duke was everywhere and that he escaped was a miracle. He rallied the troops when broken and made a stand which saved the army from being entirely cut to pieces. I had the honour of being with him the whole day except when he sometimes sent me with orders. Nothing was ever like the fire, both cannon and small arms. Dettingen was play to it.[5]

Another eyewitness, an officer in the Blues, described the battle to the *Reading Mercury*:

> Cumberland was by turns on every spot of ground on the field of battle, giving his orders with the utmost resolution and firmness of mind. He exposed himself to the greatest danger like a grenadier.[6]

Henry Seymour Conway, MP, also in Cumberland's regiment and another of his aides, was similarly impressed; writing to his cousin, Horace Walpole, he described how his chief 'exposed himself wherever the fire was hottest and flying wherever he saw our troops fail to lead 'em himself and encourage 'em by his example.' But certain members of the older generation reacted more pompously to reports of Cumberland's behaviour. Henry Pelham wrote solemnly:

> ... I cannot conclude this letter without begging leave to implore your R.H. not to expose your Royal Person upon any further engagement more than the necessity of the scene and the immediate occasion shall require. Your life is of too much consequence to your Royal family, your country and your faithful servants to be equally hazarded in every action.[7]

Cumberland was probably more touched by a message from the Prince of Wales, conveying through Lord Baltimore the Prince's satisfaction at his brother's safe deliverance.

There was, in short, no criticism whatever of the Duke of Cumberland after Fontenoy. While he regrouped his troops at Lessines, the government at home was already ordering reinforcements to be sent to him as soon as possible. Reports circulated in London not only of his bravery but of the energetic measures he took to reward good service and look after his men. A trooper of the Blues who was dismounted in battle but continued to fight on foot in the ranks of the 1st Guards he rewarded with a £5 bounty from his own pocket. Another who fought in the Welsh Fusiliers was given a commission on the spot. The son of a man killed in the battle was given an ensign's commission in the Guards. A formal vote of thanks was proposed by the Lords Justice, the regency council who ruled in the King's absence, commending 'that spirit of humanity which appears in all H.R.H.'s actions and the justice he has done to those who have deserved so well of him and their country.'[8] Even Horace Walpole, ever ambivalent towards Cumberland, had to admit:

> All the letters are full of the Duke's humanity and bravery; he will be as popular with the lower class of men as he has been for three or four years with the low women.[9]

At Lessines Cumberland continued his efforts to restore order and morale among his troops, and fretted about the wounded, including two of his aides, who had both been hit in the face: William Kerr, Earl of Ancrum, a personable young Scot who served as a captain with the 1st Regiment of Foot Guards, and Charles Lord Cathcart, 3rd Foot Guards, whose father had died on the way to the West Indies in 1740. Cathcart had in fact lost an eye, and would in future be known as 'Patch'.

On 22 May, still at Lessines, Cumberland wrote to the Princess of Orange:

> Dear Sister, I hope that the hurry of business that I have been in for this last week will plead my pardon for not having writ before, but the care of the wounded & the changing of Regiments has taken up all my time.
>
> All the account that I can give is that the Allies have been within a trifle of destroying the whole French army, of taking King, Cannon & Bagage.
>
> The Right Wing did their duty & have lost between five and six thousand men, & good men they were, how to recruit them is the difficulty now.[10]

Going on to praise Königsegg ('I am as great an admirer of his as anybody can be, he seems very fond of me & I am greatly flattered by it'), he says nothing at all about Waldeck or the Dutch troops – but the inference is abundantly clear.

*51*

Fawkener told Newcastle confidentially that Cumberland and Waldeck were at odds and Cumberland criticized him mildly as 'a little obstinate and not very deep.'[11] But as the weeks passed the mutual antagonism deepened. The allies were increasingly under pressure now and Waldeck, unhappy about Cumberland's new priorities, ceased to communicate with the young Captain-General. Cumberland vented some of his frustration in a letter to his sister Amelia, describing one incident during the retreat when 'the Goats' had risked being overrun by the French; the 'Chief Goats' had left their post and anyway 'are not animals to give spirit.' 'Now you have my whole letter except the name of Goats,' he finishes, 'but that they so well deserve that I beg they may go by that name in the future.'[12]

Because of Waldeck's sulks, Cumberland could not correctly ascertain the Dutch order of battle. The heavy losses sustained by the allied armies at Fontenoy had forced them on to the defensive: in mid-June it was calculated that Saxe had 133 battalions and 204 squadrons, while the British, Hanoverians and Dutch had only 55 battalions and 55 squadrons. But many of the Dutch troops were being confined to static duties in garrison, and Cumberland could not rely on them to play an active part in the coming campaign. If the French pushed forward, as they undoubtedly would, Cumberland foresaw that he would have to withdraw north to the Antwerp area and defend a line behind the Bruges canal. However, this realistic plan was rejected by the Austrian governor-general of Brussels, the formidable Count Kaunitz, who wanted Cumberland to make his stand further south, naturally enough, to protect Brussels. Even with the reinforcements due to arrive from England, Cumberland's defensive line was likely to be dangerously stretched.

It was now, in early July, 1745, when Cumberland was struggling to reconcile the conflicting aims of the allied commanders, that a disturbing new factor entered his calculations. Charles Edward Stuart, the Young Pretender, was on the loose. He had left France for a destination as yet unknown, but the presumption was that he planned to raise a new Jacobite army in Britain.

# 7

# The Rebellion of '45

EVER SINCE THE ABORTIVE EXPEDITION OF 1744, Charles Edward Stuart had been looking for another opportunity to launch his claim on the British throne. Though officially cold-shouldered by Louis XV and his ministers, he had been living openly in Paris; but now he was convinced that his chance had come. Not only had the French trounced the British and their allies at Fontenoy, but the British themselves seemed ripe for rebellion. As always the Young Pretender was surrounded by Jacobite exiles and other sympathizers, many of them of Irish origin like Lord Clare, whose regiment had fought for France at Fontenoy. They and their agents had been stirring up Jacobite sentiments in Britain, particularly in the Highlands, where Scotsmen were even now being recruited for the cause. Moreover, George II was in Hanover and his army was in Flanders, fighting a losing battle under Cumberland. There could hardly be a better time. On 5 July (OS) he sailed from Britanny, heading for the west coast of Scotland.

The fresh upsurge in Jacobite activity had, of course, been noted in London. General Guest, the octogenarian governor of Edinburgh Castle, passed on reports of treasonable correspondence between clan chieftains and Jacobites in Paris, and further reports of active recruitment for the Jacobite regiment commanded by Lord John Drummond. But London's reaction was divided.

The Lords Justice possessed only limited powers and depended largely on long-distance orders from the King. They comprised chiefly members of the cabinet – at this time notably Henry Pelham, his brother Newcastle and Lord Granville – but also the Archbishop of Canterbury and Field-Marshal Lord Stair. Newcastle, always excitable, was prone to take the rumours of rebellion seriously, and Pelham tended to share his fears. But they were outnumbered. Stair, whose opinion as an experienced soldier was given due weight, was not disposed to believe the rumours. Lord Tweeddale, the Secretary of State for Scotland, similarly made light of the danger, despite

the worries of Sir John Cope, commander-in-chief in North Britain, whose scattered garrisons contained no more than 2,000-3,000 effective fighting men. Tweeddale's position was supported by Duncan Forbes, Laird of Culloden, who was Lord President of the Court of Session.

Initially, therefore, London's response to reports of a planned rebellion was sceptical. And Cumberland, for his part, was probably too busy to register the full extent of the danger at home.

Cumberland's problems in July, 1745, were increasing almost by the day. Saxe and his subordinate commander, Lowendal, the Danish mercenary, with their superior forces had already taken the border fortress town of Tournai and were rampaging across Flanders: Ghent and Bruges were clearly in their sights. Cumberland was obliged to retreat northwards. To keep Kaunitz happy in Brussels he set up his headquarters at nearby Vilvorden, but the bulk of his army was now strung out behind the Bruges canal. He evidently considered the possibility of making his stand at Antwerp, for he sent a promising young infantry officer seconded to engineering duties – Captain Caroline Scott, of whom we shall hear more – to survey the city's fortifications. Although Scott's report was favourable, Cumberland's hand was forced by a new threat, to the port of Ostend.

Ostend was crucial to Cumberland's communications with Britain and, backed up by Colonel Edward Braddock of the Coldstream Guards, who inspected the port, he asked for the garrison to be strengthened. The Lords Justice agreed that two battalions should be despatched immediately. Cumberland secured a promise from the old Austrian commander of the garrison that if the French approached he would open the sluices and flood the surrounding land. But the promise was never kept. The French took Ostend in early August.

With events so critical in Flanders, Cumberland had little time to reflect on the growing rumours of a Jacobite invasion, but his instinct was sure. On 28 July he wrote to Newcastle:

> I desire you, that if this pretended design of an invasion should continue, to let me come home with whatever troops are thought necessary, for it would be horrid to be employed abroad when my home was in danger, and really, should it be found proper to detach home to England troops sufficient to secure it, there will be none left to save this little scrap of country we still have here, of the Austrian Netherlands.[1]

In response Newcastle suggested that Cumberland should apply to his father in Hanover and ask for the home command.

The King, however, had failed to see the danger. Irritated by the stream of fretful communications from the Pelhams, he preferred to accept the advice of old soldiers like Stair and Wade. Besides, he felt that Hanover would be safer if the French were engaged in war elsewhere. He wanted his son to continue the campaign in Flanders while Britain's meagre home defences were augmented by 6,000 Dutch troops due under treaty.

Cumberland's view of this can only be surmised. He had seen the Dutch in battle and was not impressed. The battle for the Austrian Netherlands he considered to be a hopeless task, with too small a force and divided allies. Against the advice of Sir John Ligonier, his military mentor, he wanted to renounce the battle and continue the campaign on a more suitable front, but first the priority was to defend the home base. For Cumberland saw what his father apparently did not: that the British throne might be at stake.

Meanwhile, Charles Edward had landed on the mainland of Scotland on 23 July (OS), on the Moidart peninsula some thirty miles west of Fort William. He had sailed from France with two ships, the *Du Teillay* (commonly written *Doutelle*) and *Elisabeth*, the latter carrying most of his arms and other military supplies. But the *Elisabeth* had run into trouble at once, from none other than HMS *Lion*, the ship that had caused the Duke of Cumberland such a rude awakening one night in 1740. Now commanded by Captain Brett, *Lion* had no inkling of the *Elisabeth*'s importance to the Young Pretender and the rebellion, but after a tremendous duel off the Lizard she forced the French ship to retire, damaged.

Charles Edward had thus arrived in Scotland without his arms and ammunition, almost entirely dependent on the good will of the clans and relying on his own charm to win support for the cause. He was lucky. Within a month he had gathered 900 men to witness the raising of his standard at Glenfinnan.

The news of Charles Edward's arrival took some weeks to reach London, but soon Cumberland was being bombarded with messages of increasing urgency. Yet even now there were some who treated it all as a joke. The British minister in The Hague, Robert Trevor, wrote to Cumberland, 'I am sorry to hear that the Young Squire is gone a-shooting grouse in the Highlands.'[2] But the Young Pretender had more than grouse in his sights. Marching eastwards, still charming the clansmen out of the glens, Charles Edward's luck continued to hold. Sir John Cope, belatedly ordered to collect his scattered forces, hurried north to meet the rebel army but veered off towards Inverness – which left the way clear for the rebels to march on Edinburgh. By 17 September (OS) they had entered Edinburgh, having already taken Perth. Cope had returned south and on the 21st, in a ten-minute battle at Prestonpans, the Jacobite army achieved its first victory.

Cumberland was deeply shocked by the news from Prestonpans, and equally frustrated to be still in Flanders. At least the King was now back in

London. Having finally realized the gravity of the situation, George II had returned at the end of August. By this time both he and his ministers were sufficiently frightened to send to Flanders for ten battalions, which Cumberland personally chose and despatched to England under the trusty Ligonier. 'I hope the King will do me the favour to let me come to them,' he wrote to Ligonier.[3] 'Let me know all that can be trusted to paper.'[4] Cumberland had also asked Lord Harrington, the Secretary of State (North) and a man well liked by the King, to use his influence in the closet. After an agonizing wait, Harrington's reply arrived, dated 19 October:

> I have the pleasure to acquaint you that the King consents to your coming home the moment the troops should have entered winter quarters. The King has ordered a yacht with sufficient convoy to Willemstadt to attend your orders.[5]

Cumberland wasted no time. Such troops as were being left behind were already in winter quarters. Most of the British troops, however, were now required at home, to join the 6,000 Dutch troops waiting in the north-east of England. By 21 October Cumberland had embarked no fewer than twenty-five battalions of infantry, twenty-three squadrons of cavalry and four companies of artillery. By the 28th he himself was back in London.

By now all London was nervous, with the notable exception of the King: George II had complete faith in Cumberland and the British army to repel the upstart and his rabble. At first, however, Cumberland was given no active role and was forced to kick his heels impatiently in town. At least it gave him a chance to assess the prevailing mood.

The British people seemed on the whole to be supporting the Hanoverian cause. Although the mainly Tory shires had previously shown a tendency to sympathize with Jacobitism, their antipathy towards Papism was the stronger; with few exceptions, the areas most likely to support the rebels were in Scotland and the north of England. What was harder for Cumberland to fathom was the true state of affairs between the King and his ministers. That the Pelham brothers were disliked by the King was no secret, and the ministers generally were suspicious of the King's activities in Hanover. Pelham twice tried to persuade the King that Pitt should be brought into the ministry as Secretary of War, but George flatly rejected the suggestion, not only because he loathed Pitt but because he feared strengthening Pelham's hand.

Cumberland had no particular reason to dislike Pitt, except out of loyalty to his father. Pitt's abrasive attacks on Hanover and Hanoverians had ceased; his latest hobbyhorse was the need for a stronger navy, which seemed merely perverse when the immediate future clearly called for a land campaign. For the time being Pitt would remain in the wilderness, but Cumberland was coming to respect his abilities.

In fact the young soldier now found himself courted by politicians of every hue, hailed as a man of calm good sense and maturity. Although undoubtedly conscious of being used as a conduit to the King, he was still idealistic enough to hope for a closing of ranks and stability. 'I don't doubt but this alarm will have one good effect,' he wrote to Newcastle on 6 September, 'since it must convince the King of the zeal of his servants and in that regard will be of infinite good.'[6] Later, over the years he would become increasingly impatient with the manoeuvrings of the King's servants, with the bickering and the jostling for power, the sudden espousal and desertion of causes. But another youthful characteristic would stay with him for longer: the tendency to see all things in black and white without any shades of grey. His view of the current crisis was as straightforward as that of Major-General the Duke of Richmond, who said simply: 'We ought to serve the King and save him from destruction, whether he will or no.'[7]

The King himself continued to show remarkably steady nerves although bad news and rumours abounded. Ever since the rebels' victory at Prestonpans, their numbers had been swelling — to 5,000 infantry and about 500 cavalry by mid-October, and there was a constant fear that French reinforcements might arrive by sea. But the King's army was swelling too, with Cumberland's battalions arriving home, as well as the 6,000 Dutch. To Cumberland's astonishment he learnt that the Dutch troops, shipped to the Newcastle-on-Tyne area with Count Nassau in command, had come from Tournai; taken prisoner when their garrison was overrun by the French they had then been released on condition that they did not actually fight.

The government had enacted various measures to meet the emergency, such as suspending habeas corpus and ordering JPs to arrest papists and other suspects. A reward of £30,000 had been offered for the capture of the Young Pretender (who offered a like sum for the capture of 'the Elector of Hanover'). The lords lieutenant had been instructed to array the county militia, although this move was of dubious constitutional legality and equally dubious value; it was argued, for instance, that arming bands of men across the country might be just an indirect way of supplying the rebels. London's defence was better organized; apart from the 'train bands' or city militia, six battalions of guards had been retained in the capital and were reviewed in St James's Park by Cumberland and the King.

After Prestonpans Sir John Cope had retired to Berwick, his men demoralized by defeat at the hands of the ferocious Highlanders. Marshal Wade had now taken command of the northern army, the 10,000 British and Dutch troops from Flanders. They faced a daunting task: to hold the border against an invasion. Luckily the Jacobites had chosen to consolidate their political and logistical base in Edinburgh. Despite the Young Pretender's progress, isolated garrisons continued to hold out against him — in Forts William and Augustus, in Stirling Castle and even in Edinburgh Castle — and he had been persuaded against his own judgement to pursue a policy of caution.

But the army was not prepared for a winter campaign. The troops were ill-provided for and had little if any mobility. Wade's discontented and loquacious second-in-command, Lord Tyrawley, complained of his irresolution and muddle-headedness but admitted that the problem could not all be laid at his door:

> Bread, carriages, straw, firing and even coals for the men I have found wanting — all these for the want of foresight, and parsimony ill-judged for the public that cannot lay out half a crown.[8]

Such problems were too much for a man as old and infirm as Wade. When it became clear, at the end of October, that the rebels were preparing to move south, Wade trembled like a rabbit before a stoat. He knew the clansmen of old; he had spent years in the Highlands after the rising of 1715, building and improving roads, bridges and forts. He knew and feared their fighting skills, their efficiency with the claymore, and he knew how they could survive amid the hills and heather, even in winter, wrapped in their thick plaids and seeming to feed off their own clan loyalties and myth. In London, even in Edinburgh, such men were regarded as savages; to Wade they were real — and now he was going to have to face them.

Cumberland was well aware of the problems facing Wade. With his old friend and mentor Sir John Ligonier, who was to lead the main army in the south — 9,000 strong, to be deployed in the west midlands — he had studied all the Young Pretender's moves in the closest detail. He had also studied Wade's reports from the Highlands in the 1720s and many other government papers concerning Scottish affairs. He was well briefed on the whole background of Jacobite rebellion and Highland history. But Cumberland was obliged to remain in London until the King and his ministers had agreed how best to use his services.

Suppressing his impatience, Cumberland attended not only the anxious Privy Council meetings but the usual court levées and other receptions too. One such was held for the officers of all seven battalions of Foot Guards. Cumberland, attending as both Colonel of the 1st Regiment and Captain-General, witnessed an incident that moved the King to tears. George II bade all the officers gather round him in the throne room and asked if they were prepared to fight for the Hanoverian cause; anyone not prepared to fight should raise his left hand, those willing to fight should indicate with their right. In an instant, all the right hands went up. Though some of the officers might lack the qualities that their enthusiastic young Captain-General required, he certainly approved their loyalty to his father.

On 31 October Cumberland was present at a family reception in St James's Palace. He was wearing 'a general's coat of scarlet and gold' according to one of those present, 'much the same as his ordinary regimentals only with rather more gold.'[9] His sister Amelia was said to be gaily rather than elegantly dressed, but Caroline looked beautiful 'in pink, with flower patterns of green, yellow and silver.' Even the Prince of Wales was there; fretting as usual at his exclusion from an active role in events, yet loyally supporting the King at this time of crisis.

That same day, Charles Edward was making final preparations. On 1 November he and his army left Edinburgh, heading south.

# 8

# Carlisle and Back

THE YOUNG PRETENDER had appointed two commanders of his army, James Drummond, Duke of Perth, and Lord George Murray. The Duke of Perth — a title bestowed by the Pretender, and thus not recognized by the Hanoverians — had been brought up in exile and spoke little English; devoted to the Stuart cause, he was more enthusiastic than experienced in military matters. Murray was the opposite. He proved to be a fine soldier and leader, but his arrogant manner and suspicions over his commitment to the cause led many Jacobites to mistrust him. Not surprisingly, there was mutual dislike between the two commanders, and Charles Edward was forced to keep them apart.

Just south of Edinburgh the rebel army divided. One column, under Perth, went south-west through Peebles and Moffat; the other, under Murray, headed south-east through Lauder towards Kelso. Charles Edward himself went with Murray. It was a deliberate deception, to make the Hanoverians keep their army in the north-east of England — and it worked. Wade kept his troops in Newcastle and, confused by reports that the rebels were making for Carlisle, dithered over his response. By 8 November the Young Pretender's column had swung west and crossed the border south of Canonbie, joined one day later by his other column. The rebels were now in England, at the gates of Carlisle.

Carlisle's meagre defences could offer no hope and the citizens were unprepared for a siege; late on the 14th they hung out the white flag of surrender.

Meanwhile 800 reinforcements had arrived from France, landing at Montrose with Perth's brother, Lord John Drummond, and were marching south to join the rebel army. On the other hand, the rebels had seen widespread desertion on their way to the border: their numbers were certainly below 5,000. The Hanoverian army was four times the size, and, moreover, had begun to recover from the first shock of defeat. In Scotland

Lieutenant-General Handasyde had gathered a force of loyal Hanoverians and was already threatening the rebel base at Edinburgh.

By this time Wade had started to march westwards. But his opponent's luck still held. Snow and ice had blocked the passes and forced the northern army to turn back at Hexham. The southern army started to move north through Staffordshire, but its commander, Ligonier, was ill. At last the King and his ministers agreed that the young Captain-General should take over from Ligonier.

Cumberland reacted with commendable calmness. Instead of dashing north at once, he reviewed the situation with Ligonier himself, with Lord Stair and other advisers. While London consumed itself with nerves, he gathered reports on the rebels' numbers and likely moves. Then, even as Charles Edward moved south from Carlisle, Cumberland left London to take up his post as head of the King's southern army.

On 28 November Cumberland arrived in Lichfield with three ADCs who had been with him at Fontenoy: Henry Seymour Conway; William Kerr, Earl of Ancram; and Charles 'Patch' Cathcart. The Captain-General's arrival was greeted with delight by the troops, who regarded Fontenoy as a glorious defeat and Cumberland as a hero.

Except for one brigade of guards under Colonel Braddock, all Cumberland's force was assembled, billeted over a wide area of Staffordshire: fourteen battalions, three regiments of horse and three of dragoons. Wade, moving slowly down the eastern side of the Pennines, hampered by the reluctant Dutch, was still in Yorkshire. Almost parallel with him, the rebels were also moving south, entering Manchester on 29 November. As Conway told his cousin Horace Walpole in a letter, a decisive encounter was now inevitable.

Cumberland knew that Manchester was a Jacobite town; here Charles Edward would gain more recruits and gather his forces in preparation for his next move. This, it was rumoured, would be to march into Wales to gather more recruits and also to meet up with 5,000 French troops arriving in the Bristol Channel. But Cumberland's forward screen had broken all the bridges across the Mersey, from Warrington to Cheadle, despite the protests of local tradesmen, and blocked all the roads with fallen trees; if the rebels still meant to move south-west the going would not be easy. If, however, they moved east they would meet the combined force of Cumberland and Wade. 'They might think of trying to slip us,' Conway wrote on 30 November, 'but they are now quite out of that road.'

> They can't think of Chester while we are so near and I can't think 'em mad enough to go into Wales, where both armies must block 'em up: and

therefore they must, in my opinion, either engage us or retire immediately.[1]

He was quite wrong.

Although Cumberland was planning to force an encounter on a field of his own choosing, for a set-piece battle that would inevitably favour his own more disciplined troops, he needed an area of open land, free from the enclosures, ditches, hills and bogs that would prevent the infantry from forming up in serried ranks as they were trained to do and the cavalry from making their intimidating charge. The Duke of Richmond, who commanded the advance guard at Newcastle-under-Lyme, recommended a suitable area: near Stone, to the north of Stafford.

On the night of 2 December Cumberland dined with the Earl of Albemarle, father of his aide George Keppel, Lord Bury, who was also Colonel of the Coldstream Guards, and Thomas Anson, brother of Commodore George Anson who had completed his famous circumnavigation of the globe only a year before. Anson, whose home at Shugborough was not far from Cumberland's Lichfield headquarters, wrote to the Commodore that he found all 'in spirits and jollity' and impatient for action. The next day Cumberland gave the order to march on Stone.

On the 4th Anson wrote to his brother again, but this time with bad news. He had gone to Stone to witness the battle that morning, 'and met crowds of people coming back in consternation who cried out it was begun':

> I heard no firing. When I came I found all the troops in and about the town upon heaps. I forced my way to the Duke's quarters where I learned that the rebels were at Leek at 1 this morning and 'tis supposed will be at Derby tonight. The troops were all returning in great haste.[2]

The rebel army was indeed in Derby that night. Partly because it was a smaller force than Cumberland's, it could move more quickly. The rebels had also captured one of Cumberland's agents, John Weir, who had been forced to betray his master's plans. Anson heard exaggerated reports of the rebel numbers — 'not above 7,000, about 3-4,000 good troops, the rest rabble and boys' — and even had news of their leader:

> The Pretender's son... is something under 6 foot high, wears a plaid, walks well, a good person enough but a melancholy aspect, speaks little and was never seen to smile.[3]

Charles Edward had good reason to look gloomy. By jinking east to Derby, he had hoped to avoid a confrontation with Cumberland, perhaps even to reach London before the Hanoverian troops could catch him. But he now realized his mistake.

Cumberland had immediately turned his men back towards London. Tired as they were, his men readily did his bidding; he was 'justly their darling' according to Joseph Yorke, 'for they see he does whatever the meanest of them does and goes thro' as much fatigue.'[4] At the same time Cumberland wrote to the King, advising him to assemble the London garrison at Finchley — Ligonier suggested a defended line of field works at Barnet — and announcing his intention of making for Northampton via Lichfield. By 6 December he was at Meriden, near Coventry, when he heard that the rebels had left Derby and were withdrawing northwards. The Young Pretender had advanced on Derby against the wishes of Lord George Murray, with whom he had quarrelled. In fact, Murray had resigned on 14 November; for a time, the Jacobites had marched under the sole command of Perth.

Charles Edward had then been persuaded that Perth's religion would prejudice the cause and reluctantly reappointed Murray, who now commanded the rebels but not the wholehearted support of his master. At Derby he reasserted his belief that they should return to Scotland; they were not winning the popular support of the English and they faced annihilation at Cumberland's hands. He suggested they should regroup with Lord John Drummond's men and if necessary wait for the spring before relaunching the assault. His advice was echoed by others. Bitterly Charles Edward gave the order to withdraw.

Cumberland could hardly believe the news, but it was soon confirmed. His thoughts now turned to the pursuit. He wrote at once to Wade, requesting him to cross the Pennines into Lancashire, sending his cavalry ahead towards Preston. He himself set about raising a picked force of mounted men on horses provided by the local citizenry: 1,000 men from the infantry volunteered, including 400 of the Guards. With the two regular regiments of dragoons, by 8 December he had a force of 1,500 ready to pursue the rebels north. The Jacobites had two days' lead, but the freezing weather would slow them down. Cumberland urged his mounted column forward.

In two days they had reached Macclesfield, eighty miles from Coventry, despite icy conditions that sent the horses slithering. Here Cumberland was caught up by a government courier with orders that he should halt: there were continuing worries about a French invasion on the south coast. An expeditionary force of 10,000 French and Irish recruited troops, under the Duc de Richelieu, was gathering in the Pas de Calais; ominously, the Young Pretender's brother Henry was there also. Cumberland realized that he might be called back south with his armies, to defend London, while 'these villains may escape back unpunished into the Highlands, to our eternal shame' as he had told Wade.

Cumberland was delayed in his pursuit. Mr Stafford, an attorney with whom he had stayed three nights at Macclesfield, followed the mounted column out of town and saw how Cumberland personally led the way, even through the icy water of a river 'which was very deep but ye bottom proved good.' On the 13th he was at Preston, where he met General Oglethorpe, sent by Wade with three regiments of horse. Oglethorpe was a remarkable man; he had founded Georgia as a settlement for debtors, then returned to England in search of an heiress to marry and recruits to join the Georgian Rangers. When the Jacobite crisis arose, he had offered his Rangers for government service in the north. He had entered Preston only hours after the rebels left, and Cumberland was jubilant, convinced that the decisive encounter was imminent.

But now another courier arrived from London. Pelham and Newcastle wanted Cumberland to wait while they checked out new rumours about the French expeditionary force, said to have landed in Sussex (the 'invaders' turned out to be smugglers). Cumberland's reaction is not recorded, but Joseph Yorke wrote to his father, the Lord Chancellor, that the delay made him 'sick at my stomach and heart.' 'We have lost our opportunity,' he added.[5] The Young Pretender was at Lancaster, just thirty miles away. Jacobite stragglers had already been caught. But dutifully, curbing his impatience, Cumberland halted the pursuit.

On the 16th word came from London: he was given leave to continue. Cumberland, a report said, jumped for joy, boasting he would drive the rebels back to Scotland.

Needless to say, the rebels had moved out of Lancaster by the time Cumberland got there, but before them lay Shap Fell: steep hills and narrow tracks to be negotiated with waggons and gun carriages. Cumberland was still hopeful. He had already sent Oglethorpe's cavalry off as an advanced guard, along with the Yorkshire Hunters, Mordaunt's Dragoons and St George's Dragoons, with orders to follow the road through Hornby and Kirkby Lonsdale. He himself, with the rest of the mounted column, now took the more direct route north through Kendal.

Oglethorpe's force managed to intercept the rebels on the afternoon of the 17th, just south of Shap, but daylight was fading and a snowstorm threatened. Oglethorpe broke off contact with the enemy and returned to the nearby hamlet of Orton for the night. The following morning he stirred late and rode into Shap to find that his chief was ahead of him. Cumberland had ridden all night and was furious to hear that the General had overslept at the local vicarage, and worse, had allowed the enemy to escape the previous afternoon; he ordered a court martial, charging the General with dereliction of duty, but Oglethorpe was eventually absolved.

It was Lord George Murray and his 800-strong rearguard that Oglethorpe

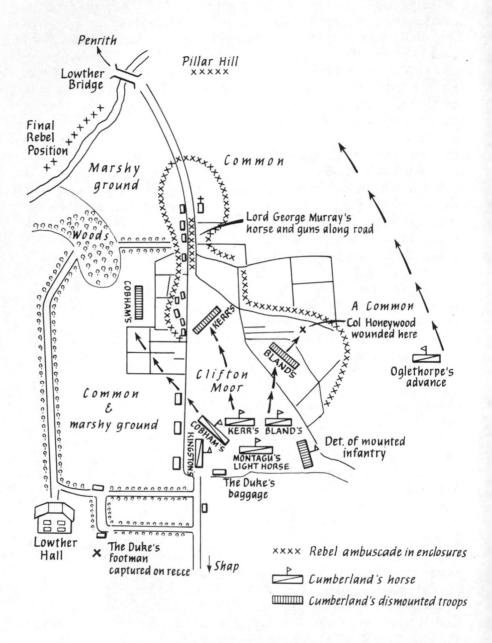

Penrith

Lowther
Bridge

Pillar Hill
× × × × ×

Final
Rebel
Position
+ + + + +
+

Marshy
ground

C o m m o n

Woods

Lord George Murray's
horse and guns along road

COBHAM'S

KERR'S

A Common
Col Honeywood
wounded here

BLAND'S

Oglethorpe's
advance

Common
&
marshy ground

Clifton
Moor

KERR'S   BLAND'S

Det. of mounted
infantry

KINGSTON'S

COBHAM'S

MONTAGU'S
LIGHT HORSE

The Duke's
baggage

Lowther
Hall

× The Duke's
footman
captured on recce

↓ Shap

× × × × Rebel ambuscade in enclosures

Cumberland's horse

Cumberland's dismounted troops

The Skirmish at Clifton

66

had tangled with, the Young Pretender having gone ahead to Penrith. Murray was facing problems not only with his sulky Commander-in-Chief but with the equally demoralized and untamed clansmen. Grateful for the snow that covered their tracks, Murray managed to chivy his rearguard as far as the small village of Clifton, three or four miles south of Penrith.

Cumberland moved cautiously now, aware that he was closing on his quarry. Commandeering Lowther Park for his troops and ordering a meal for them, he decided to make an attack that afternoon. He was warned of a possible ambush on the outskirts of Clifton and took some time to reconnoitre the position, but he decided his plan was good. At five o'clock that afternoon, the 18th, he ordered forward a good proportion of three regiments of dragoons − but on foot.

It was already completely dark. Stumbling through ditches and crashing into thorn hedges and stone walls, the troopers found their jackboots unsuited to the terrain; soon their feet were soaking and frozen, their shins barked, their hands grazed. The air jangled with the chink and clatter of their equipment and their suppressed curses.

Not surprisingly, the enemy heard them coming. The Highlanders, better camouflaged in their dark plaids, lay in wait behind walls and hedges. When some of Bland's 3rd Regiment of Dragoons opened fire too soon, the Highlanders replied at close quarters, first with fire and then with their claymores. Colonel Honeywood, the Blands' commanding officer, was among those hurt; according to one Highland account, 'We got on very well till the long man in the muckle boots came over the dyke, but his feet slipped on a turd and we got him down.'[6] Honeywood had only recently recovered from wounds received at Dettingen, but it seemed he was a survivor. Despite being hacked by claymores this night, he lived on for another forty years.

The encounter petered out into a clutch of isolated skirmishes, as men wounded and weary collapsed to the sodden ground. Both sides had lost men, Cumberland ten (as recorded in the Clifton parish register), the enemy twice as many. It would go down in history as the last battle on English soil, but it was hardly decisive. That night, as a fitful moonlight illuminated the scene, Cumberland realized that the Highlanders had escaped him.

By incredible labours, working in the dark and under fire from the dragoons, Lord George Murray had managed to save much of his artillery and baggage train. The clansmen retreated across the moor to Penrith, to join their 'Prince Charlie'. Charles Edward, however, was already moving on to Carlisle, leaving Murray and the rearguard to follow as best they could. They had no intention of staying at Carlisle, but left a garrison to hold the semi-ruined castle while they trudged back across the border. It was 20 December (OS) as the Young Pretender forded the Esk into Scotland on his twenty-fifth birthday.

Cumberland stayed the night of the 18th with a Clifton Quaker by the name of Thomas Savage, who claimed that it was his son who had warned Cumberland of the ambush. Savage found his guest to be pleasant and agreeable company and voted him 'a man of parts, very friendly and no pride in him.'[7] But the young soldier must have been feeling very frustrated that the enemy had yet again slipped out of his clutches.

At Carlisle Cumberland had to wait for the siege train to arrive with the heavy guns: ten 18-pounders, shipped from Liverpool to Whitehaven and then dragged around the coastal tracks. Not until the 27th was the first shot fired. After three days the rebels had had enough. Governor Hamilton surrendered; after a long series of judicial delays, his motley garrison of Englishmen, Frenchmen and Scotsmen was brought to trial and thirty-one (out of roughly 400) were executed.

Cumberland entered Carlisle on the last day of 1745. He was greeted with due ceremony by the Deputy Mayor and city aldermen, who gave him as good a dinner as they could lay their hands on. But Cumberland responded coolly, and did little to discourage Belford, his artillery commander, from laying claim to the cathedral bell as a right of conquest. He had decided not to continue the pursuit; though reports came that the Jacobites were meeting stiff resistance from militias in the Glasgow area, and it might have seemed a good opportunity to close the net around them, Newcastle was insistent that his presence was required in London. General Henry Hawley was sent north to take command, Wade having finally been retired. On 2 January Cumberland headed south.

London had spent the past few weeks in continuing trepidation. The rebel army's swift advance to Derby had been frightening enough: there were terrible stories about the Highlanders — 'so many fiends of hell' according to the town clerk of Derby, a Mr Bateman, who added that they 'jabbered like a band of Hottentots.'[8] But even when the rebels returned north, rumours remained that the French were still planning to launch an invasion in southern England. Cumberland had asked Ligonier to take the balance of his force back south, and now he supervised the deployment of nearly 2,000 troops in Kent and Sussex, to restore confidence in the local townspeople and militias.

In fact the French expeditionary force had been stood down as soon as word came of the Young Pretender's retreat from Derby, and, in view of the complete lack of French naval support, the whole affair may be regarded as a feint to give comfort to the Young Pretender and to divert attention from Marshal Saxe's preparations to attack Brussels.

However, Jacobite stories of panic in the streets of London are grossly exaggerated. George II remained calm throughout, and his influence helped to steady the nerves of most of those around him. Stock prices certainly fell rapidly, but the story about a run on the Bank of England on 'Black Friday' 6 December, the day the Young Pretender left Derby, is not borne out by the bank's records.[9] One of the great government bankers, Samson Gideon, wrote to fellow financier, Sir Thomas Drury, on 7 December:

> I rec'd yours of the 5th and I am sorry you have been in such consternation and do assure you the alarm of the rebels approaching had the same effect here, but being informed that H.R.H. would be in Northampton this evening we are all in better spirits. There is a perfect stagnation in our affairs here and nothing doing in stocks except 4% annuities which are under parr.[10]

Of the King's ministers, undoubtedly the most nervous had been Newcastle. It was he who had been responsible for halting Cumberland's pursuit of the rebels, and after it was all over he tried to excuse himself, giving Stephen Poyntz copies of all the ministerial correspondence so that he would see, and tell Cumberland about, the whole picture.

Cumberland was greeted in London with much relief, particularly by the King who was exasperated by Newcastle's fretting. Newcastle himself wrote, 'All the world is in love with him and he deserves it.'[11] Both the King and the politicians were eager to know what he had learnt about the rebels and the true scale of their threat to Britain's stability, and Cumberland no doubt spent much of early January recounting details of his progress. Field-Marshal Stair commented that the nation owed a great debt of gratitude to him for pursuing the rebels with such vigour, and regretted that the pursuit had been interrupted. The Common Council of the City of London voted to grant the Freedom of their City to the young Duke.

But now it was Cumberland's sojourn in London that would be curtailed.

# 9

## Pursuit in Scotland

WHEN THE YOUNG PRETENDER agreed to withdraw north, he had meant to recruit some more men, raise some more money and start his campaign again in Scotland. Edinburgh being lost to him now, he made for Glasgow, despite its known Hanoverian sympathies. Arriving on 26 December he made an effort to win the Glaswegians' approval, but in vain. A recruitment drive produced only sixty men. Charles Edward took his revenge by extracting thousands of pounds cash and supplies for his men, then moved on towards Stirling where he hoped to find Lord John Drummond and his reinforcements. Stirling, too, was known to be anti-Jacobite, but its meagre defences were unable to prevent the rebels from entering the town on 8 January. Stirling Castle, on the other hand, was held by General Blakeney, who had no intention of opening his gates to the Jacobites.

Unwisely, Charles Edward decided to lay siege to the castle. He had quarrelled again with Lord George Murray, and refused to call a proper council of war. But now came good news. Apart from the reinforcements brought by Lord John Drummond, several other shiploads of men and *matériel* had arrived from France, landed on the east coast at Peterhead and Montrose: enough, in fact, to swell his army to 8,000.

Cumberland, meanwhile, had been relying on General Hawley as supreme commander in the north. Hawley was a cavalry general, only six years younger than the man he relieved, Marshal Wade, but ruthless and rough-tongued. Yet for all his experience he was apprehensive about his responsibilities; he complained about his subordinates, his lack of provisions and the fact that 'Marshal Wade won't let me have his map.'[1] Nevertheless he managed to find his way to Edinburgh, along with 8,000 British troops. The Dutch were being sent home – a consequence of French protests and Holland's own need at this time – but they had never been much use anyway. To take their place, 5,000 Hessians were on their way, under the command of Cumberland's brother-in-law, Prince Frederick of Hesse.

Edinburgh having been retaken by Handasyde, Hawley now turned his attention to Stirling. On 15 January Lord George Murray learnt of Hawley's advance and decided to intercept him at Falkirk. On the 17th the unsuspecting Hawley fell into the trap.

'Sir, my heart is broke,' Hawley wrote to his Captain-General. 'I can't say we are quite beat today, but our left is beat and their left is beat.'[2] Hawley accused his men of 'scandalous cowardice' but it seems that he had placed too much reliance on his cavalry and had underrated the rebels' skill in movement and swordplay; the horses had shied in terror when the muskets were discharged, and while the troopers endeavoured to regain control the rebels' knives and swords had done their work. A few infantry battalions standing firm under General 'Daddy' Huske had saved the day; otherwise the rebels' victory would have been complete.

Cumberland wasted no time in recriminations. As soon as the news reached him, he knew he must go to Scotland. He left St James's Palace at 1 am on 25 January.

On 26 January the Archbishop of York, Thomas Herring, was at Wetherby when a breathless King's messenger interrupted his visitation to announce the impending arrival of the Duke of Cumberland. The Archbishop jumped into his coach and raced back to York, beating Cumberland by just ten minutes. There was no mistaking the young soldier's mood. Cumberland told Herring that he had been given a free hand by the King and his ministers; he was to take command of Hawley's army and use whatever means he thought necessary to eliminate the Jacobite menace.

At 3 am on the 30th Cumberland was in Edinburgh, after further stops in Newcastle and in Berwick, where he had stayed long enough to receive the freedom of the city. It had been a record-breaking journey: the poet Gray compared him to a cannon shot. Hawley had sent a message that he had prepared rooms at Holyrood House, and, after inspecting the soldiers' quarters, Cumberland finally went to his bed.

After just three hours' rest, Cumberland was up and conferring with Hawley and Huske. His immediate task, he had already decided, was to raise the siege at Stirling. His long-term objective was equally clear, as he had told the Archbishop; it was his duty to crush the rebels once and for all — rid the country of the Pretender's son, and so thoroughly stamp on his supporters that the validity of the Protestant Hanoverian accession would never more be in doubt. What was less clear was how to achieve this end.

Cumberland had considerable respect for the Scots, not merely the educated city folk, but the Highlanders too. He knew from reading government papers that they were a law unto themselves, that the most common means of livelihood was cattle-stealing, that protection money was the chieftains' usual form of income, that efforts to disarm the Highlanders after the rebellion of 1715 had been futile. He had read Wade's report of his attempts during 1725-33 to consolidate government control in the Highlands. Wade and his generals had built hundreds of miles of roadway, at a cost of £70 a mile, and fifty-odd bridges, but received no thanks from the clansmen of Perth or Dalmally. On the contrary, the Highlanders felt exposed by such open arteries of traffic and feared intruders with their alien ideas and customs that would inevitably weaken clan ties. 'Their notions of virtue and vice are very different from the more civilized part of mankind,' commented Captain Edward Burt, who had served under Wade and written a gloss to his report.[3] An even more telling comment was made by Professor Blackwell of Aberdeen, in a paper on the state of Scotland, who said that inhabitants of the east-coast towns knew more about the American colonies than about the West Highlands.[4]

Wade had realized, however, that the key to controlling the Highlands was not only good communications but sturdy forts, and he added (among others) Fort Augustus, at the southern end of Loch Ness. At the other end of the Great Glen was Fort George, at Inverness, but the most important was Fort William: easy to supply by sea from Liverpool and with a commanding strategic position. The English garrisons hated life in these forts. 'We are miserable, ill-lodged and ill-fed,' wrote one soldier at Fort William:

No fire or provisions but what the officers must provide themselves, for the men have oatmeal and ale and are now salting up beef for the Spring half-year.... Neither Fort William or Fort George have water within the works. I have nothing at all to do. No books and so raining for 40 days I have been here − not one dry.[5]

Another letter written in May, 1745, described a journey through the West Highlands when the snow still lay on the peaks − 'the mountains stand all round like a parcel of sugar loaves on a grocer's counter' − but the writer's comments on the people he met were less poetic. 'I got nothing to eat but what I carried with me, at night no bed to lie on. You may well call this a cursed country.'[6]

Naturally Cumberland was most interested in the Highlanders' fighting ability. At Prestonpans, he was told, the rebel Highlanders had fought like savages, armed with scythes on sticks for lack of muskets, wielding their huge two-edged swords like flails, hacking at men and horses with their axes and daggers. Back in 1743 he had seen for himself the aptitude the Highlanders showed for the claymore and Lochaber axe, when Colonel Sempill brought a few of his men to St James's Palace for a demonstration before the King. Along with the rest of the court, Cumberland had also seen them dance, long-limbed and graceful, but silent and proud — so proud, indeed, that the golden guineas given them by the King for their pains were regarded as an insult and passed on to royal flunkeys at the door as they departed.

Sempill's Highlanders had come from the independent companies raised by Wade. Formed into a regiment, the Royal Highlanders (now the Black Watch) had fought in the British army at Fontenoy. Cumberland was told about their special 'tactic' of throwing themselves to the ground to avoid the French musketry — a drill unknown to the English army manual — but he wisely refrained from interfering. He had also been very favourably impressed by their Commanding Officer, Sir Robert Munro. Sadly, Munro and his brother had been among those killed at Falkirk.

Ever since the start of the present crisis, hundreds of loyal Highlanders had been recruited by, among others, Duncan Forbes at Inverness and John Campbell, Earl of Loudoun, in Perthshire and Argyll. Cumberland knew, therefore, that he had on his side a well of valuable local knowledge. Properly co-ordinated, and used particularly for wide-ranging reconnaissance, he felt confident that they would prevent the rebel Highlanders from flaunting their native subterfuge to much effect. There was no uniform for them, as such, but all wore blue bonnets with the black cockade of Hanover and a distinguishing red or yellow cross of ribbon.

Cumberland's own regiment of Foot Guards had been left in London, much to their disappointment. In addition to Hawley's northern army and elements of the force with which he had taken Carlisle, notably the company of artillery under Major Belford and Captain Desaguliers, he had the Hessian contingent, to be employed in the Edinburgh area initially, and would soon receive further reinforcements from the south: two more battalions of infantry, the newly raised Kingston's Light Horse to be his bodyguard, and Cobham's Dragoons. He also had the support of the Royal Navy. While one squadron sailed to and fro among the Western Isles, keeping watch on the myriad bays and lochs, another squadron under Admiral Byng cruised up and down the east coast, paying especial attention to the Firth of Forth.

His staff was virtually unchanged from Fontenoy, though William Kerr, Earl of Ancram, formerly one of his ADCs, had been promoted to a cavalry command. Lord Bury was in Edinburgh already, as was his father the Earl of Albemarle, who was to lead Cumberland's front line at Culloden. 'Patch' Cathcart was also there, and Joseph Yorke and Henry Seymour Conway, along with 'the old boy' as the other ADCs called Studholme Hodgson; he was all of fifteen years older than the rest of them. Another aide, who had first served Cumberland at Dettingen, then again at Fontenoy, and now had arrived in Scotland too, was the Hon. John Fitzwilliam from Dublin, son of the fifth Viscount Fitzwilliam. David Watson, the engineer who had helped to take Carlisle and whose military career would now be closely entwined with that of the Duke, had been at Falkirk and as a result of his courage and leadership had been promoted lieutenant-colonel.

Curiously, the young Captain-General did not seem to blame Hawley for the fiasco at Falkirk, though there was no doubt that Hawley had allowed himself to be taken by surprise. However, he did try to soften the harsh disciplinary measures that the General was inflicting on his men, some of whom had already been hanged for desertion or shot for cowardice. Even by the brutal standards of the day his ruthlessness was excessive, and over the coming months he would certainly earn his nickname, 'Hangman Hawley'.

Just hours after his night arrival at Holyrood Cumberland had plunged into urgent tactical discussions with Hawley and Huske. Although Blakeney and his garrison at Stirling were making a gallant stand, they could not hold out for long; according to government agents, the Young Pretender had acquired not only massive reinforcements but also some heavy siege guns. But the King's son could not omit the formal niceties; he was obliged to receive a visitation from the local dignitaries, address the assembled ministers of the Church of Scotland, and that evening he held a levee at Holyrood House.

His presence had excited particular attention from the young ladies of Edinburgh, who had not long since been ogling the Young Pretender; he was judged to be less elegant in his person than Charles Edward, but his affable and lively manner won him many admirers. One Miss Kerr made a special hit with him; she was exhibiting Hanoverian favours on her bosom.

'The arrival of H.R.H. has done the business,' commented Andrew Fletcher, the Lord Justice Clerk, adding that Cumberland had 'animated the army and struck the rebels with terror and confusion.'[7] Indeed, the mere news of his presence had boosted morale among the Hanoverian force, already moving out for Linlithgow on the road to Stirling. Marching columns of men recalled stories they had heard of Cumberland's courage at Dettingen, his leadership at Fontenoy, his determination, his efforts to raise standards, even among the officers. The Jacobites, by contrast, took fright. Lord George Murray advised Charles Edward that, as Stirling Castle showed no signs of yielding, the rebel army should withdraw into the Highlands.

Soon after five on the morning of 31 January Cumberland was leaving Edinburgh, now in the hands of General Bligh. In a magnificent coach drawn by twelve horses, lent by the Earl of Hopetoun, he was driven to the city gate. Hardly dwelling a minute over the formal ceremony at the gate, he mounted The Lizard, his grey charger, and to great applause, with pipers playing 'Highland Laddie' he rode off towards Linlithgow. There he inspected the camp, remarked critically on the officers' laxness, which did not add to his popularity among the seniors, and called a meeting of his commanders. His plan, he said, would involve the whole force; the rebels were encamped beneath the walls of Stirling Castle and there he intended to rout them. He had changed the normal order of battle after hearing the details of Falkirk, relegating all cavalry to the third line 'because by all accounts the rebels don't fear that [the cavalry] as they do our fire, and on that alone I must depend.'[8] Adding the usual exhortations, he gave the order to move out at three o'clock the following morning, 1 February. In the interval he managed to catch up on a couple of hours' sleep.

The rebels, however, had gone. Cumberland could scarcely believe it. Not a shot had been fired, but the rebels had gone.

Once again the Young Pretender had been forced to accept the advice of Lord George Murray; he and his army had fled in extreme haste, taking with them only the most portable supplies.

Cheated of his quarry once again, the young Captain-General could barely contain his disappointment. Though General Blakeney and his garrison were undoubtedly glad to see the new arrivals, Cumberland was furious at himself for missing the opportunity. Still, he found some compensation in the huge mass of rebel documents that had been abandoned, as well as artillery and other supplies. While he issued new orders to pursue the rebels through the snow-covered hills to Perth, he began to wonder if the whole rebellion had fizzled out. Perhaps Charles Edward was already taking ship back to France. Cumberland wrote to the Duke of Bedford, First Lord of the Admiralty, expressing his fear that the rebels might escape by sea and his concern at his own lack of control over the Royal Navy patrols. The Admiralty promptly directed all captains of His Majesty's ships in Scottish waters to report to Cumberland and carry out his instructions.

Cumberland's frustration was as nothing compared to his opponent's depression. In the headlong flight from Stirling many of the rebels had simply deserted. Charles Edward had no idea where to go next, or what to do with the remaining force of Jacobites; he lashed out at his advisers and quarrelled yet again with Lord George Murray. At heart perhaps he knew that he was being boxed into a corner. When Murray put forward a plan to split the force in two, with one division heading through the mountains and the other taking the coastal route, to meet up again at Inverness, he raised only weak objections. With the Hanoverians continuing the chase from Stirling, he knew that he had little choice in the matter. He took the mountain route for Inverness.

Cumberland was still not convinced that the rebels meant to fight on, but he urged his force to pursue them at least to Perth, arriving there on 6 February. The evidence that the rebels had just left lay all around, including, much to the amusement of Cumberland and his ADCs, some very personal letters from Lady Kilmarnock to her Jacobite husband, whom she addressed as 'Life, honey, jewel, only joy and love etc' according to Conway, who also quoted her as complaining that she had had 'a fistula in ano and had been exposed to a man to have it cut.'[9]

At Perth, the general feeling among Cumberland's aides was, as Conway wrote to his cousin Horace Walpole, that there was 'nothing more to do.' He went on: 'I am willing to conclude we shall not stay long. Adieu, make London as ready as you can for our reception.'[10] Once again, Conway had come to the wrong conclusion. Cumberland had decided that the campaign must go on until he had definite proof that the rebels were disbanded and the Young Pretender gone, or until he could rout them himself.

With grim determination, Cumberland returned to Edinburgh to plan the next phase of the operation. While he had been marching on Stirling and then Perth, the 5,000 Hessians had arrived to take the place of the Dutch, and he wanted to confer with their commander, his brother-in-law, Prince Frederick of Hesse. But arriving back in Edinburgh on 15 February, Cumberland was much shaken by the news from London. The Whig administration had resigned as one body and the country was without a cabinet. Pelham and Newcastle had been pressing the King to appoint Pitt the Secretary of War, but the King had refused; he regarded Pitt as a dangerous maverick and could never forgive him for sneering at Hanover. The Pelhams had found the King increasingly difficult to work with, and finally hit on the idea of resignation as a means by which to force his hand. And it worked. The King tried to persuade Granville and the Earl of Bath to form a new ministry, but without Whig support they could not survive. Within two or three days the King gave in, though for the time being Pitt was still excluded.

Cumberland was back in Perth when he heard the Whigs had been returned to office. He was delighted. Always more of a realist than his father, he also knew that the Whigs would give him firm political backing for his campaign in Scotland. Dining with his officers, he proposed a toast: 'To the Ministry: and no more changes.'[11]

By now Cumberland had taken a firm grip on the southern Highlands. The Hessians would control the area around Stirling, Perth and Crieff; some of the Argyll Militia he sent up the Tay to hold Blair Atholl, and the rest were sent on to Aberdeen under General Bland. Humphrey Bland had been appointed the senior infantry commander; a general of much experience, he had written the classic contemporary manual of military discipline, carried by almost every officer in his knapsack. Cumberland himself would take the bulk of the army by the coastal route to Aberdeen, and eventually to Inverness, where Duncan Forbes and Loudoun were waiting with their loyal Highlanders.

Cumberland set out on 20 February. It became ever clearer to him as he moved north that many of the clans and families had hedged their bets, enlisting on both sides. He already knew that Lord George Murray and his brother William, the Jacobite Duke of Atholl, were supporters of Charles Edward, but their brother James was a government supporter (and the *Hanoverian* Duke of Atholl). The Campbells, from Argyll and Perthshire, were widely thought to be using the conflict to increase their territorial strength and influence. The Campbells of Ardkinglas and Lochnell had declared themselves for the Jacobites. The Duke of Argyll, head of the senior branch of the clan, was theoretically a government man, but his allegiance was mistrusted at Westminster; Tweeddale, the Secretary of State for Scotland, considered him unreliable and Cumberland was wary of his advice. John Campbell, Earl of Loudoun, on the other hand, had proved his loyalty by helping to raise a sizeable militia. The Frasers, the Gordons, the Mackenzies and many others were divided. The Laird of Mackintosh was a government man but his wife had given Charles Edward a warm welcome when he reached Moy Hall, a few miles south-east of Inverness on 16 February.

'There is no trusting to any people in the country to give intelligence,' Joseph Yorke told his father, the Lord Chancellor. 'The Presbyterian ministers are the only people we can trust.'[12] His opinion was clearly shared by his chief.

Arriving at Montrose on the 24th, Cumberland received word of strenuous rebel activity in the north. His mood of grim determination was unmistakeable. Through the Presbyterian ministers he issued a proclamation to the people of Scotland. Hand in your arms and you will go free, he announced; keep them and soldiers will come for you, no holds barred.[13] Any rebels who were found in arms would be arrested, but if they surrendered willingly they would be disarmed and sent home. The innocent would not suffer. Cumberland expressly forbade any plundering or raiding by his soldiers; if they were caught they faced the gallows. His order books are explicit; one order written at Stirling read: '*Any man who is found plundering will be hung on the spot by the provost. No soldier to presume to search for arms without an order.*'[14] Unfortunately, orders were sometimes ignored. In this savage country, in the middle of winter, with supplies uncertain, the discipline of officers and men could not be relied on.

Cumberland was well aware of the supply situation; one reason why he had chosen the coastal route was that he hoped to be resupplied by sea. Food provisions were adequate, though thanks to a crooked contractor bread was sometimes short; but just as important, in this bitterly cold winter, were clothing and particularly shoes. He'd had to issue 500 pairs of new shoes free at Perth. Although reportedly furious when he heard of plundering by his men, he could not have been surprised. He did his best, however, to repay those who had suffered, like Mrs Oliphant of Gask, who complained that an officer in the Argyll Militia, a Captain McLachlan, had demanded ten guineas from her, 'which at that time I could not command,' said Mrs Oliphant; however, one of her daughters had given him 'twelve and three out of her pocket' and the money had never been returned.[15]

If Cumberland's men behaved less than perfectly, however, the rebels had been at least as bad. Everywhere he went he heard horror stories about their violent recruiting methods and plundering raids. Lord Lewis Gordon, the Jacobite-appointed Lord Lieutenant of Banff and Aberdeen, was said to have forced out 300 men of Deeside and Strathbogie by burning their homes and property, as well as by straight abduction. Mr Robertson of Kirkmichael told of 'recruiting parties raising men by fire and sword.'[16] It was clear the rebels were desperate, but that was the only consolation Cumberland could find in the grim catalogue of woes now greeting him.

By 28 February Cumberland's forces had all reached Aberdeen, including the men under General Bland. Their Captain-General had arrived on the 26th and was already busy refining his plans for the next stage of operations. He was sure, now, that a decisive battle lay ahead. He would keep the army here for nearly six weeks, for an intense programme of training, the object of which was partly to co-ordinate the disparate regiments and companies but principally to instruct them in fire discipline.

Cumberland was convinced that victory went to those who held their fire until the appropriate moment. It required nerve; it also required trust, between the men as much as between them and their officers; in short, it required training. Having analysed the enemy's tactics at Prestonpans and Falkirk, Cumberland and his generals expected the rebels to adopt similar tactics again: to fire at longish range, then throw down their firelocks and charge with swords and daggers in both hands. Cumberland's idea was to form up battalions in three ranks by platoons, and for the platoons to fire alternately, directing their shot diagonally towards the centre and at very short range. His men had to be taught to withstand the rebels' initial fire and to remain in position even when the enemy made his terrifying charge, complete with bloodcurdling yells. They could fire only when given a specific signal to do so, usually by a particular drum roll. As contact was made, the still unbroken ranks of the front line would be transformed into a flashing wall of bayonets, each musket angled so as to avoid the rebel shield or targe.

Cumberland took a close personal interest in the training and allotted generous supplies of practice ammunition. Platoon by platoon the men were drilled, the 'awkward men' given special extra training. Whole battalions were rehearsed in their manoeuvres under the critical eye of brigade commanders. Much trouble was taken to co-ordinate drum signals

5. "The Pretender's Son" aged 17. Charles Edward Stuart. (*Gabriel Blanchet, National Portrait Gallery*)

6. The victor of Culloden at the point of crisis: "Riding The Lizard, splendid in his scarlet and gold with tricorne hat". (*John Wootton, Hopetoun House*)

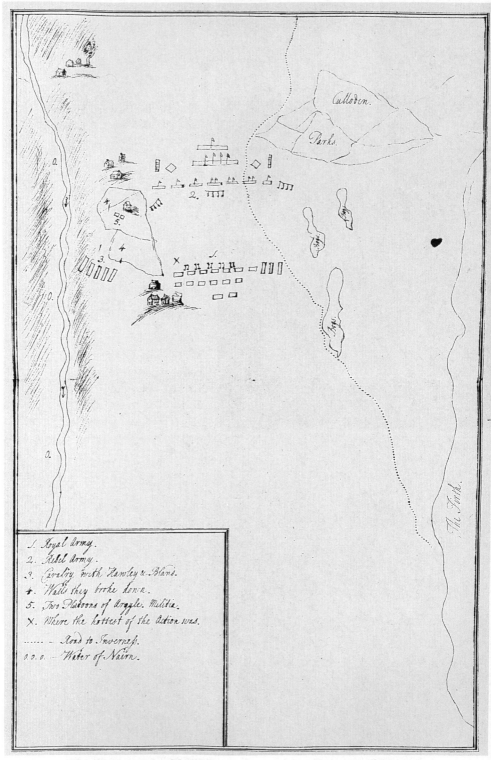

*Key (as written on the sketch):*

1. Royal Army.
2. Rebel Army.
3. Cavalry, with Hawley & Bland.
4. Walls they broke down.
5. Two Platoons of Argyle. Militia.
✗. Where the hottest of the Action was.
...... — Road to Inverness.
o.o.o. — Water of Nairn.

*Labels on map:* Culloden. Parks. The Furk.

7. This field sketch of Culloden together with an account of the battle was sent by Joseph Yorke to his father, the Lord Chancellor, from Inverness on 18 April. The Lord Chancellor sent the paper to George II who replied, "I thank you my Lord for this very pretty description of the battle".

8. The Culloden Tankard made to Cumberland's order in London by Gabriel Sleath, 1747. "We be prisoners of de Gran Monach de Great Britain," say the French.

9. The Pursuit of the Fair Sex, August, 1749: "John of Gant Mounted or Mars on his journey". The caricature celebrates the scandal of Cumberland's alleged failure to abduct a Savoyard singer from Covent Garden to Windsor. "My all is in my possession," says he. "My dear sister. Stop'e Stop'e," cries her brother.

10. The Cropper: "Fussed too much over superficial detail like dress," 1749. To facilitate marching, soldiers had their coat skirts shortened. "Short coats but long duty." "We shall run well now," says the satirist.

throughout the army, and to teach the troops to recognize them and respond as appropriate. Meanwhile their Captain-General built up a detailed picture, from his own reconnaissance of the area, of rebel positions, strength and probable strategy.

Although it was hard to ascertain details, Cumberland knew by now that Inverness had fallen to the rebels. Loudoun's militia had panicked and fled, and although Fort George had held out for two days the garrison had eventually surrendered. The fort had been ransacked then blown up. Loudoun and Forbes had disappeared with the remnants of their force, eventually to seek refuge in Skye with the McLeods. Then, after another two-day siege, Fort Augustus had also fallen. Only Fort William held out, besieged by Charles Edward's men for exactly four weeks from 7 March.

The loss of Fort William was an eventuality that Cumberland could not permit; it was 'the only fort in the Highlands that is of any consequence,' he said in a letter to General John Campbell, asking his support for Captain Caroline Scott. Scott, his favourite engineer officer, reached Fort William by sea on 4 March and, with help from the Royal Navy and two companies from Edinburgh, managed to repel the besiegers.

In mid-March Cumberland heard more bad news: two posts held by the Argyll Militia at Rannoch and Castle Menzies had been overrun by Lord George Murray's men, and a strong detachment in Blair Castle was surrounded. He was even more furious to hear, from Lord Crawford at Perth, that on account of the rebel advance Prince Frederick and the Hessian generals were planning to withdraw to Stirling. He immediately sent Joseph Yorke with a letter, worded in the strongest possible terms, countermanding the withdrawal. Two days later, on 21 March, he followed that letter with another, ordering Frederick to take four battalions and St George's Dragoons to effect the immediate relief of Colonel Agnew's battalion at Blair Castle. Fortunately Agnew managed to hold out until they arrived.

Cumberland's patience with all Scotsmen was running short. Blair Castle was the seat of the Dukes of Atholl, the home, in fact, of Lord George Murray's two brothers, the Hanoverian Duke *and* the Jacobite Duke. These people were beyond Cumberland's comprehension; he simply could not fathom their motives. He expressed increasing disillusion in letters to the Duke of Newcastle, describing 'the general villainy and infidelity of the Highlands' and mentioning in particular Lady Seaforth and the Laird of Mackintosh's wife, both 'in open rebellion'.[17] Henceforward he began to show a new implacability in dealing with the rebels. Newcastle wrote back with words of encouragement, and many others in London, such as the Lord Chancellor and Chesterfield, the Lord Lieutenant of Ireland, expressed their sympathy; but what the young soldier really wanted was firm political direction. When Newcastle promised government measures after the rebellion — 'such laws... as may effectively reduce the power of the Highlands and briefly disable France from playing this game on us whenever they please'[18]— Cumberland responded forcefully: 'Mild measures won't do.' Then, as if feeling the need to excuse his bluntness, he added a postscript to his letter:

> Pray make my compliments to Mr Pelham and don't imagine that threatening military execution and many other things are pleasing to me but nothing will go down without in this part of the world.[19]

Undoubtedly new laws were needed, but in this place of utter lawlessness the first requirement was peace, to be imposed by force.

While Cumberland was wrestling with his private doubts, his opponent was engaged in nothing more than an extended holiday at his hosts' expense, hunting, shooting and attending balls, taking no part in the military operations carried out by his generals. At one stage Charles fell ill with a fever, perhaps pneumonia; but by late March he had recovered and was resuming his life of relentless gaiety at Inverness. He seemed to have lost touch with reality. He had also lost £12,000 sent from France to bolster his supplies. The Royal Navy had caught the French ship in March as she was putting into a little port to the west of Banff.

By contrast, supplies had been reaching Cumberland with welcome regularity. And, with better weather reaching these northern latitudes at last, he was ready to make his move.

# 10

# Culloden

'WE MARCH TOMORROW, THAT'S SOMETHING; but as it's a vast way to John of Groat's home I don't know when we shall turn our faces to London.'[1] Thus Conway signalled to Walpole his master's decision to end the tedious weeks of waiting at Aberdeen and move out for the decisive battle. It was 6 April, 1746.

It must have been an exhilarating moment, breaking camp at Aberdeen after a halt of nearly six weeks. Apart from the training sessions, only one relatively small excursion had been made from Aberdeen, when Bland led a raid on a rebel detachment near Keith, the object of which had been to secure a bridge over the River Bogie at Huntly. Bland had achieved his objective, though at some cost, for the rebel detachment had turned out to number some 800 men. In fact, when Cumberland set off from Aberdeen, he believed he might very soon encounter the main rebel force.

The troops marched eagerly, heading north-east via Meldrum to the coast, where the advance guard arrived on the 9th. Cumberland kept a very firm grip on his men on the line of march. Troops caught plundering or marauding were to be hanged without court martial. Company roll calls were ordered four times daily to check for absentees. Rewards were offered for any rebel weapons handed in: a shilling for a broadsword, more than twice that for a firelock. All women accompanying the march had to stay with the baggage train behind each regiment, on pain of being whipped by the drummers; but according to one much-repeated story Cumberland himself carried the musket of one of his sergeants who was obliged to relieve his wife of her baby.

Arriving at Cullen, Cumberland stayed at the home of James Ogilvy, sixth Earl of Findlater and Seafield. A man of progressive ideas in matters of agriculture and forestry, Findlater was also interested in increasing the variety of employment in Scotland by establishing manufactures in the Highlands, and he did much to improve the lot of his tenants. Cumberland found that Findlater agreed with his ideas for fundamental reform in

Scotland, and decided that here was one of the few great lairds whom he could respect. Cullen House had been considerably damaged by the rebels, and Lady Findlater was sly enough to give Cumberland a bed in the room with worst damage, no doubt hoping he would endorse their claim for £8,000 compensation from the government.

His army, strung out along the coast from Banff to Cullen, had regained contact with the all-important convoy of supply vessels, which had rounded Kinnairds Head under the protection of HMS *Fox*. Cumberland was determined to stay as self-sufficient as possible, to reduce the temptation for his troops to go foraging; besides, the rebels had already plundered everything they could find.

On the morning of 12 April Cumberland was up very early, issuing orders for the day's advance. Anticipating that he might have to force a crossing of the Spey, he took an advance guard of cavalry and grenadiers and went to investigate. At the approach of this formidable array, the enemy on the far bank of the Spey took fright; they burnt their wattle huts and fled. HMS *Fox* arrived off the mouth of the river and her guns gave the rebels extra speed. Fortunately the river was shallow enough to wade across and Cumberland's whole army was able to ford the water without much difficulty. The omens seemed good. He ordered an issue of brandy to warm his hardy troops.

For the next two days progress was uneventful. Leading the way was a troop of dragoons, covered by infantry pickets. Then came the five infantry brigades marching in three columns, a strong flank-guard of sixty men on the landward side. Including the fifteen battalions of infantry, three weak regiments of cavalry and a company of artillery with ten guns, there were some 8,000 men in all, fewer than Cumberland might have hoped, because he had felt obliged to leave a sizeable detachment to protect Aberdeen, but nevertheless a force to be reckoned with. 'We were a fine sight,' wrote one soldier afterwards. 'He that had seen [the Duke of Cumberland] reviewing the lines on their long march could see pleasure in his eyes.'[2] The first hint of resistance came as they approached Nairn on the 14th; a body of mounted rebels tried to separate the advance guard from the main force, but a spirited cavalry action drove them off.

Reaching Nairn that evening, Cumberland called a full day's halt for the next day. Inverness was now only fifteen miles away. From his reconnaissance patrols he knew the rebels to be consolidating their numbers in and around the town – about 7,000, it was estimated – and he knew the long-awaited encounter was imminent. He wanted to draw up detailed battle plans with his commanders and check the terrain.

It so happened that the next day, 15 April, 1746, would be his twenty-fifth birthday.

Cumberland's opponent, Charles Edward, just four months his senior, had heard of the Hanoverian army's approach only on the 13th. Turning for advice to his Irish friend, Colonel John O'Sullivan, he assembled his clansmen hurriedly on Culloden Moor, about four miles east of Inverness. He would use Culloden House, the home of the absent Duncan Forbes, as his headquarters.

Culloden Moor was a stretch of open ground lying between the Moray Firth and the River Nairn, part divided by low stone walls into enclosures, part hilly, part boggy. It was a thoroughly unsuitable place for a battle, as Lord George Murray remarked when he arrived. By then it was too late to move, for the rebels expected an attack to come on the morning of the 15th.

No attack came. Cumberland had ordered his unit commanders to take their men through their drill yet again. He ordered extra rations to be prepared and loaded on to the wagons, enough for four days: he personally would pay for an extra piece of cheese for each man. The infantry would need twenty-four rounds of ammunition per man, the dragoons eight. Then he ordered a special issue of brandy to all troops, paid for out of his own pocket. Well pleased with his preparations, he rode through the lines of tents with words of praise and encouragement, acknowledging the men's cheers and birthday greetings delightedly. Many had been with him at Fontenoy, and hailed him almost as a friend: 'Billy!' and 'Flanders! Flanders!' they called out to him, as if reminding themselves of past glories. He took a special interest in the loyal Highlanders, including some Sutherland men with Monro's Company. Seeing the 'bundles of sticks' under their arms he remarked that he could provide 'better instruments of war than those'. Politely the staff officer explained: 'Those are their bagpipes, the Highlanders' music in peace and war; wanting these, all other instruments are of no avail.'[3]

That night Cumberland slept at the Provost's house in Nairn, oblivious to the foolhardy step his opponent had taken. For Charles Edward, proceeding on the unprofessional assumption that the Hanoverian troops would be drunk after partaking of the celebratory tot, had decided to launch a night advance over unreconnoitred ground.

In two columns the rebels moved east towards Nairn, intending to encircle Cumberland's camp. But the men were ravenously hungry. Charles Edward's secretary, Murray of Broughton, was ill and his replacement, John Hay, had bungled the ordering of provisions. In the dark some of the rebels crept away in search of food. The rest stumbled on reluctantly, until it was clear that daylight would come before they reached their objective; without the element of surprise their plan had no chance of success. The raid was called off halfway to Nairn. Wearily the men turned back. Some were so overcome by exhaustion they collapsed in ditches to sleep. Many woke only to the stampede of battle around them.

Cumberland's force was assembled by dawn. Soon after four o'clock the advance guard had moved off, led by Colonel David Watson: the Campbells of the Argyll Militia and a picket of Kingston's Horse under Lord Robert Manners. An hour later the rest followed. The infantry marched in three parallel columns, with the Moray Firth to their right where Admiral Byng's ships moved restlessly to and fro, anticipating action. Albemarle and Sempill commanded the right column, 'Daddy' Huske the left and Mordaunt the centre. The cavalry, taking the landward flank, was now commanded by Bland, while Hawley acted as Cumberland's second-in-command. The artillery under Colonel William Belford was positioned at regular intervals between the infantry battalions. It was an orderly and intimidating spectacle, the ranks of scarlet snaking through a grey morning, keeping pace with the brisk drumbeats. A strong wind blew from the north-east, propelling them towards Inverness, and an occasional downpour meant that the men had to clasp their firelocks to their chests, folded under the lapels of their coats to protect them from rain.

Cumberland was mystified at the enemy's absence. His night pickets had reported hearing distant noises which might have been the rebels, but today there was no sign of them. Fearing an ambush, he left the main road early but the ground was boggy and uneven, and the men found it impossible to keep rank; he ordered them back to the road. Not till eleven o'clock was the rebel force sighted on Culloden Moor.

The Captain-General immediately deployed his columns and watched with pleasure as they moved into position as they had been taught: three lines deep, with each battalion in the second line covering gaps between the front-line battalions, where the artillery were in place, and the dragoons with the reserve battalions behind. Then, riding The Lizard, splendid in his scarlet and gold frock-coat, his tricorn tipped low over his nose in characteristic fashion, Cumberland inspected each line and addressed each battalion in turn, challenging any faint-hearts to withdraw. No one did. Now they stood in the chill and the rain, silently waiting for the rebels to make their customary headlong charge.

Lord George Murray was leading the Atholl men, on the right of the rebels' front line. On his right flank there were enclosures, surrounded by stone walls and a turf dyke, which fell steeply away to the River Nairn. O'Sullivan had insisted that no horse could ride up these slopes, but Murray was not convinced. He knew the rebels' left flank was safe; towards the Firth there was boggy and treacherous ground that would prevent a cavalry charge, and the higher walls of Culloden Park would offer some protection. But he was worried about the sloping enclosures.

Cumberland had seen the possibilities at once. He ordered Hawley and Bland forward with the dragoons and two platoons of Argyll Militia, to feel their way into the dead ground of the Nairn Valley and then if possible up the slope. While they set off he asked Lord Bury to ascertain the position of the enemy's artillery; it meant riding to within a hundred yards of the rebels' front line, but Bury rode off calmly and returned minutes later with the vital information. Now Belford could direct his guns with pinpoint accuracy.

The enemy guns opened fire first. Cumberland authorized Belford to reply. The rebels were chafing with impatience, unaccustomed to these set-piece battles and the need for fire discipline. Now they came under murderous fire from Cumberland's guns. Peal after peal of thunder rolled across the hills, split by screams of agony as the gunshot penetrated flesh. Still restrained by their commanders, the clansmen were dropping in scores. Suddenly to their right there was a new threat. The Campbells had crept up the slope and the dragoons were following. The Highlanders could hold out no longer. Without waiting for the command, the Atholl men and their neighbours broke into a run, screaming their clan cries as they charged at the Hanoverian front line.

Cumberland had positioned himself behind the front line towards their right, but as the rebel charge developed he galloped towards this new threat, urging men to hold their fire as trained. The rebels were 'within a hundred yards of our men, firing their pistols and brandishing their swords,' he himself recorded, when he gave the order to return fire:

> The Royals and Pulteney's hardly took their firelocks from their shoulders. Then their whole first line came down. On the left Bligh's and Sempill's fired on those who had outflanked their bayonets: the Highlanders enraged at making no impression threw stones at our men.[4]

For a time it looked as if the clansmen would break through the front line. Barrel's and Munro's came under severe pressure, and many men fell; but the gaps were filled immediately by Wolfe's, Sempill's and Bligh's. The Macdonalds, on the enemy's left wing, led by the so-called Duke of Perth, hurled themselves at Pulteney's and the Royals, but without success. Kingston's Light Horse and Cobham's Dragoons went in to help.

Meanwhile the Campbells had dismantled a section of the stone wall and swarmed through, closely followed by the dragoons. The horses had negotiated the slope with ease but the four-foot wall at the top had at first defeated them. Now Bland sent the dragoons around the rebels' right rear flank. Even through the fog of war, it was clear the battle was won. It had lasted just half an hour.

Charles Edward, who had stayed well to the rear of his army, had already left the battlefield. He was led away to safety, while behind him on Culloden Moor the ragged cheers of Cumberland's men mingled with the cries of the dying.

# *11*

# Aftermath

THE BATTLE OF CULLODEN had lasted barely half an hour. It was without doubt the decisive encounter that Cumberland had meant it to be. The battlefield was stained with the blood of almost 2,000 dead and dying rebel soldiers, whereas Cumberland had lost just 350. The Young Pretender had escaped, it was true, and Lord George Murray had made an orderly retreat with some of his men, but the Stuart cause had died upon Culloden Moor.

Cumberland was elated. 'Well done, my brave boys!' he called out to his victorious battalions as they left the battlefield. To Colonel Wolfe's regiment he called out his thanks: 'You have done the business!' he cried. 'Well done, my brave Campbells!' he called to the Argyll Militia, praising their flanking manoeuvre. And they cheered him in return, throwing their hats in the air and telling each other that if only the Duke had been at Prestonpans and Falkirk things would have been very different.

Later that afternoon, having already sent Bury south to tell the King of his victory, Cumberland entered Inverness to the sound of church bells and cheering crowds. But the first euphoria of victory was wearing off. There were all the wounded to be cared for, and prisoners to be dealt with – like Brigadier Stapleton, an Irishman, and his mixed Irish-French unit. The wounded Stapleton was dying, but Cumberland assured his unit of fair treatment; they had fought legitimately in his opinion in the service of a foreign country, France, and for that reason deserved honourable treatment. Towards the rebel Highlanders, English Jacobites and other Britons who had chosen to fight for the Young Pretender, Cumberland had less merciful intentions. In his eyes they were traitors to the King and the Union.

Furthermore, it had been clear to Cumberland ever since he reached Scotland that no mere battle could solve problems of lawlessness and thraldom to the clans. His long-term objective was to ensure that a lasting, loyal, Hanoverian peace was brought to the Highlands and islands. The clan system, the feuds and the barbaric justice must be abolished. That meant comprehensive new legislation must be enacted, new administrators appointed, and strenuous efforts made to persuade the Highlanders of the benefits of London rule. Cumberland knew he had the backing of men like Newcastle, Chesterfield, Hardwicke and of course his father, who would support him to the hilt, but the priority was to disarm the hostile clans, if necessary by force.

Thus the Battle of Culloden marked not a conclusion but a new start in Scottish affairs. In the myths later cultivated by Jacobite ladies and others with a taste for romance, it was the beginning of the time of butchery. It was a time of harsh repression, certainly, for which Cumberland was held responsible, although it was not he who made policy decisions but men in London, in Edinburgh and Glasgow.

At first Cumberland's victory was hailed with gratitude throughout Hanoverian England. 'I am extremely pleased with the countenance and behaviour of the troops,' the King wrote. 'I hope you will let them know it.'[1] Sir John Ligonier, too, wrote with fulsome congratulations, to which Cumberland replied: 'I must own you have hit my weak side when you say that the honour of troops is restored. That pleases beyond all the honours done me.'[2] For honours aplenty were being heaped on his head. Parliament offered him thanks on behalf of the nation, along with an annuity of £25,000 for life. Handel set to work on an oratorio inspired by Cumberland's feat, called *Judas Maccabaeus* after the Jewish patriot. Poets and other scribblers put pen to paper; the newspapers were flooded with offerings such as

> The lily, thistle and the rose
> All droop and fade, all die away.
> Sweet William only rules today.[3]

William Collins, mentor of Keats, was moved to write about 'Pale red Culloden' and 'Illustrious William! Britannia's guardian named...'[4] But Britannia saved the fullest demonstrations of her gratitude for when the young hero eventually returned south.

The Young Pretender left Culloden Moor in a state of stunned disbelief. When Lord George Murray reassembled a few units of his men and urged him to fight on, Charles Edward's response was unambiguous. He would fight no more. His Highlanders melted away into the hills, and he wanted only to do the same. From now on he was a fugitive.

For as long as the Young Pretender remained on British soil, Cumberland believed that the Jacobite seed might still germinate. Naturally the fugitive Charles Edward was to be sought out; there was still the £30,000 reward on offer for his capture. But his generals and commanders were sought too, and such of his followers who persisted in their misguided beliefs. Cumberland's orders were clear. If the rebel soldiers willingly surrendered, his officers should give them a certificate of receipt for their arms and they should be allowed to go home in peace. Otherwise, he proclaimed throughout the Highlands, his officers would be justified in enforcing 'military execution' at the point of the sword.

The lawyers demurred at this. In London and Edinburgh there were legal men who argued that Cumberland's policy would be acceptable in a state of war, but as this did not pertain at present his orders could be construed as illegal. Their prissy, academic arguments were met by scorn from the young soldier. He was fighting a war against subversion, against a hidden enemy; tough measures were vital. He repeated his orders to all his commanders. Later in April his secretary Fawkener wrote on his behalf to Lord Crawford at Perth:

> I am to inform you that H.R.H. treats all prisoners born subjects of His Majesty as traitors and rebels: and all others as prisoners of war. H.R.H. would have you observe the same rule and I am also to recommend to your Lordship on the part of H.R.H. to be diligent in inquiring after persons who have been in arms against His Majesty and to seize all such, as well as arms that be or have been in the arms of such. Likewise that if you hear of any persons yet in arms against His Majesty you endeavour to put them to the sword.[5]

It was harsh, certainly, but Cumberland did give the rebel Highlanders a chance. If they chose to continue to resist they would have to take the consequences – and, of course, many of them did. But as a result the myth-makers found ammunition to use against the victor of Culloden.

In later years one lie in particular would blacken Cumberland's name. Among the papers found on a prisoner was an order signed by Lord George Murray on 14 April – *before* the battle – that no quarter should be given to the Hanoverians. The lie was that Cumberland had forged this, to justify reprisals against rebels found in arms. Cumberland had no reason to forge anything. That the order existed is proven by many individual accounts, such as the letter from Lieutenant Hugh Ross of the 13th Foot to the Mayor of Newcastle:

> There was one of their orderly books found after the battle wherein the order the night before we fought was to not give quarter to man or woman, to cut all out prisoners' throats and murder everyone from there to London.[6]

This undoubtedly applied to the night march. And James Wolfe wrote in similar vein: 'The rebels besides their inclination had orders not to give quarter to our men.'[7] Even more convincing proof is an article in the *General Evening Post* later that year, on 12 August, explaining the inaction of the French troops at Culloden: their commander claimed that he had preferred to resign himself and his men into the hands of the Duke of Cumberland rather than carry out so shocking an order; his directions were to fight, not commit murder.

Undoubtedly, when news of this enemy order spread among Cumberland's men their indignation would have increased and their attitude towards captured rebels would have hardened. Undoubtedly, too, there were individual acts of vicious and totally unjustified revenge. But the Jacobite claim that Cumberland organized a systematic campaign of reprisals against men, women and children is patently false.

There were many other such stories in the years to come, their object always to vilify the man responsible for the Jacobites' defeat at Culloden. After two hundred and fifty years, it is not easy for the historian to refute these lies in detail, but some of them are simply ridiculous — such as the one concerning James Wolfe. Cumberland is said to have ordered Wolfe to shoot a wounded rebel on the battlefield, and Wolfe is said to have refused. That Cumberland, who had shown such concern for the rights of prisoners and wounded men at Fontenoy, should have ordered anyone to shoot a wounded Highlander is unlikely, to say the least, and if Wolfe had refused a direct order from his Commander-in-Chief he would have faced a court martial. Wolfe certainly never mentioned such an incident in any of the copious accounts he later gave of Culloden; on the contrary, his writings betray only the highest respect for his chief, and Cumberland for his part thought very highly of Wolfe.

In fact, the irony is that Cumberland did all he could to restrain his men, to prevent them from wreaking vengeance on the subversive Highlanders. He remonstrated with 'Hangman' Hawley for his excessive zeal with the noose and execution squad. He reined in his own instinctive desire to punish the rebels indiscriminately for their disloyalty to his father. But his distaste for the task he could not hide.

In immediate celebration of victory, Cumberland rewarded all those who had captured rebel colours with sixteen guineas. In fact, every man who had served at Culloden was given a cash reward. According to the bounty roll, 376 sergeants got 19s 0½d each — this at a time when sergeants received net pay of about 1s a day — 6,602 privates 9s 6¾d each, and 402 corporals and 252 drummers something in between, while the Argyll Militia and twenty subaltern officers divided £100 between them. The Duke also devoted the sum of £1,640 to the relief of widows and orphans of men killed at Culloden and Falkirk, and used another £1,000 to set up a special fund to reward acts of outstanding merit. Sizeable donations were also made to the regimental infirmaries and to a fund for the purchase of extra blankets, breeches, shirts, stockings and caps – all thanks to the generosity of the Lord Mayor of London.

But the Captain-General was rebuked by his father for sending the captured enemy colours down to Edinburgh to be burnt; they were, he said, the business of the hangman. This upset the King, who had wanted the colours to be paraded in triumph through the streets of London and then retained as war trophies. Cumberland apologized, but the colours had by then been destroyed.

At first Cumberland and his staff worked with enthusiasm and energy, buoyed up by their victory. He urged the regimental surgeons to greater efforts in finding and treating their wounded, many of whom had crawled away from the battlefield. He emptied the Inverness gaols, many of whose inhabitants told terrible stories of Jacobite barbarity, in preparation for rebel prisoners. Meanwhile the dragoons were rounding up all rebels still found in arms in the area of Inverness, and the cavalry pursued remnants of the Young Pretender's army into the hills.

On 23 April Cumberland wrote to the Duke of Newcastle that he hoped his work would be finished within a few weeks; thereafter, all would be up to the politicians. For this reason he sent Lord Findlater down to London:

> He is thoroughly master of the laws as they now stand, and of those which will be absolutely necessary to be done by Parliament this summer. I would to God I could be in town to explain a number of things that can't be explained in writing.[8]

That last phrase is interesting; not only does it express the young man's innate caution, it also suggests that he knew the Jacobites had sympathizers in high positions in London – and one hazards a guess that he might have been thinking of the Duke of Argyll. Not only in London, in fact: 'I believe the greatest blow to all the Jacobites would be for the King to move all the judiciary from Edinburgh to Glasgow for the former is the seat of the rebellion.'[9]

On the 25th Duncan Forbes arrived in Inverness, the 'Old President' as he was known, Lord President of the Court of Session. He and Loudoun had found refuge with the MacLeods in Skye, and he brought news that his and Loudoun's militias were now working to subdue the rebels in the west. But Forbes was a pious, long-winded lawyer and his outlook accorded not a bit with Cumberland's. The young soldier found him unrealistic, believing that leniency would be the better policy towards the clansmen, when the evidence was that they were using violence and subversion to resist the King's orders. He nevertheless agreed to Forbes's request that he make one more proclamation about the surrender of arms under amnesty, though he did not think it would be effective. Forbes appreciated his forbearance and admitted that he was surprised to find such patience in a man so young and active.

However, Cumberland's patience soon began to wear very thin. He was receiving news from the Netherlands, where Saxe had launched his new campaign; having overrun Brussels in the winter he was now threatening Antwerp. Cumberland felt it his duty as a soldier to return to Europe, yet he clearly could not while the remnants of the Jacobite threat persisted in Scotland. The Highlanders continued to resist, the lawyers continued to argue, and his own men were becoming impossible to control; much of his time was wasted in dealing with cases of indiscipline. One day no fewer than twelve officers were absent from their picket duties, and every day men were indulging in their predatory instincts – thieving, despoiling, and ravaging the countryside in the name of the Hanoverian army. If caught they faced severe punishments: up to 1000 lashes was not uncommon. But they were undeterred. They found Inverness dull, particularly in comparison with cities like Bruges and Ghent, where many of them had found consolation after the glorious defeat of Fontenoy. Lord George Sackville was exceptional in noticing the beauties of a Highland spring.

In May Cumberland decided to move down the Great Glen to Fort Augustus. Loudoun's militia had already chased the rebels out and an advance party was now sent ahead to prepare the way. At the south end of Loch Ness, Fort Augustus was in a commanding position, with easy access to both Inverness and Fort William. Although intelligence was hard to come by, it seemed that the Young Pretender had fled west towards the sea lochs and islands. The Royal Navy was patrolling these waters, and there had already been a skirmish in early May when a French privateer, the *Mars*, was spotted off the Moidart Peninsula. Now Cumberland resolved to tighten the net around the fugitive. A few days later, leaving only a few companies in Inverness, he led his main force south-west down the glen. They arrived at Fort Augustus on 23 May.

If Inverness had been boring, Fort Augustus was worse. There was nothing here to keep the men amused. In fact there was nothing here at all, bar the beauty of the sparkling River Oich amid steep hills. The fort and barracks had been destroyed during the various encounters between government and rebel troops and Cumberland himself was obliged to live, apparently quite contentedly, in a 'green turf hut, a green bower of branches, heather and sods built for him as a rustic pavilion.'[10] His men had their sailcloth tents, of course, and the weather now was milder; they were in no danger of starving, with the supplies he had brought from Inverness and all the cattle rounded up by his men, lifted both lawfully and otherwise from the surrounding farms. But Cumberland's chief problem now was how to maintain discipline and morale.

His intention was, of course, to keep everyone busy, partly by making repairs to the fort and partly by enforcing the King's law in the surrounding hills. He sent out large detachments to scour the glens, and two companies of Royal Scots Fusiliers went with General John Campbell to join forces with the navy, on patrol among the Western Isles. Campbell's zeal was to prove excessive, matched only by that of Captain John Ferguson of HMS *Furnace*; together they and their men would wreak havoc among the island clans − killing, pillaging, raping, and forcibly disarming even anti-Jacobites like the MacLeods and the Macdonalds of Sleat. It was some weeks before Cumberland heard of their antics and, although he strongly disapproved, by then the damage was done. By then, too, his own frustration was getting the better of him.

At first, to his gratification, some rebels began to submit. According to The MacLeod:

> The Duke is well enough pleased with delivery of arms in Brae Lochaber, Badenoch and Macintosh's country and I believe no more harm will be done to that quarter. As to their operation some mistakes I believe have happened, made by officers out on command.[11]

Here indeed he had touched the heart of the matter. Whatever orders Cumberland issued, he was unable to control the men who carried them out. Once they left Fort Augustus and his restraining presence, if the men chose to slaughter and plunder and wreak revenge on the rebel Highlanders, to misinterpret his orders or ignore them entirely, their chief could no nothing to prevent them. Until more and better communications were built, the same problem would face anyone trying to control this lawless place.

The MacLeod's brother-in-law, Sir Alexander Macdonald, was equally sure where the blame should fall:

> Was there as much goodness in proportion to their rank in the other officers as their commander is possessed of, his stay at Fort Augustus would have been as agreeable a sojourn as any in the world.[12]

On the other hand, Cumberland was insistent that the law had to be enforced by military means, as he told Forbes; and Forbes for his part agreed that 'no severity that is necessary ought to be dispensed with.'[13] The niceties of what was legally necessary no doubt escaped many of the men. Besides, their chief too was getting impatient. A week after arriving at Fort Augustus he decided that strong measures were needed.

Cumberland deployed his men with care. General John Campbell was to search the districts of Sunart and Morvern, south of Moidart, while further to the north a huge sweep would be made by over a thousand men under Lord George Sackville, Colonel Cornwallis and Captain Caroline Scott. To co-ordinate the sweep, Cumberland himself moved temporarily to Fort William. Once he was satisfied that they knew their task, 'to root out the remainder of the rebels that are in arms,'[14], he returned to his base at Fort Augustus. Here he deployed another raiding party, as a Mr Ashe Lee told the new Secretary at War, Henry Fox:

> Such is the obstinacy of some [rebels] that they choose to starve rather than surrender. H.R.H., wearied with this abuse of his lenity, sent Major Lockhart into Glen Moriston with 140 men two days ago to do military execution. He is just returned: killed about 17, burnt above 400 houses and drove home 1400 head of cattle. Some of the killed were hung up by their heels with labels expressing the reason for it.[15]

Military execution was Cumberland's new tactic, and he obviously intended to advertise the fact.

However, life at Fort Augustus was not entirely an orgy of blood lust. While Cumberland sat in his rustic pavilion, sifting intelligence reports from incoming patrols, attempting to evaluate information about rebel activity and rumours of the Young Pretender's whereabouts, attending to all the routine matters of supply and communicating ever more impatiently with the wavering politicians in London, he devised some excellent sport for his men. Lord George Sackville's account cannot be bettered:

> The Duke endeavours to divert the camp every evening by giving plates to be run for by the little horses taken from the rebels, sometimes the ladies ride and sometimes the men, but as saddles are not allowed of, you may imagine few go round the course without tumbling, especially the ladies who are commonly half drunk to raise their spirits.
>
> We had yesterday a more serious race, between a horse of the Duke's and Captain Boscawen, and everybody was as much in earnest as I hear they are at Newmarket. Boscawen won the first heat and the Duke the two others, to the great joy of the soldiers, who upon his winning huzza'd as if they had gained a victory.[16]

The picture is clear enough: yet even here the Jacobite lies attempted to

Fort Augustus July y[e] 10th 1746     426

Major Generall Campbell & Comodore
Smith hearing that you have pursued
the Pretenders Son till you drove him into
the Isle of Sky where you will be arived
by this time & as I am sure that by your
Vigilance & endeavours youll not let him
escape I send Captain Hodson one of my
aide Camp that I may be the better
informed how he[is] taken or kill'd in
the attempt & I desire youll let him
know all that concern it & trust him
as one that come from me  your affectio[n]
friend
                              William
P.S. Sir Alexander Macdonald
goes with Cap[t] Hodson

                              X

                110                        8.8

*A near run thing*
Fort Augustus, July 10th, Cumberland to General John Campbell. He is sending his ADC Captain Studholme Hodgson with Sir Alexander Macdonald of Sleat to pick up the Pretender's son, dead or alive, in Skye. Lady Margaret Macdonald, his wife, and Kingsburgh denied them their quarry.

smear the Duke, suggesting that it was the women and not the horses that were bare-backed! The simple truth is that there was a shortage of saddles and harness for the captured galloways; and Cumberland made of necessity a virtue — except in the eyes of his enemies, of course.

Charles Edward was by now on the island of South Uist, in the Outer Hebrides, but even here he was not safe. The islanders wanted rid of him; his presence was a threat to their livelihood, for who knew when the rampaging troops and marines would arrive? Moved from place to place, surrounded by a tiny band of retainers, he was being hunted down like a rabbit. A young woman by the name of Flora Macdonald was asked to help him, and reluctantly she agreed. With General Campbell close on their heels, they escaped to Skye at the end of June.

Cumberland received the news with glee. Most of Skye's inhabitants were loyal Hanoverians and Whigs. He was sure that Commodore Smith's squadron and General Campbell's men would soon close the net on their prey. On 10 July he wrote a cheerful letter to Campbell:

> Hearing that you have pursued the Pretender's son till you drove him into the Isle of Skye, where you will be arrived by this time, and as I am sure that by your vigilance and endeavours you'll not let him escape, I send Captain Hodgson, one of my aides de camp, that I may be the better inform'd how he be taken or kill'd in the attempt, and I desire you'll let him know all that concern it and trust him as one that comes from me, your affectionate friend William.[17]

But on the 13th Hodgson returned, bringing several important prisoners but not Charles Edward.

It was a bitter disappointment for Cumberland but it made no difference to his decision. He had done all that any man could do in Scotland; he had filled the Highlands with the King's Army, scoured the rebels from the glens, and sent the Young Pretender packing. The final stages of the campaign could be safely left to Albemarle. The Duke of Cumberland was leaving Scotland.

# *12*

# Conquering Hero

THE WELCOME AWAITING CUMBERLAND IN LONDON was overwhelming. He had become a national hero. Thanks to him, the Jacobite threat had been crushed and the Hanoverian supremacy guaranteed. Just as important in many people's eyes: he had driven the Highland savages back to their glens.

Cumberland left Fort Augustus on 18 July, escorted by a detachment of Kingston's Light Horse, along with three of his aides. They arrived at Edinburgh on the 21st, met at the West Gate by cheering crowds and bands waiting to escort them through the city to Holyrood. The Lord Provost and city council had been suspended, tainted by contact with the rebels, and there was no formal reception committee to greet the hero, but he agreed to receive a delegation from the city guilds who presented him with a commemorative gold box. Despite his haste to return south, he found time for another meeting with Duncan Forbes, who by now had accepted the young soldier's arguments for legislative reform combined with military severity. Indeed, the ageing lawyer had developed a considerable respect for Cumberland. Writing to the Duke of Newcastle at about this time, he remarked:

> I never saw talents united in any one which promise so complete a hero and so sure a stay to the Crown and to the Constitution against foreign forces and intestine rebellion.... If I was to talk to his father on the subject I could not possibly do it without what would seem rank flattery.[1]

Cumberland also fitted in an inspection of Colonel Lee's Edinburgh Regiment, one company of which he was sending to Stirling as the Hessians were returning to the Continent. Early on the morning of 22 July he resumed his journey south.

At York on the 23rd he was met by the Archbishop again, along with the

Dean and Chapter. This time he could not avoid a formal reception, when the Archbishop extolled his virtues at tedious length and the Lord Mayor presented him with the freedom of the city: but he managed to escape that same evening and rode off steadily southwards. He was deliberately travelling light, to escape notice when he reached London, and made such good time that he arrived in the capital ahead of the messenger who had been sent to announce him.

It was about two o'clock on the afternoon of the 25th when he rode in a postchaise through the gates of Kensington Palace, taking everyone by surprise. But word soon spread of his arrival. Church bells were rung, gun salutes fired and huge crowds assembled in the streets. According to the Marchioness Grey, Cumberland was virtually a prisoner in the palace for several days 'for the mob will devour him with fondness.' She went on: 'They were extremely loyal and drunk in honour of his name last night, and we had as great illuminations as upon news of his victory.'[2] Everyone put lighted candles in the windows of London, or if they did not their windows were broken by the mob.

On 6 August Cumberland received the Freedom of the City of London and a service of thanksgiving was held at St Paul's Cathedral at which Handel's 'Conquering Hero', written in his honour, was heard for the first time. Over the whole country inns were renamed 'The Duke of Cumberland' and his fat pink face peered down from innumerable signs. He was elected Chancellor of the Universities of Aberdeen and St Andrews, and later, in the following January, was awarded the Freedom of Edinburgh. A gold medal was struck for Culloden, one of the first campaign awards in the British army, showing Cumberland in profile — very much the 'martial boy' of the broadsheets — and Apollo on the reverse with a dead dragon and the motto *Actum est ilicet periit* ('The deed is done, it is past').

Cumberland's army had its share of the adulation and celebration of course, but with most of the Culloden troops still in Scotland it was his own regiment of Foot Guards that paraded in Hyde Park and staged reconstructions of the battle for the edification and amusement of Londoners. The park's Tyburn Gate was renamed Cumberland Gate and countless toasts were raised to his name. In the manner of the day, an officers' dining club was founded, the Cumberland Society, to meet annually for dinner on the Duke's birthday; its membership was very select, totalling just twenty-five to match the young hero's years, and its first president was the Marquess of Granby, serving with Kingston's Horse. Granby had been at Fort Augustus and boasted proudly of the Highlanders' surprise that his horses could gallop over the steep heather-clad hillsides. Kingston's, which had in all but name provided

Cumberland's bodyguard in Scotland, would now be recreated the Duke of Cumberland's (15th) Regiment of Dragoons, with the Duke as their Colonel.

Another society founded in Cumberland's honour is still in existence today. The bellringers of London, who had pealed so enthusiastically at his victory and again at his return to the capital, banded together and called themselves the Society of Royal Cumberland Youths. At their annual dinner their President wears a medallion round his neck showing Cumberland on horseback, surrounded by the legend *Pro Patria et Amico* ('For Country and Comradeship').

But of all the tributes and honours paid him after Culloden, there is no doubting that Cumberland derived the deepest and most lasting pleasure from George II's gift of the post of Ranger and Keeper of Windsor Great Park, together with a not very commodious lodge in considerable disrepair. It was a mark of the King's approval, and as such worth more to a loyal son than all the gold boxes in the kingdom. It was also a mark of personal affection, for the King well knew how Cumberland loved Windsor. And as we shall see, it was to Windsor that the Duke would always return to recuperate when fate and the world turned against him.

Amid the celebrations that summer of 1746, there were already signs of dissidence. As the weeks passed and the nation's happy mood subsided, the Jacobites began to spread their lies. Ultimately they still hoped to reverse the damage done at Culloden, and to this end they strove to blacken Cumberland's name. Although there were many other men they might have chosen as targets, like Lord Chesterfield, who proposed even more vigorous and implacable measures against the Highlanders, Cumberland was seen as the greatest threat. He was the King's son, the hero, the head of the Hanoverian army on which all laurels had been piled.

At first the subversives contented themselves with satire. As far back as May some Tory wit had suggested that Cumberland was an appropriate candidate for the livery of the ancient guild of butchers. Now the scribblers and caricaturists fastened on the image and expanded it. Increasingly he was depicted as the ruthless bully who had unleashed his savage troops on innocent clansmen. Word spread south of the roughshod manner in which Scott and Ferguson had broken the spirit of the Highlanders and islanders, and Cumberland was blamed. The flames of petty misunderstandings were fanned into righteous indignation, such as the story that Cumberland had punished the Provost of Inverness, a Whig and Hanoverian, for helping the Jacobite wounded; this nonsense was roundly condemned as such by the sister of Duncan Forbes, Mrs Fraser of Achnagairn, who asserted that 'All these mischiefs is not to be laid at the Duke's charge but the vile informers which they are daily plagued with.'[3] Unfortunately there was not always a Mrs Fraser around to defend the Duke's reputation.

One of the most notorious tales against Cumberland was based on circumstantial evidence which suggested he had aided General Hawley in the plundering of an old woman's household effects. While in Aberdeen, Cumberland, along with his secretary Fawkener and assistant secretary, Edward Mason, had found a billet in No.45 Guestrow, the house of the Whig advocate Alexander Thomson. Hawley was billeted next door, with a Mrs Gordon. When they left Aberdeen, Cumberland gave the Thomsons' staff a tip of six guineas, but Hawley had taken a dislike to Mrs Gordon and left only orders to his aide, James Wolfe, to pack up anything of value in her house and send it down to London. Mrs Gordon was understandably furious, especially as Cumberland had personally assured her that her house would not be plundered. But apparently her china was spotted some time later for sale in a London shop by one of Mrs Gordon's friends, a Miss Jackson, who enquired of the shopkeeper where he had obtained it and his answer was supposedly that he had got it from a prostitute who had been given it by the Duke of Cumberland!

So much for the myth, repeated with embellishments in *The Lyon in Mourning*, that repository of most Jacobite tales. It is true that the china, and much else, had been packed up and shipped to London on Hawley's orders, but when Stephen Poyntz, who not only was Cumberland's governor but also held a post in H.M. Customs, read the ship's manifest he immediately smelt a rat. He already knew of crates arriving from Scotland which purported to hold Cumberland's personal effects but which, on investigation, were found to contain 'crucifix, copes, vestments, beads and trumpery consigned from the titular Primate of Scotland who is with the rebels.'[4] Clearly some impudent person had hoped to save Catholic contraband by smuggling it out of Scotland with the Duke's own consignment. Now Poyntz had found Mrs Gordon's household goods. He immediately wrote to Fawkener, admitting his suspicions; he had heard gossip in London that some officers' loot was being passed off as Cumberland's property. On 20 May Fawkener wrote back:

> I had, to say truth, forgot the two boxes of china ware. It was not intended they should be sent to London in the Duke's name.... The things might as well have been left, and I am sure the Duke would have been better pleased if they had; but he did not seem to give any order in it. It might be right the things should be plundered but that officer [Hawley] might I think have forborn appropriating any part of them as he lodged in the House.[5]

In other words, Cumberland had nothing whatever to do with Hawley's looting, and the china ended up in his possession by mistake. But as Fawkener's letter makes clear — "Tis good to take where we can, as it is some alleviation of our own losses' — contemporary attitudes towards plunder were less strict than today. If a rascally old general like Hawley was feathering his nest, he was by no means alone; and there was very little that his young chief could do to stop him.

Another concomitant aspect of victory was, of course, the trial and punishment of prisoners. At Culloden, some 500-600 rebels had been captured and many more had been added to their number since. By no means all were imprisoned by Cumberland and his men; once the die had fallen, many a laird and provost saw fit to throw the local trouble-makers into prison on suspicion of aiding the Jacobites.

In total, 3,471 prisoners were taken, many of them shipped south to Tilbury to await their fate in London, and surprisingly, despite the usual appalling prison conditions and an outbreak of gaol fever on the prison ships, the vast majority survived. Nor did many receive the death penalty: just 80 were executed, mostly by hanging. Four rebel peers were sentenced to the axe, being noble, but one of them (Lord Cromarty) was later reprieved. Lord Kilmarnock had been captured during the battle and Lord Balmerino surrendered; Lord Lovat, however, had been found by Captain Ferguson's men, hiding in a hollow tree trunk on an island in Loch Morar, and led prisoner to Cumberland at Fort Augustus. Here he had the impudence to ask for mercy on the grounds that he had once been in favour at Court, and had carried Cumberland as a baby in his arms so that a doting grandfather, George I, could embrace him in the gardens of Hampton Court. At his trial in London, however, he was betrayed by Murray of Broughton, the Young Pretender's secretary, who turned King's Evidence to save his own hide.

Another 935 prisoners were sentenced to transportation, usually to the colonies of America or the West Indies; some 200 were banished, over 1200 exchanged or released as prisoners of war, 88 died while in prison, at least 30 escaped, and 76 won a conditional pardon.[6] The remaining hundreds cannot be accounted for, perhaps due to poor records.

Meanwhile the cause of all their woes still lurked in the glens of Scotland. Cumberland had left Albemarle in charge of the northern army, no longer trusting Hawley, but Albemarle did not relish his new position. If the energetic young Duke had failed to suppress the rebels or catch Charles Edward Stuart, then William Anne Keppel, second Earl of Albemarle, doubted his own ability to succeed. He would, he wrote,

be split upon the rocks that have in different ways undone four of my predecessors, as it is absolutely impossible for the person that commands here to do his duty like an honest man and be well with the people and ministers at court who we hear already begin to screen some of these rebellious rascals.[7]

He was in fact facing all the same problems that Cumberland had experienced in controlling the troops as well as suppressing the rebels, without much help from London. He wrote repeatedly to Newcastle expressing his distaste for Scotland and her inhabitants.

On 13 August, with Cumberland's permission, Albemarle broke up the camp at Fort Augustus and dispersed the weary battalions to winter quarters. He himself returned to Edinburgh with the headquarters staff, but many of his men, largely shoeless and in rags, now found themselves facing another cruel Scottish winter. The officers would all have echoed the complaints of George Sackville at Dundee, who regretted 'that the Duke thinks it necessary to keep us all at our posts for I should have been very glad of a month at Knole.'[8] All over the Highlands men gave vent to their frustration by plundering and laying waste to farms and homes, even those of loyal Hanoverians, or by going absent without leave and numerous acts of indiscipline. In Aberdeen the Earl of Ancram feared the local populace would rise in revolt at the troops' disorderly conduct.

The men would scarcely have believed it but Cumberland was equally frustrated. He had left Scotland in Albemarle's hands not because he felt he had completely subdued the rebellious clans, but because he thought himself required again in Flanders as commander of the allied armies. Marshal Saxe was still rampaging across Flanders and threatening Holland; Ligonier had been sent to help stiffen allied resistance but now Cumberland thought he should take over. However, while there was any risk at all that the Jacobites might rise again, the King and his ministers wanted him at home.

Reluctant but obedient, he spent the summer in London. At least he was able to speak in person and in confidence with the nation's law-makers about the question of new legislation in Scotland. He remained suspicious of Argyll, whom Albemarle also mistrusted, and wanted to clip his wings, and he found ready allies in two prominent Lowland Scots, Hume Campbell and his twin brother Lord Marchmont. According to Campbell, Cumberland was 'very aware of all that look like Jacobites as he thinks all the Duke of Argyll's friends are.'[9] In particular Cumberland was furious at Argyll's opposition to a bill to abolish the heritable jurisdiction of the clan chiefs. The clan loyalties had to be broken, and the system of clan justice was contrary to the King's law; when Argyll tried to justify the old ways he was undoubtedly trying to protect his own interests. After discussing details of the bill with Cumberland, Campbell remarked that he was 'very kind and reasonable and knew the facts.'[10] But even with the support of Hume Campbell and his brother, as well as that of Findlater and Duncan Forbes, Cumberland's suggestions met a lukewarm response from the ministers. Argyll's influence not only in Scotland but in London was such that he could not lose; in the end, he won very considerable monetary compensation for the loss of his jurisdiction.

Other legal measures in which Cumberland took an interest included acts of Parliament intended to disarm the rebels once and for all; to oblige all ministers of religion to swear an oath of loyalty and to outlaw the wearing of the kilt, the plaid over the shoulder and any form of tartan cloth. Simple as it seemed, this last act did more to demoralize the rebel Highlanders than all the other measures.

On the more positive side, Cumberland took steps to continue the work begun by Wade. He despatched his chief engineer, William Skinner, to design and build a new Fort George and to restore Forts William and Augustus. David Watson, who had been not only at Carlisle but also at Falkirk and Culloden, remained in Scotland to supervise the rebuilding of other defensive works at Inversnaid and Edinburgh; and in the following year was appointed superintendent of a scheme he himself had submitted, to carry out a complete topographical survey of the Highlands. This invaluable task, mapping the hills and glens at two inches to the mile, would involve eight years' work and the services of men like Paul Sandby, William Roy, Manson and Dundas. Sandby's brother Thomas was equally useful to Cumberland; he had attended the Battle of Culloden and drawn a sketch of the battlefield, as well as views of Fort Augustus and other sites of military interest. These maps and the Sandby sketches were just some of the huge collection of similar items amassed by Cumberland over the years, the maps now in the British Museum, the views in the Print Room at Windsor.

This enforced spell in London also allowed Cumberland to assess recent events in Westminster and on the international scene. Pitt had finally joined the administration, taking over as Paymaster General of the Forces in May, shortly after the appointment of Henry Fox to the post that Pitt had coveted, that of Secretary at War. But Pitt had learned to behave himself. In March he had even supported the Pelhams in proposing subsidies for the allied armies, including £400,000 for Austria and £310,000 for the maintenance of the 18,000 Hanoverian troops. As a result the King found him slightly less of an irritant. Besides, when cynics sneered that Pitt took the paymastership for the personal dividends that would notoriously accrue, he publicly renounced them all and accepted only his proper salary. To men of honour, this was a favourable sign.

Much more worrying was the news from the Continent. As Cumberland had feared, the Austrian Netherlands had fallen to Saxe. Although Austrian troops had repelled the French in northern Italy and even attacked Provence, in northern Europe it seemed the allied forces were unable to co-ordinate a response to Saxe. By the time Cumberland returned to London, Ligonier had already left with a handful of battalions, to pick up the cavalry regiments that had never been brought home, as well as the Hessian and Hanoverian contingents now in British pay, and to join Charles of Lorraine's army on the River Meuse near Liège. But the Dutch had embarked on negotiations with the French, hoping to secure neutrality. This news threw Pelham's ministry into confusion. He himself favoured peace and economy; his brother Newcastle and the King were for a better peace through victory in Europe. While the Earl of Sandwich, Ambassador in The Hague, was told to monitor the Franco-Dutch negotiations, Newcastle invited Cumberland to advise on strategy. Naturally, he favoured a strong military solution.

One glimmer of hope lay in the fact that Philip V of Spain had died in July; his son Ferdinand VI would quietly secede from the war, so that France effectively lost her only important ally. Another, more distant glimmer lay across the Atlantic, where British colonial forces had captured Louisburg and the French-held Cape Breton Island. Already there was talk in London of building on this success by sending further troops to North America.

It all served to increase Cumberland's restlessness as he spent his days in the ordinary pursuits of English court life. In July he went to the races at Ascot, his first public appearance since Culloden, and was immediately surrounded by a jostling throng which according to the poet Gray wanted only 'to gaze on the young hero like a crowd at a bear baiting.'[11] He attended the trials in Westminster Hall of the rebel peers. He attended levees and receptions, and stifled any boredom he felt at repeating over and over the stories of his victory at Culloden.

And then came the news that he had half dreaded, half longed to hear. Charles Edward Stuart had escaped to France. Word reached Albemarle within four days, thanks to an efficient network of agents throughout the Highlands, and was swiftly transmitted to London. But at least the nation had been spared the grim eventuality of putting the Young Pretender on trial.

The French had regarded Charles Edward's antics in Scotland merely as a useful distraction from the campaign in Europe: a risky sideshow from which they preferred to remain aloof. While the Royal Navy patrolled Scottish waters with such vigour, they had not been overkeen to rescue the fugitive, though back in May the *Mars* had managed to embark several of his supporters, including the mortally ill Duke of Perth. Lord George Murray had found his own way to safety.

Eventually it was the Young Pretender's own followers in France who sent two French privateers to help him. On the evening of 19 September, 1746, the ships' crews made contact with Charles Edward's men, and late that night he was embarked in Loch nan Uamh, very close to the spot where he had landed fourteen months earlier. Ten days later he was back in France. Behind him he left only romantic legends; ahead he faced the emptiness of exile.

# 13

# Back to Europe

IRONICALLY, EVEN AS Charles Edward Stuart arrived back in Britanny, a combined operation by the Royal Navy and six battalions of the British Army had launched an attack on the Breton port of Lorient. It had been planned to send troops under General Sinclair to consolidate the gains in North America; but after months of dithering Pelham's ministry had sent them instead to raid the main naval base of the French East India Company. Cumberland had been against the expedition. In his opinion the troops should have been sent to Flanders where they could offer direct resistance to Saxe. Newcastle, however, argued that a diversion in Britanny might weaken Saxe's resolve in the Low Countries, and Cumberland found his advice overruled.

The expedition was a complete fiasco. The French defences soon drove off the attackers. Two of Sinclair's battalions panicked under fire and abandoned their guns. A boatload of soldiers capsized, drowning twenty-five men. Eventually the operation was called off and Admiral Lestock turned his convoy back for home, only to run into gales that blew him off course to southern Ireland. Much later, in April, 1747, four of Sinclair's battalions and the artillery company fetched up in Holland, where Cumberland believed they should have been sent in the first place.

The fundamental problem was that Pelham's ministry could not decide on a strategy by which to fight the French. For so long as London had concentrated on the immediate threat posed by the Jacobite rebellion the whole administration had united in the national interest. Even the Prince of Wales had given his whole-hearted backing to the campaign to excise the rebels. Now, however, the King and his ministers found themselves in disagreement. France was advancing in Flanders. She was also menacing British colonies in North America and in India. How best could France be controlled?

Pelham himself was hoping the Franco-Dutch talks would lead to neutrality for Holland, and ultimately, by deflecting French interests, produce peace in Europe. His hopes were shared by Harrington, as Secretary of State (North), and Chesterfield. Pitt also favoured peace, in Europe at least, though he had supported the Britanny raid; he was beginning to look overseas at the burgeoning British empire and he championed the efforts of the Duke of Bedford, First Lord of the Admiralty, who wanted to exploit the colonists' success in Cape Breton Island. Newcastle and Hardwicke believed that peace in Europe would come only when France was forced to acknowledge the legitimacy of the Austrian succession, which meant continuing the war. The King, characteristically, wanted a military solution; but according to Pelham he was ill 'of his old distemper'[1] − a delicate reference, presumably, to George II's haemorrhoids − and wanted only to leave the decisions to someone else.

Cumberland, for his part, sought to finish the fight he had begun eighteen months earlier; he was convinced that the French would be stopped only by superior force. But until the nation's great leaders could settle on a policy, he felt himself to be in limbo. He turned his attention to army reform, to prepare the troops for the battle he was sure lay ahead.

His first efforts were concentrated on his new regiment of dragoons, formerly Kingston's Light Horse, which would now supply him with a personal cavalry guard, not replacing but supplementing the 1st Guards. In action they would carry out reconnaissance duties in particular. Cumberland's enthusiasm for the dragoons and for every detail of their establishment is vividly conveyed by the regiment's standing orders:

> Dragoons have a multiplicity of things to do more than a foot soldier − they must not be cluttered up with heavy and unnecessary equipment...
> Their horses to be hunter types and nimble...
> No officer is supposed ever to fight himself any more than to defend his head. His business is to see the men fight and do well...

He laid great stress on the officers' duty to ensure their men's welfare at all times. He also took a close interest in their uniforms: red coats faced and lined with the green of his own livery, and gold lace on the eight drummers' coats, making them four times as expensive as those for the Greys and Inniskillings.

However, as Cumberland well knew, the country's mood had changed; with the rebellion over and the battle won, it seemed to the British taxpayer that an army was an unnecessary luxury. Thus it may have been to help ease approval of his new regiment through the Treasury that Cumberland agreed to cuts in the cavalry establishment overall. Two regiments of horse were reduced to dragoons and Wade's Horse was put on to the Irish establishment.

More sensationally, two troops of Horse Grenadier Guards were disbanded. Cumberland was careful to discuss the cuts with the King and the government, and according to Pelham the reduction of the Horse Grenadiers was a voluntary gesture. It had been offered of the King's free will, Fox explained to Fawkener, and not on ministerial advice for 'nobody could ever think of meddling without the entire concurrence of H.M.'[2] But His Majesty was tending more and more to leave matters of detail to his son.

Detail was Cumberland's forte; in years to come he would devote considerable time and effort to the details of army reform. Broadly, however, his objectives were to improve discipline and to change the system of purchase, whereby officers bought their commissions and then recovered their costs by methods both honest and dishonest, often to the detriment of their own men. Cumberland wanted officers to be commissioned and promoted according to merit. Ability and loyalty should be the sole criteria for promotion. But this novel idea met with fierce resistance. Many officers saw Cumberland as a threat to their comfortable positions. Moreover, about forty army officers were also MPs, with all the extra privileges and influence bestowed by Westminster. The young Duke faced an uphill task in persuading them to accept his reforms.

Apart from the professional defects of the officer corps, the army's greatest failing in Cumberland's eyes was its totally inadequate training procedures. During the long years of peace under Walpole, the army had been run down and scattered. Outside London and the main fleet bases there was no barracks capable of holding a battalion; scattered garrisons, prone to indiscipline, were billeted at random in ale-houses and inns, with small detachments used to police the coastline in support of the excise officers and held available in case of civil disturbance. Under such circumstances, no squadron of cavalry could be trained to stand against cannon fire and musket shot, or horses accustomed to the crack and roar of battle; no infantry could learn to hold their positions and their fire until the order came. What Cumberland wanted was a system of peacetime exercises, regularly performed and inspected, for the whole army. But this, of course, depended on the co-operation of the officers.

There had been previous attempts to raise army standards, but they had met with only sporadic success. The Woolwich Academy had been founded as recently as 1741, to train gentlemen cadets for the Royal Artillery; but when the Duke was invited to inspect them in 1744 he had found them in bad order, ill disciplined with no proper uniform and no place of parade. An academy for engineers, founded in the same year, had made still less progress. He hoped to found a similar school for infantry and cavalry officers. Although Cumberland managed to make substantial improvements to the artillery, for engineers he would always remain reliant on a few talented individuals.

However, after Dettingen, Fontenoy and now Culloden, Cumberland had a very clear grasp of what was needed, and, with the King's support, he would gradually manage to introduce some of the men and the measures that the army required. But now, in the autumn of 1746, his efforts were about to be curtailed.

In October Sir John Ligonier was defeated by Saxe at Roucoux, near Liège. At last the administration agreed that Cumberland must return to the Continent and challenge the French.

In November, at the state opening of Parliament, the King's speech reinforced the impression that the government was at last united. Even Pitt agreed to the employment of Hessian and Hanoverian troops as mercenaries, which allowed the British expeditionary contingent to be kept down to 15,000. Financial provisions were granted to the Electors of Cologne, Mainz and Bavaria and to the King of Sardinia, to keep them out of the French camp. Efforts were made to enlist Russian military support, which would help to restrain Prussia.

Cumberland, elated by this evidence of a new resolve, could hardly wait for the start of the new campaign season. At the end of November he wrote to thank Newcastle for helping to bring about the change of policy, and assured him he would do all in his power to make it successful:

> What I may want in experience or capacity will be searched for in the Generals that are to serve me. No pains shall be spared by me for answering the view the King and my friends had in placing me in the very station that I wished to be in.[3]

And, he added, 'I shall be ready to go over whenever it may be thought necessary.' But much still depended upon securing the active participation of Holland.

Early in December Cumberland left for The Hague, accompanied by Fawkener, to see his brother-in-law the Prince of Orange and to hear from Sandwich how the Franco-Dutch negotiations were going. He found the Dutch politicians as elusive and indecisive as did Marlborough before him but by 3 January, 1747, he was telling Newcastle: 'All goes quickly, considering the want of government.'[4] Presumably he meant that the peace talks were faltering, for the Dutch hawks, the more belligerent Orange party under Bentinck, had gained an edge in Holland.

Cumberland had less trouble with the Austrian ministers in The Hague, who shared his belief that the French would be stopped only by force. Maria

Theresa, the Queen of Hungary as Cumberland called her, readily agreed that he should resume his former position in command of the allied force. He began to organize the various elements into a cohesive whole. The Austro-Hungarian contingent, led by a Hungarian commander, Marshal Batthyány, would be the largest: 60,000 men, although a proportion of them would not be available until late spring. The Hessians and Hanoverians, subsidised by Britain, would provide 6,000 and 18,000 men respectively. With the 15,000 British troops, this meant that Cumberland had nearly 100,000 men. It was a formidable army, but it faced an even stronger enemy, for Saxe was estimated to have 150,000 men.

At last, partly because Bentinck's party had overthrown the timorous republican régime that had constricted the Prince of Orange, the Dutch agreed to stand firm against France. Holland undertook to provide 40,000 troops to the allied army. Fawkener confided to Stone, Newcastle's secretary:

> All people here attribute whatever has been done to the Duke's presence and I think with great reason. He is the surest pledge we could have given that we are in earnest and his talents improve all advantages and conjunctions.[5]

Leaving Sandwich to sign the agreements committing Holland to the conflict, early in January, 1747, Cumberland returned to London in triumph.

He did not remain in London long. After reporting to the King and his ministers, he eagerly returned to the Continent at the beginning of February to finalize arrangements for the coming campaign. He knew it would not be easy. Saxe seemed to be unstoppable; he had almost reached the Dutch frontier, and the faltering peace talks at Breda only added momentum to his military bandwagon. Saxe's main force was concentrated in the area of Louvain and Malines, with detached corps to the left at Ghent and to the right at Liège on the River Meuse, threatening Maastricht. His next move might be on a flank or in the centre or at any point in between. He might choose to advance down the Meuse into the heart of Holland.

Cumberland believed that his only hope lay in striking first, but he had reckoned without the lethargy of his allies. The allied forces had been in widely scattered winter quarters; it would take over a month to assemble them all. He also needed to arrange supplies to meet the requirements of a vast number of men and horses, far in excess of the numbers that fought under Marlborough. To add to his problems, he found that the Dutch troops had again been placed under Waldeck. Furthermore, the allies required their commander-in-chief to consult his subordinate commanders in a council of war before making any major decision, and the subordinate commanders had

11. George Townshend, the Duke's former ADC, had a flair for caricature.
1. Newcastle. 2. Lyttelton. 3. The Duke. 4. Henry Fox.

12. "No man has done more for racing in England": Barnard Smith lunges a horse in front of the Duke, Sir Thomas Rich and the Earl of Albemarle. The artist stand slightly apart. (*Thomas Sandby, Windsor Castle*)

13.  The disastrous German Campaign of 1757: "Rare Turnips Ho! The root of all evil." The Duke is in the cart, Pitt and Fox on the right.

14.  Cumberland tries to hold the political balance after the fall of Pitt and Newcastle, exclaiming, "O Damn that heavy boot," referring to Bute and the Princess Dowager of Wales. "Preserve the Equilibrium, Uncle," says the Duke of York; 1762.

15. "Cumberland entertained his guests with a 'Mandarin Junk'." The hull of the Chinese junk is hauled from the Thames to Virginia Water in the Presence of the Duke. (*T & P Sandby, The British Museum*)

16. Cypron and her Brood. On the extreme right is her colt foal, King Herod, held by a groom. Cypron was bought by Cumberland from the Sykes stud in Yorkshire. (*Sawrey Gilpin, St James's Palace*)

17. Marske, sire of Eclipse, aged 20. Bought from Mr Hutton of Marske in Yorkshire by the Duke. *(George Stubbs, Arundel Castle)*

18. "Eclipse first, the rest nowhere." By Marske out of Spiletta, foaled 1764 at Cranbourne Lodge, Spiletta having missed the previous year. Eclipse stood 15.3h, being an inch higher over the loin than at the withers. He had an exceptionally long back. *(George Stubbs)*

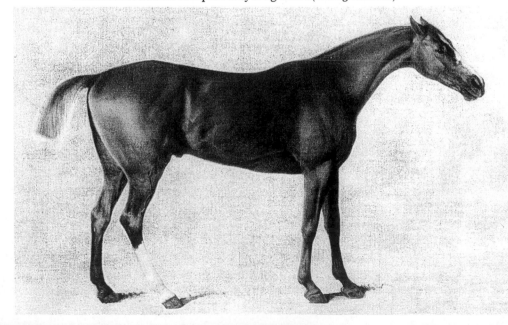

to consult their subordinates in national councils of war. It was a recipe for disaster.

Even the terrain was in Saxe's favour. The rivers mostly ran northwards in this area, which would help to carry his military supplies. There was a great high road running east from Louvain to Maastricht, offering speedy communications if he chose to attack that city. So Saxe could afford to relax in Brussels, indulging in extravagant dalliance, in no hurry to resume the conflict. As he explained later:

> My aim was to ruin the enemies' army once I had taken Flanders. I would do it by adopting a suitable position and allowing time to take its course.[6]

His opponent, by contrast, scurried round attempting to rouse the allied armies and their commanders out of hibernation. But in vain. As February gave way to March, the allied armies were still far from prepared for the opening of the new campaign season.

Suppressing his impatience Cumberland passed his time reviewing the initial British force of 13,587 men, later to be joined by a further brigade; he also approved the raising of three independent light companies, recruited locally but paid for by London. The British artillery contingent, under Colonel Belford, was a cause for some satisfaction. There were five companies or brigades, with a formidable array of guns including twelve-pounders, two 8-inch howitzers and six royal mortars. The engineers, too, had exceeded expectations, producing a 'brigade' of six engineers-in-ordinary and eight engineers-extraordinary with Dougal Campbell as their Chief Engineer (like the gunners, the engineers had no army rank). The engineers were supported by a company of miners, about forty-strong, with its own complement of officers; the miners would help to build field fortifications and emplacements for artillery pieces. The whole ordnance train, including thirty pontoons for bridging purposes, would require 1,500 horses to move it.

Another sixty horses comprised the equipage of Lord Albemarle, now a lieutenant-general and Cumberland's senior British infantry general; it was a somewhat grand establishment and far from necessary; not for nothing was Albemarle dubbed 'the spendthrift earl.' To his enormous relief, Albemarle had been allowed to hand over the post of commander-in-chief in North Britain to Humphrey Bland; the burden of subduing the rebellious Highland spirit now fell on other shoulders. He had joined Cumberland in Holland with renewed enthusiasm for battle.

Ligonier, a full general, had command of the British cavalry, with Hawley as his subordinate, and Ligonier also acted as Cumberland's deputy and chief of staff in certain circumstances. From Ligonier not only did Cumberland borrow a Dutch lady friend in the shape of 'La Berkenrode' but, more importantly for the army, he took on Colonel Jeffery Amherst. A man of great initiative and courage, Amherst now assumed special responsibility for intelligence gathering; one indication of how seriously he took his job is the £80,000 secret service money that he spent during 1747 (by comparison, Fawkener had spent just £35,000 during the Fontenoy campaign).

Albemarle's son, Lord Bury, was again on Cumberland's personal staff, along with Hodgson and Yorke, and also Major Caroline Scott. Joining them were two younger aides: Captains George Townshend and Lord Howe, both soldiers of great promise. In addition Cumberland had the faithful Robert Napier as his military secretary and adjutant general, and two quartermasters general, Colonels Stewart and Forbes. To advise him on matters of discipline, he could call on the Judge Advocate General, Thomas Cokayne, and the Provost Marshal, Daniel Dupuy, who exercised considerable summary powers of punishment over the British contingent. Equally important, in their own way, were the wagon-master general, John Douglas, who organized transport, and Orby Hunter, who controlled finances and was responsible not only to the Captain-General but to the Treasury in London.

Cumberland's medical staff was headed by Dr John Pringle, in charge of the base hospital, with Dr Charles Wintringham running a 'flying hospital' that linked the regimental medical teams. Jonathan Shipley continued to hold the post of chaplain to the commander-in-chief; his duties included not merely the holding of divine service in camp and in garrison − a regular commitment in Cumberland's orders − but also the duty of supervising the regimental chaplains and seeing to the welfare of the sick and wounded. Physicians and chaplains alike would be stretched to the limit before the year was out.

And as always Cumberland was accompanied by Sir Everard Fawkener, head of his civilian secretariat, on whose experience and diligence the young Captain-General could depend. Fawkener was kept particularly busy now, with the diplomatic negotiations between his chief and the various foreign representatives, but also with a huge traffic in despatches to and from London. Pelham, Newcastle, Fox and Chesterfield all had to be kept informed of Cumberland's plans and movements, and all four men conducted a private correspondence with him in parallel with, but not always tallying with, the official exchanges. Newcastle was the most demanding; his own letters often ran to fifteen pages or more, containing all kinds of court and ministerial gossip which a busy commander in the field could well have done without.

March gave way to April and the allied forces were only just beginning to assemble at Breda and Tilburg. At Bois-le-Duc, a few miles north of Tilburg, the Royal Artillery's regimental orders for 7 April show that they were preparing for a visit by Cumberland:

> The regiments and artillery to be reviewed tomorrow morning early by H.R.H. the Duke. The officers of the Garrison to be ready at the Coffee House to wait on the Duke in their regimentals.

The regiments were the four battalions of infantry of Houghton's Brigade, which, together with the five companies of artillery and three battalions of Hanoverians, all at Bois-le-Duc, were to be reviewed on 8 April.

Cumberland ordered trial shoots by the British artillery and saw both grape and round shot fired at a rate of ten rounds per minute. He saw the howitzers firing shells with a new percussion fuse. In a competition between the Imperial (Austrian) Artillery and the British gunners, he saw the latter prove themselves the more accurate at knocking down iron plates. At an earlier inspection of his own regiment, he had assessed their parade skills as indifferent; but on 8 April he was very pleased to see the Guards Brigade carry out the first twenty-two movements of their drill in impressive silence, without a word of command, relying just on drumbeat, flam or ruffle. Later he would order the Guards' methods to be adopted throughout the infantry.

On 26 April Cumberland, accompanied by Amherst, made an inspection of the Austrian contingent at Roermond. It was unconventionally marshalled, which Amherst believed to be a deliberate attempt to disguise the fact that the Austrian troops were under strength. He counted forty-seven battalions (fifty-four had been promised) and sixty-one squadrons (one hundred promised); including about 2,000 irregulars, mainly Hungarian and Slav, he computed the total at 28,000 men, the battalions being less than 500 and the squadrons below 100 each. But Cumberland seems not to have protested. Following the inspection he dined with Marshal Batthyány and his senior commanders, Generals Daun, Baranyay and Trips.

According to Ligonier, the Duke had fallen victim to Batthyány's Hungarian charm. What seems to have happened is that Cumberland found Batthyány shared his interest in the breeding of horses, and at the dinner table, no doubt well lubricated with arrack or gin, their talk soon turned from military shop to the possibility of Batthyány supplying new blood for the Duke's stable. Cumberland also persuaded Batthyány to supply meat on the hoof from Hungary, to help feed his troops at a time when Holland's supplies were scarce, and advanced money to pay for the meat on behalf of his regimental commanders.

If Cumberland found Batthyány the most cordial foreign commander, Waldeck was already proving to be a thorn in his flesh. On 15 April, at a full council of war, Waldeck had expressed great apprehension at reports that Saxe's left wing, led by the Danish General Lowendal, was moving out of Bruges and heading north. By the 18th Lowendal's corps, 25,000 strong, was undoubtedly on the move and Waldeck was urgently calling for help in Dutch Flanders. Cumberland wanted to defend Antwerp, and especially the nearby fort of Bergen op Zoom, but further to the east he was also worried about Maastricht, where Albemarle and Scott even now were reconnoitring the state of the garrison and defences. He summoned Batthyány for another council of war. The Austrians, it was decided, should move west from Roermond and the rest of the allied forces should move south from their bases around Breda, converging on the Dutch border around Baarle. Waldeck complained that they would not arrive soon enough. Cumberland had already issued orders to increase mobility, forbidding officers to take unnecessary items of clothing or equipment into battle and above all restricting the carriages and coaches that clogged up the highways; there was no more he could do. Waldeck had himself been slow to assemble the Dutch forces; if he was in trouble now it was his own fault.

Nevertheless Cumberland sent forward a brigade of troops that had served in the Lorient fiasco; newly arrived in Holland, commanded by a General Fuller and including the Royal Scots and 42nd Highlanders among their number, they were a force to be reckoned with. They crossed the Scheldt north of Antwerp and moved south-west towards Hulst to reinforce the garrison under General La Rocque.

Lowendal and the French had grown overconfident. In a series of bloody encounters with the British troops, they were beaten back. For the time being, Cumberland had managed to contain the threat.

# 14

# The Affair of Laffeldt

DESPITE HIS TROOPS' SUCCESS at the end of April, Cumberland knew that Saxe had yet to show his hand. He also feared that the French might be goaded by defeat into making another attempt on Hulst and decided to send Caroline Scott to ascertain the situation while he himself moved headquarters to Westmael, north-east of Antwerp.

Scott returned from Hulst on 8 May with the very tidings the Duke had feared. French troop movements suggested that another attack was imminent. Cumberland called a hurried council of war and, despite Waldeck's trepidation and Batthyány's pleas not to expose himself to danger, announced that he himself would go to Hulst. Sending Studholme Hodgson on ahead, he ordered his coach to be prepared that night, and in the early hours of the following morning, accompanied by Caroline Scott, Joseph Yorke and General Purmania from the Dutch service, he set off in the dark from Westmael. Reaching the wide estuary of the River Scheldt they embarked on a Royal Navy bomb ketch, on which they passed a most uncomfortable night, then resumed their journey on land at first light on the 10th.

Almost at once they encountered elements of General Fuller's brigade, retreating in disorder. To his dismay Cumberland learnt that Fort Sandberg and La Rocque's whole garrison at Hulst had surrendered at one o'clock on the 9th with scarcely a shot being fired. Hodgson told the Duke that the Dutch garrison troops were already dispersed across the countryside in total disarray, and the British, being vastly outnumbered, had seen no alternative but retreat.

In a cold fury, Cumberland set about restoring order. Fortunately the Royal Navy was waiting in the wings, partly for just such an eventuality and partly as escort to the supply ships still arriving from England, and soon the troops were being embarked and ferried back across the Schelde. Fuller was suspended from duty pending an enquiry, though privately Cumberland thought La Rocque was to blame; mutual recriminations between Fuller and La Rocque would drag on for months, souring Anglo-Dutch relations and making Cumberland's task even more difficult.

The Duke's options were rapidly decreasing. While Lowendal swept the remnants of the allied forces back north, Saxe was laying siege to Antwerp and still his right flank threatened Maastricht. Cumberland ordered Fuller's regrouped brigade to support the garrison of Bergen op Zoom and sent the Coldstream Guards to maintain a British toehold at Flushing, while he considered how best to meet the French threat further east.

At least there was one ray of hope amid the gloom. The emergency had united the Dutch. In a wave of patriotism, the provinces or *stadts* of Holland proclaimed William IV *stadtholder*, or overall ruler. Now, instead of dealing piecemeal with each *stadt*'s leaders, Cumberland merely had to consult his brother-in-law. Unfortunately their relationship promptly deteriorated. William of Orange had little grasp of military affairs and, naturally enough, was concerned only with Dutch interests; blinkered to the wider European picture, he resented any move that Cumberland made in other theatres of the war. Princess Anne, for her part, begrudged the extra burden now placed on her husband's unsteady shoulders and tended to hold her brother responsible.

After a few days at Westmael Cumberland realized that Antwerp and the River Scheldt could not be saved. French reinforcements at Antwerp meant that Saxe intended to maintain his siege and, very probably, consolidate his forces before launching a new attack. To loud protestations from the Dutch, Cumberland announced his decision to move south-east. But his main objective now was to protect Maastricht, he explained to the allied commanders; this great fortified town on the River Meuse could be the key to the defence of Holland. Waldeck seemed to be convinced, and the council of war duly approved Cumberland's order that he should reinforce the defence of Maastricht with six battalions.

Meanwhile Cumberland set about shifting the rest of the allied forces gradually eastwards. With the spring and warmer weather, grass for the horses became lusher and more abundant; foraging parties found their task easier. But the Captain-General was anxious to keep his forces in trim. He ordered a halt from time to time, to allow for vigorous training sessions, particularly in the Royal Artillery, his current pride and joy:

> The Colonel desires that those officers who are not perfect in the manual exercise will as soon as possible make themselves so.[1]

He stressed the importance of maintaining security:

No officer or soldier to give the length or dimension of any of the guns to anyone without leave of the Colonel.[2]

He organized a complicated programme of front-line reliefs, to ensure that no one became stale and equally that each national force played its part. He frequently rode around inspecting his outlying detachments, even though the French were less than fifteen miles away, behind the River Dyle. If Saxe wanted to play a waiting game, his young opponent was content to let him.

In mid-May some splendid news arrived from London: Admiral Anson had defeated the French fleet off Finisterre. From now on the French would be hard pressed to continue their supply convoys across the Atlantic. Cumberland delightedly approved the firing of a *feu de joie* throughout the whole army to celebrate this great victory. But now he ran into trouble closer at hand. Waldeck, he discovered, had not obeyed instructions to reinforce Maastricht; in fact, he had directly countermanded the Commander-in-Chief's order. Nor was that all. Although Cumberland was able to control both his nerve and his troops, some of the other allied generals were getting edgy. However, he refused to be downhearted. He continued to hold field days for the British infantry, instructing all battalions to standardize their tactical drill system on the pattern of the Guards. Later, on the King's orders, this was committed to paper by Napier and promulgated throughout the army: the first standard field service regulation.

By early June, however, Cumberland himself felt his confidence to be ebbing. He could not expect this huge army which he was now commanding to remain intact and controllable throughout the summer; he had to convince the allied generals that the French were not invincible.

Suddenly Saxe's right wing was reported to be moving north from Liège along the Meuse. This was Cumberland's chance. On 6 June (OS) he gave orders to all forces to converge on Maastricht. According to the diary of a Royal Artillery officer by the name of Wood, the men marched steadily south-east, tension mounting all the time. On the 14th they were at Diest. On the 17th, after passing through 'a Very Pleasant Part of the Country' they stopped for the night 'in a Large open Plain within 18 Miles of Mastrick.' Wood's diary goes on (all dates Old Style):

*June ye 19.* March'd by 4 oClock Morning and Came to our Quarters by 4 in the Afternoon, within 6 miles of Mastrick. March'd about 12 Miles....
*June the 20, 1747. Battle Mastrick.* March'd by 3 oClock in the Morning and Left Mastrick 1 Mile to ye left. About 12 oClock ye French Hussars attack'd our Hussars on a Hill, whereof proceeded a Smart Engage't. In a little time, made ym retreat into a village where they had a Battery of 5 or 6 Guns, but the English Immediately brought up to the top of the

Hill six 6 pounders. A Great Many Shots fir'd on both Sides, we blew up one of their Batterys with a Shell and kil'd a Great Many of them.... By reason the Village was so thick with trees, they Killed but two of our men that Evening, 1 Bombardier and 1 Mattross. It rained so prodigious hard that at last both Parties left off Firing, in the mean time we Detach'd two Pieces of Cannon to Every Reg't, as far as they would allow of number they was Short Sixes and Long three pounders. Draw'd the rest of the Heavy Cannon into the Park and in the night Erected Batterys for our 12 and 9 pounders faceing the Village, and prepar'd our selves in Readiness for an Engagement the Next Day. Lay on our Arms all that night in the Open Field, continued Rayning all night. Nothing to be Got to Eat. Prince of Waldeck Com'd the Dutch, Marechal Bathiani the Austrians and Bavarians.

*Sunday June ye 21, 1747.* Battle Mas'ick Plain. The English begun Cannonading from our Batterys that was Erected in the night, we begun about 5 oClock Morning, the French begun about 6 oClock, and Continued Cannonading untill half an hour after 8 oClock, then the French advanc'd, accordingly the English, Hanoverians and Hessians advanced with two Pieces of Cannon with Every Regm't. Advanc'd and fir'd at one Another for three Hours and a half as fast as we could load. At half an hour after 11 oClock they at last retreated, we following with Loud Huzzas, but the Dutch horse gave way and the Austerians Never Comeing to Back us, and a large boddy of both horse and Foot Comeing from the right to the Assistance of the French, and as they say the French King Comeing up along with [them]. Inspir'd them with new Life and Courage, which Caus'd them Immediately to turn and Advance on us, most Furiously, and they realy behav'd Very Well, tho we Cut them Down with Grape Shot from our Batterys of 12 Pounders. Ye [French] Did not Seem to mind it, but fil'd up their Intervals that we made with Grape Shot as they Advanc'd. Being over Power'd we was at Last oblig'd to retreat Something faster than we Advanc'd and in our retreating we left 9 three Pounders, 6 Short Six pounders, 1 Long six Pounder with three Colours and a Kittle Drum.

Our Army lost about 6 Thous'd, the French 10 Thous'd men, the Hanoverians lost 6 pieces of Cannon, as to the Loss of Men on both Sides I cannot tell as Yet. Sr. Jon. Ligonier was Taken Prisoner and Several officers of Distinction, we Lost More of the Artillery People that Day than Ever was known at any Battle before.[3]

What Wood called the 'Battle Mas'ick Plain' — better known as the battle of Val or the 'affair of Laffeldt' as Cumberland himself called it — had turned out to be a greater numerical confrontation than Waterloo. However much experts debate the actual effective strength of the opposing armies that day, it was a massive encounter for the period. But neither commander had the means to control his huge army, so on both sides the bulk of the forces were simply never engaged. Saxe's massed columns, used in succession so that they 'fil'd up their Intervals that we made with Grape Shot' had eventually battered through an over-extended allied line, which had been too slow to occupy the intended defensive position in front of Maastricht. But, having broken through, Saxe failed to exploit his success.

As the allied armies regrouped beside the River Meuse, Cumberland realized that Maastricht was safe. Saxe had withdrawn his forces; having suffered double the casualties of the allies, clearly he had decided the great fortified town was not worth the price that Cumberland had wanted him to pay. This was, however, the Duke's only consolation in defeat.

The original alarm had been raised when the Austro-Hungarians under Generals Daun and Wolfenbuttel ran into a thin forward line of French Hussars near Tongres. In the ensuing skirmish, the allied troops failed to press home their advantage, which allowed Saxe time to send in reinforcements. Cumberland had called a council of war for the evening of 29 June (NS), at which it was decided to interpose the whole allied army between Maastricht and Saxe's main force at Louvain. But allied progress had been slow, and Saxe had shown an unsuspected turn of speed. By the time Cumberland's force arrived at Maastricht, the selected battle ground sketched out by Caroline Scott was occupied by the French. The allies were thus obliged to take up poor second-best positions during the night of 1/2 July (NS), stretched out for six miles along a concave line that took in four or five small hamlets. The British, Hanoverian and Hessian infantry and the Royal Artillery were placed here in the centre, with the cavalry away on the left flank towards Maastricht itself, together with the Austrian light troops under General Trips. To the right, connecting with the Austrian main body, were the Dutch.

Saxe had meanwhile taken advantage of both the night and a low ridge to hide his movements, so that on the morning of the 2nd he was able to unleash his columns on the villages of Laffeldt and Vlytingen. Cumberland took up position behind Vlytingen and sent a message to Batthyány asking for reinforcements. It was about now that Cumberland's German ADC, Colonel Schweizer, had his head blown off by a cannon ball, just as the Duke turned to speak to him. Batthyány's battalions failed to appear. Under extreme pressure from Saxe's repeated attacks, Cumberland again sent to Batthyány for help, asking him to launch a flank attack from the west. Batthyány's response was cunning; he asked Cumberland to seek a second opinion from a senior Hanoverian general, who readily acquiesced in the Austrian commander's opinion: such an attack was inadvisable, if not impossible. The Austrians would advance part of the way, but no further.

Cumberland had no time to argue. By this time the Dutch had come under heavy artillery fire from the French and some squadrons were already crumbling. The Duke rode to the commander of the Dutch cavalry and tried to rally them, but in vain. He was nearly taken prisoner in the mêlée. Perceiving the line to be broken he gave the order to withdraw. Ligonier, with three regiments of British cavalry, fought off an attempt to pursue the allied troops — but in the process he himself was captured, among many others.

And so Maastricht was safe, albeit at a terrible cost in men and equipment, as Wood's record shows. George Townshend, whom Cumberland asked to take the despatches back to London, noted in his own diary:

> The action was long and severe: many respectable officers were brought out severely wounded, to the great concern of H.R.H. who stood the whole action under a heavy fire from the enemy's artillery until the troops were obliged to abandon it. The Dutch on the right made but a feeble resistance behind Vlytingen.[4]

Joseph Yorke was more succinct. 'H.R.H. did wonders,' he wrote. 'I believe in my conscience the strength of his own arm saved him from being a prisoner.'[5] In the cavalry mêlée, apparently, Cumberland had cut off the hand of a French dragoon who was threatening him with his sword.

Indeed, the French had taken worse casualties than the allies, and Louis XV — who, as Wood rightly heard, had arrived at the battle ground to urge on his troops — had been devastated at the loss of life. He summoned Ligonier and spoke with feeling about the need for peace, then sent him on parole back to the allied lines.

Cumberland was overjoyed to see his old colleague safe and sound. He embraced him warmly and listened with interest to Ligonier's reports of life in the French camp, particularly his interview with the King of France. Louis XV had declared that in his opinion the Austrians had played their usual role of spectators. But the Duke was even more relieved to hear that the French wanted to talk peace. He immediately opened a correspondence with Saxe on terms for ending the war.

In London George II received the bad news with composure, though like the French king he was particularly curious about the Austrians' inaction; he noted that Cumberland's official despatch made no attempt to explain it and asked for a report. Unfortunately Cumberland's reply is missing, if indeed he made one, but he never seems to have held a grudge against Batthyány who remained a lifelong friend.

Otherwise there was little reaction in London to the news from Europe. Cumberland was truly, as Horace Walpole declared, a man of 'vast vigilance and activity. For bravery H.R.H. is certainly no Stewart but literally loves to be in the act of fighting and for this the army adores him.'[6] But Walpole also wrote that people were growing weary of hearing about Cumberland's heroism; 'His prowess is so well established that it grows time for him to exert other qualities of a general.'[7] This was the only hint of criticism, however, implying that the Captain-General now needed to wield his authority more forcefully. Henry Pelham was pleased to hear of the French king's overtures for peace. 'It is our only hope,' he remarked at the time, 'and I am glad to find the Duke of that opinion.'[8] But his brother Newcastle regarded Cumberland as an unsuitable person through whom to conduct the peace negotiations; he wanted Sandwich.

One reason for London's indifference was that a general election had been held in June. The results, while strengthening Pelham's hand, had as usual set every man of position to wondering how the changes would affect himself. Of most widespread interest was the recent intervention by the Prince of Wales, who had declared his intention to back the Tories: in effect, to challenge the King. Pitt, formerly in the Leicester House set, had turned to Newcastle for a new seat in Parliament and was duly returned as MP for Seaford in Sussex; the King still regarded him with hostile eyes but accepted that Pelham found him an asset to the ministry.

In fact it was now Newcastle who, so Cumberland was told, 'went so often into the closet and said something which upset everything.'[9] Pelham did not want the matter of Cumberland's role in the peace negotiations to be referred for a decision by the cabinet, but his brother insisted that the business should be handled by Sandwich. The other ministers 'don't care to speak their minds,' Pelham said.[10] Finally he persuaded Chesterfield to urge the King to go against Newcastle's advice, and the King agreed: Cumberland was to be the chief negotiator, though Newcastle jealously refused to brief anyone but Sandwich.

Thus the peace talks at Breda, formerly between the French and Dutch, were joined by the British. And, as if to add point to the negotiations, France now resumed the offensive in northern Flanders.

It was in mid-July that Cumberland heard that Lowendal's army, now reinforced to 35,000, was threatening Bergen op Zoom. The French idea of peace, apparently, had never included the Scheldt. The Dutch were desperate for help and Cumberland sent all he could spare, including gunners, engineers and British infantry, but in accordance with orders from London he personally was obliged to remain on the Meuse. He despatched Yorke to be liaison officer with the Prince of Orange, who had taken the loss of Laffeldt in his stride and was now pushing on with the war. For two months Cumberland was forced to remain idle, mesmerized like all Europe by the persistence of Lowendal's assault. The Dutch, strengthened by Austrian as well as British detachments, repeatedly drove off the French attacks, but on 27 August (NS) Cumberland received a gloomy report from one Major Walters of the Austrian artillery. It seemed that the allied garrison in Bergen op Zoom, led by old General Cronstrom, was expected to give in.

Far from giving in, however, the garrison fought back with all they had when Lowendal made his long-awaited assault on the fortress itself on 16 September. But the end was inevitable. After a terrible slaughter, in which the French lost some 500 men and the Austrians and Dutch some 2,000 killed in the initial assault, and many more wounded, Lowendal captured the fortress and thus took control of Bergen op Zoom. The River Scheldt was now entirely in French hands.

Cumberland's reaction to this French victory is not recorded; but after a summer spent mostly in idle manoeuvres by the Meuse he must have felt acutely disappointed, to say the least. His father was equally dejected, according to letters from London, though the Duke cannot have derived much comfort from the thought. Pelham told him:

> I look upon you, sir, as the bulwark and true support of His Majesty, his family and your country, but what can you do alone? The King has said no one could have done better in your situation.[11]

Then, to his astonishment, he discovered that the peace talks with France were to be continued. Pelham was concerned at the financial cost of the war in Europe, and he was supported by Pitt who held out greater hope of weakening France by attacking her interests in North America. Thus, at the end of the campaign season, Cumberland left for England while Sandwich sought to find common ground among the allies for a settlement with France.

It had not been a successful season for the Duke.

# 15

# Negotiations

CUMBERLAND WAS NO DOUBT happy enough to be back in London in the autumn of 1747. No one blamed him for the summer's failures, and Newcastle, for all his insistence on controlling the peace talks through Sandwich, greeted him as if he were still the young hero of Culloden. There had been reports of unrest in Scotland and elsewhere, and Newcastle, always a victim of his own lurid imaginings, was among those who feared another Jacobite rebellion. He sought out Cumberland repeatedly and plied him with a mixture of flattery and doubts. But Cumberland gave his fears short shrift. He discovered from Humphrey Bland in Edinburgh that out of ten letters he had written to Newcastle, not one had been answered. The unrest he had reported derived less from Jacobitism than from resentment of the harsh imposition of the new laws. What was true, however, was that the French navy seemed to be preparing for conflict.

In September, 1746, the French naval commander La Bourdonnais had led an attack on the English East India Company's base of Fort St George, Madras, and the weak British garrison had surrendered. (All news from India took six or nine months, or even more, to reach London.) Obviously the French wanted to exploit this success in India as well as make good the loss of Louisburg, and now planned to sail reinforcements either to India or across the Atlantic.

Following Admiral Anson's victory in May that year, one of his captains had pursued and caught a huge convoy of French ships taking supplies to the West Indies. Such tactics clearly hurt French trade and thus encouraged the Admiralty to devise another attack on the enemy fleet. This time the attack was led by Rear-Admiral Hawke: on 14 October he achieved another clear victory over the French East Indiamen, again off Finisterre. If France held the winning hand in Europe, Britannia ruled the waves.

In November the Admiralty also decided to despatch Admiral Boscawen to retake Madras, with a fleet carrying for the first time regular British troops to fight in India; previously the garrisons had consisted of private soldiers, recruited and paid by the East India Company itself. The troops had posed a problem; Cumberland needed all available manpower in Europe. However, Fox, the Secretary at War, had come up with a scheme to raise twelve independent companies which, under the command of Major Monson, would join one company of the Royal Artillery and some individual engineers on the expedition to India. Some men came from the garrison battalions in Portsmouth, but many of them were Highlanders and Jacobite rebels released from gaols in Carlisle and York, and their numbers were topped up with British army deserters freed from the Savoy prison in London. Cumberland apparently gave his approval to the scheme, though he may well have doubted the Highlanders' abilities to take on the experienced French troops under Dupleix, particularly in that notorious climate. In the months and years to come, he would take an increasing interest in how the men fared in India.

Stimulated by the naval successes and taking courage from Cumberland's confidence, Newcastle began to see hope for Britain's cause at the peace conference. However, he still feared a renewed outbreak of Jacobitism — to such a degree that he persuaded Cumberland to allow five battalions to be summoned back to England that autumn, to ensure internal security in the south-east.

But, while Pelham and others sought to negotiate an end to the war, Cumberland spent most of the winter of 1747-48 discussing plans for a resumption of the campaign against Saxe. Newcastle was determined that Sandwich, still in The Hague, should have as strong a hand as possible when negotiations re-opened with the French; when Cumberland suggested that Russia might be pursuaded to back the allied cause, Newcastle eagerly seized the idea. General Mordaunt was despatched to Russia to fetch a contingent. Meanwhile Sandwich sent back sanguine forecasts of Dutch capabilities which led Cumberland and Newcastle to expect a combined allied army that would once again exceed 100,000 men, despite the fact that half the Austrian force had been withdrawn.

Chesterfield, who in November, 1746, had succeeded Harrington as the Secretary of State (North), ought to have been involved in these discussions; but he was against any idea of recommencing the conflict. He also felt a growing antagonism towards Newcastle who he felt — and with reason — had elbowed him out of his proper sphere. It was no surprise to anyone when he resigned in February, 1748. His position was promptly taken by Newcastle, who wanted his old post to go to Sandwich; but here the King asserted himself, appointing the Duke of Bedford instead.

And so Cumberland found himself approaching the start of a new campaign season. The winter had passed all too quickly. Though dutifully attending formal and informal ministerial meetings he had wanted to spend more time at Windsor, where the six Hungarian horses from Batthyány were attending his pleasure. Now he was returning to Holland with hope and determination; but his experience of the Dutch had taught him to be cautious. He hoped to force a favourable end to the war. He hoped the peace negotiations, to be re-opened the following month not at Breda but at Aix-la-Chapelle, would bear fruit. But he was unconvinced.

The first blow to Cumberland's hopes was a totally unexpected demand from the Dutch for a huge subsidy to continue the war. This demand reached the Duke at Harwich, where his crossing was delayed by fierce February gales. With further instructions from London in his pocket, he finally embarked for The Hague. His immediate task was to reduce the Dutch pecuniary demands and persuade them to defend their country seriously, by suggesting that he should command the field army while his brother-in-law took command of the garrison troops. But the Dutch would neither answer his questions nor accept his orders. Contesting his right to command, refusing to reveal strength returns, pleading national bankruptcy, the Dutch leaders were heedlessly unhelpful.

Cumberland did not hide from Sandwich his disappointment at the way he had failed to indicate the prevailing mood in Holland, and indeed had consistently overestimated Dutch commitment to the fight. Newcastle regarded Sandwich's actions as deliberate deceit. Cumberland was more forgiving. But now he faced the additional problem of raising the necessary troops to take the place of the Dutch. Compounding his other difficulties he was also short of two of his most reliable staff: Robert Napier was sick and Sir Everard Fawkener had stayed behind in London on family matters (he had recently married for the first time, at the age of sixty-three).

At this point Cumberland himself fell ill with a serious kidney infection. 'H.R.H. is greatly to be pitied,' Yorke wrote shortly afterwards to his father:

> Great is the load he has to bear and, stout as he is, it has greatly depressed him, for I attribute that terrible illness which had like to have deprived him of his inestimable life in a degree to the ruinous situation that he found our affairs in.[1]

Conway wrote in similar vein to his cousin Walpole, adding:

> We are in a woeful scrape and should be much obliged to those, be they military or civil, who can get us out of it.[2]

Only one man was more depressed, and that was Newcastle, who had come to look upon Cumberland as the infallible hero. Having feasted on Sandwich's false reports and spun elaborate stories to his brother and Pitt, Newcastle felt that he was in trouble for urging the continuation of the campaign. 'Nothing can be more unfortunate than my present position,' he wrote to Cumberland on 4 March, 1748.

> Pushed in every corner by busy meddling uninformed men; loaded with all the omissions of others − nothing but your R.H.'s courage can thoroughly extricate me. I satisfy myself I shall receive such orders from you as will satisfy the reasonable and well intentioned and silence those who are not so.[3]

It is doubtful whether Cumberland had much time to feel sorry for Newcastle. He was at his wits' end. Still weak from his illness, he somehow had to raise an army before the campaign season opened; either that or persuade the Dutch to change their minds.

As it happened, Cumberland's sister Anne had just produced a son and heir, the future William V, and the Prince of Orange was in high good humour. He invited Cumberland to become the infant's godfather, and Cumberland readily agreed. But this show of family affection was only temporary; soon the Captain-General found himself loitering vainly in the Dutch court.

As the weeks passed Cumberland's problems multiplied. The reinforcements on their way from England were storm-bound on the wrong side of the Channel. The artillery was incomplete due to the slackness of the Master General of the Ordnance. Ligonier had no magazines to support a field army. The Dutch would not relieve his own troops from garrison duty at Breda in time to let them march across country to Maastricht, which Cumberland remained sure was the key to the defence of Holland. Saxe and his huge forces were waking up from hibernation; at any time he might strike.

Cumberland concluded that peace was the only solution, and sooner rather than later. In the short term Britain would be able to flaunt her naval prowess, but in the longer term it was probable that superior land forces would give France the upper hand again. The Duke was concerned above all that Britain should not face direct and humiliating defeat in the field by Saxe. He suspected from what Sandwich had told him that Puysieux, the French representative at Aix-la-Chapelle, was deliberately holding out as if to win time for Saxe. But Sandwich was receiving conflicting instructions from Newcastle in London and from Cumberland in The Hague. Inevitably muddle and suspicions grew. Although Sandwich described Cumberland in the warmest terms to Bedford, mentioning 'the great kindness with which he has treated me'[4] he liked to pretend, whenever Newcastle took him to task for his somewhat ingenuous attitudes, that he was only citing Cumberland's own views. And Newcastle continued to write his incessant letters to the Duke, sometimes as many as four in a single day, each reflecting a change of mood.

In April, to his consternation, Cumberland at The Hague learnt that Saxe had laid siege to Maastricht with a huge army estimated at 100,000 men. Urgent communications passed between The Hague and London. The peace talks must be resolved, and soon. At Aix-la-Chapelle, Sandwich was bombarded with last-minute instructions. On 30 April (NS) he signed the so-called Preliminary Articles to the peace treaty, agreeing to an armistice. But twelve days later Saxe entered Maastricht. The fighting was over.

Newcastle, of course, was not happy. He rebuked Sandwich for signing the Preliminaries at Aix-la-Chapelle when several points had remained to be settled. Sandwich retorted that Cumberland had required it. Possibly Sandwich was just attempting to defend himself, but equally possibly he had decided that Cumberland knew best. As Bedford had said in a recent letter, 'Everyone who knows him [Cumberland] must own that his judgement, as well in council as in the field, is infinitely superior to what will be expected of one of his years.'[5]

However, Cumberland himself was dissatisfied: above all he had wanted to force an armistice *before* Maastricht fell to the enemy. He did not entirely blame Sandwich, however; nor did he believe that Puysieux had deliberately misled the British. He suspected that the French had simply been unable to control Marshal Saxe. Sandwich now assured him that the definitive peace treaty would be signed within a few weeks, and Cumberland hoped to be able to reverse the damage; he decided to remain in The Hague. But now a new problem arose. George II had decided that it was time he visited his Electorate. In vain Cumberland and the ministers pressed him to defer the visit; this was a time of crisis for Britain and he was required at home. But the King insisted. He left London at the end of the parliamentary session in April. Moreover, he wanted Newcastle to join him in Hanover, and reluctantly Newcastle had agreed, though postponing the trip until June.

Cumberland's life at The Hague would now become even more complicated, receiving the King's orders from Hanover and the orders of the Lord Justices from London, which did not always tally. However, he accepted the situation with a good grace and invited Newcastle to visit him on his way to Hanover. To his own surprise, Newcastle thoroughly enjoyed the break in Holland, where Cumberland invited him to inspect the troops. 'The finest troops, the greatest general,' Newcastle exclaimed as he danced along the ranks, and astonished everyone by picking out a man from Sussex. He had long discussions with Cumberland on politics, diplomacy and military affairs, and made himself so amiable and sensible a companion that Cumberland was almost sorry to see him leave.

However, once in Hanover, Newcastle's fears and suspicions returned. He thought everyone in London was plotting against him and sought constant reassurance from Cumberland. Then, it seems, he even accused Cumberland of disloyalty. Although Cumberland destroyed the letters containing these accusations, we may judge from what was said in them by the responses he sent to Newcastle at the end of July:

> It is with the most sincere sorrow that I write this letter, though I hope you are undeceived before this can reach you, as I really thought our friendship was too well known to us both and built on so real and true a foundation that it could not have been so easily overturned. For God's sake have more confidence in your behaviour towards me and a little more allowance for your friends. I in no way deserve the suspicions your last two letters are full of. I hope to see you and that this will be our last dispute.[6]

And to confirm his friendly attitude Cumberland sent one of his staff officers to Calais, to smooth the arrival of the Duchess of Newcastle who was on her way to join her husband in Hanover. The storm of suspicions subsided as fast as it had arisen.

While the peace negotiations dragged on Cumberland maintained his army in Holland, a paltry 30,000 men of whom the vast majority were British or in British pay. It was his way of demonstrating that France should not take the peace for granted. But, although he kept the troops actively employed on field days, drilling and rehearsing manoeuvres, he knew Saxe with his 100,000 men still constituted a grave threat. He was impatient for the treaty to be settled.

France was less impatient; it was in her interests to hold out for better terms. Saxe's capture of Maastricht had turned out to be an invaluable bargaining counter. Almost as useful was the news that an attack by the Royal Navy had been repulsed at the French naval base of Ile de Bourbon (Reunion). Pusyieux felt confident in demanding not just a reduction in allied forces in Europe but also a straight exchange: Madras for Louisburg.

In August Cumberland went to Hanover to discuss the French terms with his father and Newcastle, leaving the army in Ligonier's capable hands. He was still nervous of Saxe's intentions. But the King and his Secretary of State were reassured that the armistice was holding; furthermore, they had come round to the view that Britain could no longer afford this war, and Cumberland found himself discussing a plan for the reduction of the army. Although he did not share their belief in France's peaceable intentions, he settled to the task with a will and in September went on to London to secure ministerial approval.

Pelham was indisposed and could not see the Duke when he arrived from Hanover, so Cumberland worked instead with Henry Fox, the Secretary at War. The discussions went well, and both men ended with a high regard for the other's abilities. As Fox later commented to his friend Charles Hanbury Williams, a diplomat, Cumberland had 'not only more sense but more court art too than all the ministers put together.'[7]

Before returning to the Continent Cumberland then called on Princess Amelia, who was delighted to see him apparently recovered from his illness of the previous February. 'My brother is home in perfect health thank God,' she wrote to Newcastle in Hanover. 'He is in good humour with everybody and they with him.' Then, indicating that Newcastle's suspicions had reached her ears too, she added:

I find he commends you mightily, which gives me great satisfaction for he is no flatterer − your brother is also well pleased with you, if you would not interpret every letter he writes to you other than he means − if people differ with you it is not out of ill will. How false are your suspicions regarding your friends here. How can you be so childish? Forgive me for being so frank.[8]

Soon afterwards Cumberland was on his way back to Holland. If the treaty were not signed soon, he would be left with only the most contemptible remnants of an army with which to defy Saxe. He could not even count on the Hessian and Hanoverian contingents any longer. But at Eindhoven on 19 October (NS) the news reached him from Sandwich: the Treaty of Aix-la-Chapelle had finally been signed.

To Cumberland it seemed a less than honourable resolution of the war. Maria Theresa had still not recovered Silesia from Frederick of Prussia and the colonial squabbles had not been settled. Britain, France and Spain all reverted to the positions they had held before war broke out. France agreed to withdraw from Flanders, but recovered Cape Breton Island in return for Madras. And Britain's army was to be broken up. His personal regrets were offset, however, by two factors in particular. Firstly, the Treaty contained a clause by which Versailles pledged once and for all to renounce support for the Jacobite cause. And secondly, Saxe's conquests had been reversed at a mere flourish of the pen. Although France hailed him as a great military genius and piled honours and rewards at his feet, Saxe's efforts had been in vain. Within two years he was dead.

# 16

# Army Reform

THE TREATY OF AIX-LA-CHAPELLE, for all its faults, was greeted with jubilation in London. But a rueful Cumberland was convinced that it marked no more than an interlude in the world-wide struggle between Britain and France. That winter, although his royal presence was required at many of the long series of celebrations to mark the peace, he faced the sad task of dismantling his army. But if he doubted in his heart the wisdom of the reductions, he carried out the King's orders without complaint. Several times over the coming ten or twelve weeks he travelled between Europe and England, organizing the dispersal of his 'Flanderkins' as he called the men, and attempting to find new employment for them. His hope was that British expansion in North America, which would inevitably mean conflict with the French colonists, would offer new opportunities for loyal Hanoverian troops, and he began to press their services on all who made policy decisions concerning manpower in the colonies and India.

When George II returned from Hanover that autumn, reluctantly as ever, his support was immediately enlisted by his son. All told, some 40,000 men would have to be demobilized, and the King agreed that they deserved help; he would insert a paragraph in his speech for the opening of Parliament to encourage anyone prepared to offer employment to former soldiers. But Pelham's swingeing cuts in the nation's military budget affected the navy too; very soon the country would be awash with former servicemen, all too probably with idle hands. Cumberland and Pelham evidently clashed on the subject, for Pelham criticized the Duke's attitude as 'very military and not prepared to make allowance for other people.'[1] However, Cumberland was careful not to exceed the bounds of propriety and Pelham was soon telling his brother of Cumberland's amiable acceptance of the situation.

By January, 1749, Cumberland had completed the task of dismantling the army in Europe; he had dispatched the foreign mercenaries and seen to the embarkation of the last remaining British troops. His next task was to oversee the necessary reductions. The new British establishment was to be just above the pre-war figure, at 18,900: that is, 4,500 cavalry and 14,400 infantry. The infantry figure would include an artillery regiment of ten companies, with a cadet company of forty-four at Woolwich. Four battalions would be stationed at Gibraltar and another four at Minorca; and a new system was introduced to rotate the garrison battalions to prevent them getting stale. Four regular battalions would serve across the Atlantic, but the locally raised regiments of colonists who had fought with such success for Cape Breton Island would be disbanded. Similarly, no regular troops were to be retained in India. Although the Highlanders who sailed out to India with Boscawen had very nearly scored a victory at Pondicherry, an important French base south of Madras, they had eventually been beaten back. Now they were encouraged to transfer to the European levies of the East India company.

Ireland's establishment was to be increased over the pre-war figures: but this was possible only because Ireland was prepared to pay. Scotland would be garrisoned by seven battalions, with seventy men to a company. All ten regiments of marines were to be disbanded along with the five independent companies of Highlanders. But Cumberland had realized that the latter's special local knowledge must not be wasted, and he instructed Humphrey Bland to mix regulars and Highlanders 'on all posts and detachments' before the disbandment of the Scotsmen in the spring, so that they could show the regulars all the byroads and cross-country paths so beloved of the clansman. While encouraging the Highlanders to re-enlist if possible, he urged them to adopt breeches. The kilt had been outlawed and, besides, according to Henry Fox, Cumberland refused to believe 'that a man without breeches was warmer than a man in a thin plaid, could live and lye abroad in a cold climate and suffer less than one in a thick Yorkshire cloth watch-coat.'[2]

The whole strength gave Cumberland a force of just seven battalions of guards and forty-nine battalions of the line to juggle with, but he retained a degree of flexibility: in case of war, he could order augmentations to their company establishments. The cavalry remained unchanged except that the Horse Grenadiers were cut and the dragoon regiments were increased at the expense of Horse.

Two of his proposals proved controversial and had to be dropped. The first was to retain his own regiment of Light Horse. Both the King and Newcastle had approved but Pelham was opposed; he explained that if he put such a proposal to the House of Commons there would be a 'most disagreeable debate on an impertinent and personal motion by ill-designing people.'[3] Cumberland argued that the regiments, formerly Kingston's, had a fine record of service and that its particular tactical experience in the Highlands gave it a unique value to the army in case of civil unrest; he even offered to resign as colonel if that was what bothered the Prime Minister.

But, retorting that such a small unit could scarcely make a difference in a national emergency, Pelham won the day.

The other controversy had more substance to it. Cumberland wanted to disband Bragg's Regiment, the 28th Foot, on the grounds of consistently poor service in the war; to take their place he intended to retain Conway's, the 48th Foot. This appalled the traditionalists such as Bedford, urged on by the Duke of Dorset, Lord Lieutenant of Ireland, who protested strongly at such a breach of the time-honoured principle of seniority. Cumberland replied to Bedford with characteristic openness:

> My reason for proposing the reduction was to oblige the Old Corps to be more careful for the future and not to trust entirely to their seniority but their merit. The negligence and disorder of the Regiment has been most remarkable during this war.[4]

Bedford's office, however, deliberately leaked the planned reduction, which up till then had been kept secret. 'They gave copies to all and sundry,' Fox informed Napier. 'In two days it was in the newspapers – the Duke was overwhelmed with solicitations.'[5] Bowing to the pressure of the great lords, Cumberland suggested that the way to keep Bragg's within the Irish establishment was to reduce each company of the other twenty-six battalions in Ireland by one man, and this was accepted.

Having bowed to the inevitable, Cumberland was determined to use this time of transition to introduce some improvements of his own. He had learnt much from observing both allied troops and those of his opponent, Saxe, as well as from close attention to the problems of the British forces. Now he intended to encourage not only better discipline and training but more cohesion between battalions. His ultimate aim was to make this a professional army.

As Captain-General of the British Army, he was involved in all business concerning the army not only at home but in the colonies and fortresses of America, the West Indies and the Mediterranean. His experience had been entirely in the North European theatre, but he took a close interest in the overseas theatres too. From the Duke of Bedford, formerly First Lord of the Admiralty and now Secretary of State (South) with responsibility for all colonial affairs, he began to hear details of the difficulties facing those who had settled in North America and the Caribbean. In the latter area the climate itself was a threat, compounded by ungovernable privateering and by squabbles with the Spanish, French and even Dutch settlers in the islands. But in North America, from Newfoundland south to Georgia, the main difficulty, it seemed to Cumberland, was a simple lack of security. No settlement could hope to expand and prosper when the French continually provoked demarcation disputes and Indian raids interrupted communications. He was confident that the three regular battalions now preparing for departure to North America would help to impose some order for the colonists; but, still concerned for the welfare of his disbanded troops, he discussed with Bedford and the Earl of Halifax, responsible for Trade and Plantations, the possibility of sending former soldiers to settle in Nova Scotia – not merely to strengthen the territory against encroachments but to populate this former French possession with Britons, mainly from the Highland companies. Pelham refused to permit any scheme that required public funding, but a new scheme, backed with private funds, won his grudging approval and much more enthusiastic and generous support from Cumberland: he personally provided the men with boots.

He showed similar practical generosity towards his former troops at Windsor. Ever since 1746, when the King had appointed him Ranger of Windsor Great Park, Cumberland had been supervising improvements: new plantings, new drives and bridges and more meticulous efforts devoted to general maintenance. But he had also been mulling over other plans. Prompted perhaps by his sister Amelia's creation of the Richmond Park ponds, perhaps by discussions with Thomas Sandby, the military draughtsman who had accompanied him throughout the Scottish and Flanders campaigns, he had developed the idea of building a great lake in the park, some five miles south of Windsor Castle where a stream called Virginia Water ran through marshy ground. Now Cumberland saw a chance both to implement his plans for what would be the largest artificial lake in England and to give employment to hundreds of demobilized soldiers.

It was a massive project which would continue for years. Cumberland appointed Sandby Deputy Ranger of the Forest, with his own lodge, to supervise the draining and digging work that would require such heavy labour, and then the construction of an 18ft dam across the stream to create the lake itself. Later Sandby's brother Paul was brought in to help with the landscaping, the clearing and planting of trees and the creation of features such as grottoes and waterfalls that were then in such vogue. Architects and engineers, surveyors and gardeners, all were required to embellish the project and all in turn required able-bodied men to carry out the work. John Vardy, who had been clerk of works at Kensington Palace, was now appointed to draw up a survey map of the area: he alone provided work for thirty demobilized soldiers at a weekly wage of seven shillings each.

Another project that Cumberland had undertaken, which had in fact begun as soon as he acquired the rangership, was the rebuilding of Great Lodge. Originally built by Charles II, it had fallen into considerable disrepair. But Cumberland was not deterred. The house, soon to become known as Cumberland Lodge, was to be totally refurbished, with a stable wing capable of housing sixty horses and stable staff and room for carriages and saddlery. Towards the southern end of the Great Park, this reconstruction work would give employment to still more former soldiers, encamped on Breakheart Hill overlooking the lake.

The huge scale of the works at Windsor would keep Cumberland nearly as busy as the men, and over the coming years he would spend more and more time here, discussing problems and directing the work, while continuing to enjoy the hunt and other pastimes in the forest. Frequent rumours implied that these included the pursuit of the fairer sex. Back in 1746, after returning from Scotland, Cumberland was said by the poet Thomas Gray to have set up house in the lodge with 'three whores and three aides de camp'.[6] Which of the men went short of a companion one is left to guess. There are also suggestions that Cumberland had taken up with a soldier's daughter from Scotland, and it is remotely possible that this was Sarah Burt, daughter of a certain Colonel Burt who belonged to the Cumberland Society Dining Club. According to the parish registers, Sarah Burt died at Windsor in 1754. The progeny referred to in the *Complete Peerage*, however, are much more likely those of Cumberland's nephew Henry, a notorious womanizer who succeeded to the dukedom after his death. In fact, no reliable evidence exists to indicate that our Duke of Cumberland felt any inclination to share his life with a woman, let alone commit himself to marriage. One may speculate that he intended to postpone such pleasures until later in life, like his friend Henry Fox who did not marry until nearly thirty-nine, or like Sir Everard Fawkener who had just taken a young wife at sixty-three. But there is no foundation for such conjecture; history must be content merely to wonder.

In the spring of 1749, Cumberland was still attending public celebrations of the peace. Despite the surfeit of festivities, he was young enough to enjoy such jollification and regularly attended events like a gala performance at the opera and a jubilee masquerade in the Venetian manner. The latter occasion at Ranelagh required him to don fancy dress, and though details are lacking it seems he cut an unwitting figure of fun; he looked so immensely corpulent that Horace Walpole likened him to Cacafogo, the drunken captain in John Fletcher's comedy, *Rule a Wife and Have a Wife*. He had certainly acquired enormous girth; all portraits of him, however flattering, by now showed a man of greater bulk than could be disguised as dignity. Though his appetite was never poor, he was a notably active and energetic man, and it may be that his obesity was due to some glandular malfunction.

He was observed rather more to his advantage at a magnificent fireworks display in St James's Park some weeks later, which he superintended in great detail. A hundred and one Royal Artillery gun teams and the fireworkers of the Ordnance, combined with all the arts of French and Italian display technicians and Handel's genius for joyful music, produced such a splendour for the eye and delight to the ear as the citizens of London had never previously experienced. Unfortunately, sparks from the thousand exploding rockets set fire to one wing of the counterfeit wooden palace, built in Palladian style. The French architect, in a fit of hysterics, assaulted the senior official of the Ordnance Board, Sir Charles Frederick, and had to be dragged off his victim by onlookers; Cumberland ordered him to be placed under arrest until he calmed down. But the fire had taken hold and, although the King personally supervised the work of the fire tenders, several fatal casualties ensued.

The flimsy peace achieved at Aix-la-Chapelle was hardly worth all the revelry. While France had adopted a conciliatory posture in Europe, in overseas territories she still indulged in familiar aggression, and Cumberland was under no illusion that the army might at any time be required to play an active role. But the new political climate was hostile to all matters military, and Pelham's attitude to public spending made it hard for the Duke to acquire the ministerial support he needed for his army reforms.

Pelham's lack of interest in the armed forces did at least permit the King, through Cumberland, to reward loyalty and merit in a way that the system of purchase did not allow. Names came to him, of course, through the Secretary at War (Henry Fox since 1746), but the King seldom approved appointments without consulting his son first. Undoubtedly he relied increasingly on Cumberland's professional views and personal acquaintance with the candidates for promotion. Pelham admitted that if ever he made a suggestion, the King regarded it as 'meddling'. Otherwise most military administration was a matter of precedent. A mere handful of clerks, with a meagre filing system, worked in the War Office to find out how such-and-such a question was resolved in the days of William III, or even, in points concerning home defence, in the days of Queen Elizabeth. If the War Office clerks could not turn up an answer, they would ask their colleagues at the Treasury, and, irrespective of changes in operational requirements and the cost of living, new pay scales and methods of provision and support for men, horses and equipment would be prescribed. Only in the long term could such a clumsy and outdated system be reformed. In the shorter term Cumberland would have to learn the art of achieving the possible; working through the usual channels, particularly the annual Army Act, and persuading ministers to back him.

In his favour Cumberland was able to use the findings of a 1746 parliamentary enquiry into the army's financial management, which had concluded that the 1st Foot Guards, the largest (with twenty-eight companies) and most prestigious regiment in the army, and the regiment of able to prove the value of military bands to troops both on campaign and in camp, and demonstrated how the use of drum and fife helped to co-ordinate manoeuvres when verbal commands might not be appropriate.

But a tide of resentment was flowing against the Duke from within the army. Some officers were indignant at the new discipline he required of them, and used scorn as their only available weapon. They mocked him for his 'Hyde Park mentality' meaning that he fussed too much over superficial detail like uniforms and bands and efficient drilling on parade in the royal parks. They could not see the point of his reforms or if they did they pretended not to. He made demands of his officers; he wanted them to be professional, to be at their posts at the proper time, to set standards of restraint and orderly conduct for the men to follow. When he forced several senior officers to resign, including Colonels Townshend, Fitzroy and Lord Henry Beauclerk, for having gone absent without leave, they took offence. The army had traditionally allowed them to come and go more or less as they pleased; this new strict régime was not what they had expected when they joined the British Army. Townshend, the Duke's former ADC, who had a flair for caricature and had circulated some rather cruel sketches, was to nurse a grudge against Cumberland for the rest of his life. And Cumberland's pressure on Beauclerk to resign was less than tactful, considering the Beauclerk parliamentary interest in Windsor. But as one modern historian has noted: 'The Duke of Cumberland paid scant regard to interest and looked for the deserving.'[7]

Pitt, as Paymaster General of the Forces, was presently toeing the Pelham line. But many others at Westminster were not, and as always they focused their discontent on the Prince of Wales at Leicester House. Two men in particular emerged as leaders of the Prince's party: Lord Egmont and George Bubb Dodington, who had just resigned — some said defected — from a junior position in the government. One of their more coherent suggestions was that the standing army should be broken up entirely and replaced with locally raised militias. In this they found vehement support from Townshend. Another proposal emanating from Leicester House was that many officers below the rank of colonel should be made ineligible as parliamentary candidates: the implication was that Cumberland habitually used the forty-odd officers who were also MPs to prop up the government.

Clearly, a storm was brewing and it broke during the annual debate on the Army Act in the spring of 1749.

Cumberland's intention to alter the Articles of War had been signalled the previous year, for it was in 1748 that Fox referred certain proposed amendments to the Solicitor General for his advice. However, by the time the latter's views were prepared the storm had already burst.

The Duke's first aim was, as we have seen, to exact higher standards from

The Duke's first aim was, as we have seen, to exact higher standards from his officers; this achieved, the performance of the men would improve automatically. Writing to Loudoun, Cumberland remarked of Otway's Regiment that 'It was composed of a set of ignorant, undisciplined officers: and till you make an example of the officers you will never make a Regiment.'[8] But to enforce the new requirements he had to build them into military law. Even with keen young officers like James Wolfe and Robert Monckton, the army needed a stronger disciplinary framework.

Undoubtedly by today's standards the army code was tough. A man found guilty of desertion faced the death sentence, and the same penalty was available for proven disobedience to orders. Even minor offences very often resulted in 200 lashes or more, though these were administered in the presence of a surgeon and there are astonishingly few cases of men dying under the lash. But it must be remembered that the criminal law of the mid-eighteenth century exacted the death penalty for a great many offences, like stealing a sheep or picking pockets; this was a period when the London crowds at Tyburn could sometimes enjoy up to forty executions in a single day. That Cumberland's reputation for harshness is unfair is revealed by the many extant order books; on numerous occasions he ordered a court martial sentence to be reduced or suggested that a desertion charge be reduced to one of being absent without leave (which did not carry the death penalty), or recommended pardon if a man promised to serve in the colonies or if he had clearly been led into the crime by another. In some cases, however, the King overturned his son's pleas for mercy, as in the case of a sergeant found guilty of forgery in Edinburgh; this was too heinous an offence for the King to spare his life.

Considering the brutality of the age, Cumberland was in fact remarkably fair-minded, as shown by his manuscript notes on the draft revision of the Articles of War put before Parliament in 1749. At one point he noted that 'Members of Courts Martial are not judges. A C.M. is a Court of honour and equity.' And against a section entitled *Redressing of Wrong* he wrote:

Something ought to be added for to oblige the complainer to apply regularly to his superiors by steps till he is redressed, and that no one may be prevented from bringing his grievance even to the King after he has first properly and quickly applied to his particular superior.[9]

Broadly the changes that Cumberland sought to introduce were intended to tighten up both disciplinary measures and officers' powers and status. Under Section 2, Article IV, officers could now face charges for being absent from parade. In Article V came an important new definition concerning obedience to valid orders: 'any lawful command of his superior officer'. Elsewhere it was firmly stated that if an officer was to have the protection of military law, he had to be shown to be acting 'in the execution of his office.'[10]

These and numerous other changes were decided upon only after long discussions throughout the winter of 1748-9 with Fox, Newcastle, Bedford and Hardwicke. But when Fox finally introduced the amended Army Act in the Commons there was immediate and prolonged uproar. It was orchestrated, of course, by the Leicester House set and the discontented officers. The debate went on for weeks and extended to the Lords. Egmont rose to attack Cumberland in all but name, claiming that the new regulations were so harsh they could be applied only in war, not in peacetime. He suggested that the Captain-General was seeking to create an army responsible only to himself, that he planned to intimidate the nation as Marius had done in Ancient Rome, with the implication that he ultimately intended to seize power for himself. But Hardwicke in the Lords and Pitt in the Commons helped to overcome the opposition. Pitt argued that it was not for Parliament to interfere in day-to-day administration of the army; finance and general policy were Commons business, detail and discipline were not. Furthermore, he added that Cumberland had been realistic and public-spirited in agreeing to the reductions, allowing the annual cost of the army to be cut to less than £1 million; and for good measure he declared in his view the quality of discipline in a 'regular army' commanded by Cumberland was worth 5,000 men.

The debate continued outside Parliament, with broadsheets and pamphleteers extending the arguments beyond Westminster. Unfortunately, the running was made mainly by the Tories and former Jacobites, as well as the Prince of Wales's supporters, and Cumberland was frequently represented in an unattractive light. He was criticized for his sultry affairs, for keeping low company, for associating with Fox and Sandwich, both members of the notorious Hell Fire Club at Wycombe. Stories were resurrected of his supposed cruelty in suppressing the rebels and clansmen in Scotland. Sensational as the reports were, however, the public had heard enough of 'the 45' and attempts to defend the Duke were too feeble to counter the accusations. No matter that he had saved the nation from the Young Pretender, had wrought improvements to communications in the Highlands, had won the affection and loyalty of the common soldier, and now was trying to create a better army in the national interest: the taunts and sneers were louder than any reasoned defence.

But gradually Westminster found in favour of Cumberland's suggested reforms. Though committees were set up to consider some of his changes in greater detail, and some minor modifications were made – and agreed by the Duke to be improvements – at last his stronger legal framework was passed as an Act of Parliament. He wrote to his former ADC, Joseph Yorke, now Secretary at the Embassy in Paris:

> The weak and virulent minority had diverted and tired themselves out with dividing upon every clause for near six weeks together – but which we carried through, thank God, without any material alteration.[11]

Delighted at his success, and knowing now that his officers would be obliged to spend the summer implementing his reforms, Cumberland took himself off to Windsor again to review progress on his lake.

Discipline and the lake
– at the same time!
(1748-9).

# 17

# Windsor

'H.R.H. THE DUKE is grown a great planter,' wrote Henry Fox to Governor Cornwallis of Nova Scotia. And it was true.

Dividing his time between the supervision of army reforms and directing work on Virginia Water, Cumberland would spend most of the next two years or so at Windsor, his eye for detail as acute in matters of landscape as of regimental uniform. Now, like his mother before him, he began to take a close interest in the fashionable pursuit of horticulture. While the Sandby brothers designed and dug the great lake and created all the romantic embellishments, Cumberland engaged as his gardener a man with the appropriate name of Robert Greening. The son of the royal gardener at Kensington Palace and well schooled in the contemporary styles by Queen Caroline herself, Greening with his knowledge of plants fired Cumberland to greater heights of creativity. He had ordered the felling of great numbers of trees, partly to make paddocks for deer and partly to open up vistas – and incidentally to help meet costs by selling the timber – but now he started planting new trees, both mature specimens and young saplings raised from seed.

The mature oaks and elms were sometimes transported from as far away as Yorkshire, where a special machine invented by one John Doe was used to dig them up with a sufficient rootball to survive the transplantation. But the seeds came from even further afield. As Fox's letter to Cornwallis shows, Cumberland was hoping to acquire seeds from the governors of all British colonies in North America. The Secretary at War's letter went on:

> [The Duke] bids me to tell you that he shall be obliged to you if you will send him seeds of all the trees in Nova Scotia which we have not here, particularly evergreens. These seeds must be gathered to ripe, put up in sand and the earlier next Autumn they are sent the better.[1]

And to Governor Glynne of South Carolina, Sir Everard Fawkener wrote:

> H.R.H. being now a little at leisure turns his thoughts to the study of the culture of plants and forest trees and is laying out by all the ways he can to come at a variety of the more useful and beautiful ones for the improvement and adorning of Windsor Great Park.[2]

But with his letter Fawkener sent a definite list of specimens required, unlike the carte blanche offered to Cornwallis. Ten years later the consignments were still reaching Cumberland, even from the West Indies, the last apparently being in 1760 when General Amherst sent some fifty-one varieties of seed, including sumach, kalmia, tulip trees and bird cherries.

Nor did Cumberland confine his interest in exotic plants to trees; quite early on, according to one list, he had already received 136 different species including 35 different roses, and some time later he imported 2,500 strawberry plants from Holland for the kitchen gardens of Cumberland Lodge.

The trees were planted in artistic clumps, in belts or rows, according to the design Cumberland worked on with Sandby and Greening. The Duke himself was already familiar with the great garden created by Newcastle a few miles away at Claremont, Esher, and the new work by Henry Flitcroft at Woburn, the home of the Duke of Bedford, where Cumberland often stayed with Princess Amelia; he certainly would have made some personal suggestions to the planting schemes.

It was a lengthy and expensive business but for Cumberland it was clearly a labour of love. Not only did he love the place itself, he enjoyed seeing his former soldiers find honest work in and around the park. Roads were resurfaced and bridges strengthened, palings and gates were erected for the deer paddocks, rides were opened up and ditches dug. Just one stretch of road linking Cumberland Lodge with the nearby village of Englefield Green, although broader than usual at eighteen feet, cost £125 to resurface. Initial repairs to the lodge, the laying out of the ten-acre kitchen gardens and the construction of a stable wing for sixty horses and stable staff, with room for carriages and saddlery, were estimated to have cost the Duke £1,380 already. In later years he had Flitcroft design some hot-houses nearly as long as the stable block, with a heating system for the pineapples and other exotic fruits and flowers. In total it is estimated that all the work on the lodge and the park had cost him £12,000 by 1750 − and that was before many of the extra features were added, like the fine baroque stone boat-house built by John Vardy beside the Great Pond, and the rustic temple, the cascade, the grottos, the bowling green, the dairy, dog kennels and much else.

Many Londoners who read the Jacobite propaganda and thereby acquired an image of the Duke as idle, dissolute and pampered would have gaped in wonder at this indefatigable figure who constantly rode round Windsor Great Park consulting with engineers and surveyors, directing operations and encouraging the men, often mud-spattered from the excavation work around the lake and the clay-and-sand dam. But this was what he loved best, the bustle of purposeful activity in the open air, on horseback, surrounded by men far removed from the mischief of the city. As the winter of 1749-50 approached, and the King returned from his usual summer visit to Hanover, it was with some reluctance that Cumberland took himself back to London.

The country had been at peace for a full year by now, though Cumberland continued to keep a close eye on Scotland. Bland, as commander of the seven-battalion garrison in North Britain, was taking his duties seriously, possibly too seriously, enforcing the Disarming Acts with an inflexible hand and confiscating the land and property even of those who had never supported the rebellion. But Cumberland was receiving reports not merely from Bland but from more disinterested men such as David Watson, still conducting his survey and laying out roads, and the overall picture was clearly of a nation subdued. Within two years, the King's ministers, advised by Cumberland, would have passed an Act of Grace to ease the pressure on Scotland. Gradually the ban on Highland dress would cease to be enforced, until the very concept of tartan was all but forgotten, only to be resurrected a century later by the Victorians.

Watson was one of the few individual engineers in whom Cumberland could have any confidence, and the Duke was anxious to improve standards among the Royal Engineers as he had for the Royal Artillery. Since 1748 he had become in fact, though not in name, head of both artillery and engineers; the King had decided not to replace the Duke of Montagu as Master General of the Ordnance, and merely appointed Ligonier as Lieutenant-General. But now Cumberland heard from Müller, the professor at Woolwich, that Ligonier had failed to impose his undoubted authority on the gunner cadets. Evidently an unruly bunch, they required the very firmest handling and Cumberland paid particular attention to the commissioning and promoting of their officers; he obtained the King's agreement to granting the gunner officers army rank, by an act passed in 1751, and at the same time made sure that the purchase system was never allowed in the Artillery. By making frequent personal inspections, in London, Windsor or Woolwich itself, he kept the gunners on their toes; and in return for their hard work he listened to their pleas for more and better equipment. As *de facto* Master General of the Ordnance he supervised the development of various types of gun, and by arguing the gunners' case with the politicians during coming years he gradually won the necessary financial backing.

19. Thomas Holles, Duke of
Newcastle, was "jealous of
Cumberland". A glutton for
work and a gourmet at the table.
(*W. Hoare, National
Portrait Gallery*)

Henry Fox, Lord Holland
ıld not be relied upon".
*tional Portrait Gallery*)

21. William Pitt, Earl of Chatham, the Great Commoner. "Nothing good can be done without Pitt." (*W. Hoare, National Portrait Gallery*)

22. Charles Watson-Wentworth, 2nd Marquess of Rockingham; Newmarket crony; Prime Minister 1765-6; Repealer of the Stamp Act. (*National Portrait Gallery*)

23. "He visited Chatsworth between 15 July and 10 August." Of all
the portraits Reynolds painted of Cumberland, the one at Chatsworth
is the grandest and most impressive. (*Sir Joshua Reynolds, Chatsworth*)

24.  Marble Bust by Rysbrack, 1754. (*Private Collection*)

He had more trouble, however, with the Ordnance Board, whose members were jealous of their authority over the Engineers. Again, as Master General, in effect the Duke was responsible for fortifications and barracks, and for all the road-building and other work undertaken by the army in Scotland; but by opposing him the Ordnance Board was able to defer many of the improvements he sought to introduce on Watson's advice. In vain he argued that the fiasco at Lorient had been caused largely by incompetent engineers, whose over-optimistic advice had made the artillery batteries waste their efforts; in vain he argued that engineers had once again let their colleagues down in the assault on Pondicherry. It was not until 1757, in fact, that the Engineers were properly incorporated into the army, with professional standards, adequate training and army rank for their officers.

The rest of his reforms were proceeding roughly according to plan. The purchase system was not something that could be abolished overnight, though the King was actively opposed to purchase on principle and constantly urged his son to act. Fox declared that the King 'will never suffer his commissions to be looked upon as estates that are to make good the debts, or forfeitures, or pay damages incurred by the action of officers in their private capacity.'[3] Cumberland, however, found it possible to work within the system. He could take a chance with merit, as he had expressed it once to the Duke of Richmond when discussing the appointment of a certain young officer:

> As soon as a vacancy may happen where no great injustice may be done, I should place Captain Maggott, tho' I am not fond of bringing officers into our service over the heads of those who have done their duty well. I have been told that he was a little giddy in his youth but he may have improved, as I hope we giddy youths all shall.[4]

And, though he ordered that purchase money should be kept as low as possible, the Duke made few other interventions at this stage; he was content to wait for the climate of opinion to change in his favour.

The four battalions destined for service in North America and the West Indies had already sailed. The new rotation of battalions for garrison duty in Gibraltar and Minorca had already been instituted, despite obvious difficulties of transport and communication. Officers were beginning to take their peacetime role more seriously. Training improved and early signs of cohesion between regiments could be detected. Discipline was tightened. At last Cumberland was acquiring the professional army he wanted.

But there was constant friction, both within the army and in Parliament. In 1750 there was further acrimonious debate over the Army Act, with battle lines drawn much as before; again the King's son and the King's ministers won the day, but the opposition began to gain ground. The Leicester House set, augmented by a growing band of officers indignant at Cumberland's reforms, claimed that his devotion to the army was sinister and dangerous. They encouraged the pamphleteers to turn out more of their malign innuendoes. Stories began to circulate, much of the ammunition coming from the same old locker — the Duke was a butcher, cruel, despotic; and now he had designs on the throne itself.

Cumberland apparently regarded the insinuations as beneath contempt. He knew the King trusted him entirely; he knew himself to be innocent of the accusations. What he thought of the Prince of Wales's involvement can be imagined — at the very least Frederick was guilty of allowing Egmont and Bubb Dodington to slander him — but there is no evidence of a public confrontation between the brothers. The Duke continued his royal duties, attending all the usual functions at court and in society, and he frequently found himself face to face with Frederick, but they treated each other with perfect civility.

As if oblivious to public suspicions, Cumberland carried on with his army reforms, his improvements at Windsor and all his usual pursuits. From his early visits to Poyntz's house at Midgham, where he had watched the training of racehorses on the Berkshire hills, he had developed a keen interest in racing. Now, as well as breeding horses at Windsor he was beginning to take an interest in training them. In 1750 Captain Augustus Keppel wrote from the Mediterranean to say that he hoped to acquire some horses for Cumberland, presumably Arabs, and the beginnings of the Windsor stud can be traced to this source. Cumberland leased his own training establishment at Ilsley in Berkshire, run by Mr Head, galloping the horses on Gore's Hill near where the Queen has her stables today. His attendance at Ascot races, founded by Queen Anne, was therefore more than an idle pastime; in fact, such was his interest that he and a few like-minded friends decided to organize the sport with a little more regularity.

At that time there were race meetings all over the country; every little market town had its own races, even East Ilsley itself and Burford in the Cotswolds. Although racing was in theory controlled by a 1740 Act of Parliament, in practice the sport was rife with corruption. There was a contemporary mania for gambling, shared by Cumberland himself and his sister Amelia as well as most of their friends, but the racing law appeared to be unenforceable and there was a real social need for ordinary race-goers to be protected from the unscrupulous. In 1750 a number of influential owners assembled at the Star and Garter Inn in Pall Mall to thrash out some basic regulations. Cumberland himself was not present, but he undoubtedly influenced that meeting, which saw the founding of the Jockey Club. Though it would take nearly two years, Cumberland and his friends now took the supervision of racing more or less into their own hands.

In the first Racing Calendar issued by a Mr Pond in 1751, 'the Duke' was named first among the great owners. Where colours were listed, his were the first declared: and purple remains the royal colour to this day. By the rules, 'matches' were to be arranged at least a year ahead, and were minuted in the books held in the coffee rooms opened in Newmarket. The rules were promulgated throughout the racing fraternity: to be caught below the declared weights, for instance, was to incur forfeiture of the horse and a fine of £200, with common informers taking half the fine as reward. From now on, Cumberland's administrative genius and influence would become more and more evident in the racing world.

This quite ordinary, indeed laudable pastime was somehow twisted by his critics into further proof of his disreputable character. Yet in a contradictory way the same critics raged at his emphatic reorganization of the army. In particular his attempts to promote according to merit were ridiculed, but he went out of his way to demonstrate that he would not be moved. When he was due to inspect a cavalry regiment and heard that one officer, whom he personally had promoted from the ranks, was being cold-shouldered by his brother officers, Cumberland made his opinion plain. Asked to dine in the mess after the review was over, he said in effect: 'Certainly, provided I may sit next to So-and-so.'[5]

The Duke's assertive, forthright manner often ruffled feathers in the officer corps. But as he once explained:

It is every man's duty as commander-in-chief to ask the opinion and advice of those who can give him new lights from their Experience and knowledge of the country and service. But when they differ and do not convince, the person commanding ought certainly to follow his own opinion. I would as little be talked out of my own opinion as I would be deaf to conviction.[6]

And so, in the face of considerable hostility, Cumberland was laying the foundations of a stronger and more efficient army. During the winter of 1750-51 he prepared once again to do battle with his opponents over the annual passage of the Army Act. But at the beginning of the year there was published a blatantly libellous pamphlet, *Constitutional Queries*, part of which read as follows:

Whether a younger son of the crown should ever be invested with absolute power over the army, and at the same time by a factious connection make himself master of the fleet, our lives and fortunes might not be dependent on his will, and pleasure and the right of succession have no other security than his want of ambition.[7]

It was rumoured that the anonymous author was Egmont, by now the chief adviser of the Prince of Wales. Certainly Frederick's party journal, *The Remembrancer*, was strong against Cumberland, though the personal relationship between the brothers continued, outwardly at least, to be perfectly friendly.

The point about the navy was entirely without foundation, and the innuendoes were not new; but this tract sowed its seeds in fertile ground well tilled by the Jacobites and other Leicester House propagandists. Furthermore, Cumberland was likened to those earlier royal villains, John of Gaunt and Richard III, and accused of planning to usurp the throne. Such outright imputations had to be challenged. The whole of Parliament expressed its deep and genuine shock over the attack on a prince of untarnished loyalty. On 22 February a unanimous resolution of both Houses condemned the pamphlet as seditious libel and ordered it to be burnt by the public hangman in New Palace Yard.

But four weeks later there was a still more serious constitutional crisis, caused by the death, on 20 March, 1751, of the Prince of Wales.

# 18

# The Regency Crisis

THE PRINCE OF WALES was just forty-four when he died. He had been ill for a week or two with pneumonia, but had seemed to be rallying. The King heard the news while watching Princess Amelia at her cards. 'Why, they told me he was getting better!' he exclaimed.[1] To Princess Augusta he sent a kind enough note of condolence, but then spoilt the effect by ordering a private interment without ceremony. Neither he nor any of his other children attended the dismal obsequies on the evening of 13 April, though Cumberland cancelled his birthday levee and the anniversary dinner of the Culloden Society on the 15th.

Frederick left his widow with eight children and another expected in July. His eldest son, George, the new heir to the throne, was not yet thirteen. The King was sixty-seven; his health was generally good, but there was a constitutional necessity now to resolve the question of a regency, in case George II died before his heir came of age. The King's view was simple: Cumberland should be regent. Not only did Augusta lack political experience, but Cumberland had both experience and authority. But the King's ministers pointed out that the Duke had recently acquired, however unfairly, a most lamentable reputation and that in their opinion the country would not accept him as regent. In fact, there was a four-week tussle in Parliament on the subject, from 26 April to 22 May.

The Prince of Wales had died in the middle of the annual debate about the Army Act; and this year it had been even more of a struggle. In the Commons the opposition had moved that the post of Captain-General be abolished in time of peace, effecting thereby a saving of £16,000 a year in support of Pelham's programme of cuts. But Pelham had manfully defended Cumberland against the attacks, pointing out that the post was one of honour rather than power; that the King was by law the Commander-in-Chief, with ultimate power of life and limb in court martial cases; and that it was necessary to retain a Captain-General even in peacetime for the discipline of the army. Pitt had supported him to the hilt, but many soldier MPs, notably George Sackville, had demurred. And though Newcastle was careful to go along with his brother's line of argument, his lack of warmth towards Cumberland must have been obvious to all.

Newcastle had been jealous of Cumberland ever since 1748, when Cumberland had been dealing with Sandwich over the peace terms at Aix-la-Chapelle. Despite constant reassurance, Newcastle was convinced that Cumberland was building up a faction against him. The Duke and his sister Amelia frequently spent long weekends at Woburn, the home of the Duke of Bedford, consorting with Sandwich, now First Lord of the Admiralty, and other convivial companions whose interest in cards, cricket and amateur theatricals diverted them from serious matters of state. Such levity seemed to Newcastle to hide opportunities for intrigue. He told Hardwicke:

> The sole intent of the Woburn parties is to declare to the world that the Duke of Cumberland and Princess Amelia are determined to countenance and support the Duke of Bedford and my Lord Sandwich in opposition to me.[2]

Indeed, Sandwich and Bedford both admired Cumberland openly; Sandwich once vouchsafed to Newcastle that Cumberland 'promises to be the greatest genius of the age he lives in' and Bedford did not disagree.[3] But there is no evidence at all that Newcastle's fears had any grounding in reality. Cumberland had a soldier's contempt for the political horse-trading that Newcastle dealt in; possibly it was his very impatience with all these ridiculous suspicions that led to Newcastle's hurt feelings.

Ironically, Pelham himself had been at one of the famous Woburn parties. When his brother started complaining that Cumberland and Amelia were trying to 'excommunicate me from all society' and 'set up a new, unknown, factious young party to rival me'[4] Pelham sensibly poured scorn on the suggestions: 'Cumberland always speaks kindly and respectfully of you: at least as much as your late conduct to him and his to you can permit.'[5] To Fox, Pelham confided that he had visited Cumberland at Windsor in June, 1750, and had been most graciously received. 'The talk about domestic affairs is too ridiculous to write upon,' he added, and 'too childish to be worth taking seriously.'[6] On the other hand, Pelham was not averse to the idea of losing Bedford as Secretary of State (South). A rather solemn and humourless man himself, Pelham regarded Bedford as 'all jollity, boyishness and vanity'[7]; more to the point, he was notoriously idle.

Newcastle had then seen his chance to break up the 'factious young party'; throughout the winter he had been urging his brother to dismiss Bedford, no doubt playing on the fact that the King himself frowned on Cumberland's association with this frivolous character. Needless to say, when Cumberland heard rumours of Newcastle's intrigues he was furious, and he cannot have expected a warmer defence from Pelham's brother during the libel debate. But the King's son was bitterly disappointed when the regency debate was finally settled in favour of Augusta.

The King was crestfallen. He observed to Fox that he could not understand why Cumberland was suddenly so unpopular. 'The English nation is so changeable,' he complained. 'I don't know why they dislike him. It is brought about by the Scotch, the Jacobites and the English that do not love discipline.'[8]

Fox blamed Pitt. In the regency debate Pitt had argued against Cumberland, suggesting that the Duke might not be as loyal to Augusta and the future George III as he was to George II. Fox had been so incensed that he strode from the House without waiting for the vote.

In the end Parliament passed a bill to create the Princess Dowager Regent, but with a regency council to advise her upon the King's demise. The only consolation to the King was that Cumberland was appointed head of the council, subject to certain safeguards. The King asked Hardwicke to discuss the draft plan with Cumberland.

Concealing his disappointment, Cumberland gave the Lord Chancellor a dignified reply:

> I desire you will present my humble duty to the King and return H.M. my thanks for the honour he has done me by ordering this affair to be communicated to me. That I think it is necessary that something should be done in it and shall (*be ready to*) submit (as it is my duty) to take such part in it as His Majesty shall judge proper for me.[9]

The message is preserved in Hardwicke's handwriting, with the words in parentheses added as if the Duke had him read the message back to him and then made slight changes of emphasis; the words 'be ready to' were underlined as if to indicate the chosen alternative.

When Walpole later wrote his version of the incident, he had Cumberland tell Fox to convey these sentiments to Pelham:

> Return my thanks to the King for the plan of Regency. As for the part allotted to me I shall submit to it because he commands it, be the Regency what it will.[10]

The tone is significantly less gracious; either Fox misreported the message to Walpole, or the scribbler himself was indulging in a spot of mischief-making. But Fox knew that Cumberland was much upset by the whole episode which he felt had 'marked him down as a bad man to posterity.'[11]

It was alleged that on hearing of his brother's death Cumberland had made an offensive remark: 'It is a great blow to the country, but I hope it will recover in time.'[12] The words do, admittedly, permit a sarcastic interpretation; but the sentiment was sincere enough. Cumberland called on Augusta personally, soon after Frederick's death, and asked the children to take good care of her as good children should. Further, at the end of the year he presented her with the first carpet made by the Savonnerie-style workshop at Paddington that he had helped to establish. She was well protected by the Leicester House set, in particular by the young Scottish Earl of Bute, with whom she had developed a close relationship even before her husband's death. She had no need of further support.

The Duke's disappointment was very real, but he tried to make light of it. 'I am neither in luck nor in fashion just now,' he commented wryly to Sir Everard Fawkener; 'the time may come; if not I make myself happy as I am.'[13] Like Cincinnatus he returned to rural pursuits until such time as his country again needed his services.

He kept himself busy that summer of 1751, mostly at Windsor. With a timely kindness in July the King made him Lord Warder and Ranger of Windsor Forest, in addition to his rangership of the Great Park, with Cranbourne Lodge as an extra gift. The King had also caused a stone obelisk to be erected to commemorate his son's victory at Culloden. It stood above the newly created 'Cow Pond' (now Obelisk Pond) at the end of a long vista leading from the main south-east façade of Cumberland Lodge. It must have been with mixed feelings that the Duke constantly glimpsed this reminder of his former glory.

Cumberland was now responsible for the administration of over 90,000 acres of land stretching as far west as Wokingham, south to Frimley and south-east to Chertsey. He made Edward Mason his secretary for forest affairs, and inherited a paid staff of thirty-seven from the previous holder of the post, the Duke of St Albans; they included a Lieutenant of the Forest, rangers, five keepers and thirteen under-keepers. In addition, the forest law, laid down by strangely named bodies such as the Court of Swanimote in Wokingham, was imposed by officials with even stranger names: not merely riding foresters but agisters, verderers and regarders. Agisters, for instance, had the task of reporting cases of trespass by cattle, and a jury of regarders sat as might a bench of magistrates. But the laws were ludicrously complicated and unenforceable, as Cumberland realized when he summoned his first Court of Swanimote in 1754; so many of the proceedings were challenged that they had to be dropped. It took him till 1762 to get the first of a series of new Acts of Parliament passed that would start to make sense of the old forest laws, but in the end he managed to clarify some important points; in 1762, for example, a close season for all game was decreed for the first time. Also during Cumberland's time, many of the penalties were eased; in 1731 two deer-stealers had been hanged at Henley, but on 27 December 1761 a labourer of Frimley by the name of Richard Freeman, charged with wilfully killing a red deer in Windsor Forest, was merely fined £30.

Among the Duke's new duties was not only the upkeep of the forest itself but the maintenance of the lodges and houses where the staff lived, many of them in serious disrepair. Fences to the deer park and hay cribs for their feed needed renewing and much else needed attention, and for this Cumberland had to apply, through his Surveyor of Forests, Robert Nunn, to the Treasury. But it would seem that the income from the Treasury was never sufficient; Nunn often had to recoup expenses by selling timber to naval shipyards.

However, Cumberland was happy at Windsor. Despite his increasing weight and his bad knee, which made him less and less fit for the chase, on 12 May he rode out with the royal buckhounds just as he had done as a boy. He went to the races at Ascot, where he had already worked with the Duke of St Albans to improve the course, and now he began to raise standards for the racing itself, introducing matches between quality thoroughbreds, for instance, instead of horses better suited to hunting with buckhounds. With so many other duties to attend to, the Duke was forced to rely on Colonel Hodgson as stud manager, but whenever he could find a few hours to spare he would quickly become engrossed in the breeding of his own horses. They were usually raised in the paddocks around Cranbourne Lodge before being sent for training to Mr Head in Berkshire; only then could a decision be made whether or not to race them at Ascot and Newmarket.

He also held a cricket match that summer of 1751, to celebrate the acquisition of Cranbourne Lodge: his own eleven against a side led by Sir John Evills. The latter won by an innings, but the occasion was clearly enjoyed by all. The match over, he entertained the King to dinner at the Lodge itself. It was a biggish house, owned until 1738 by the Carteret family from whom the King had bought it, and it would continue to be the Duke's residence for as long as his own lodge was undergoing rebuilding.

Partly, perhaps, because he was now a man of considerable property, Cumberland had also started to take a keener interest in the arts. As early as 1743 he had brought the Swiss artist David Morier over to England and retained him on his staff, chiefly to paint a gallery of military portraits showing the uniforms of all the guards, marching and cavalry regiments in very close detail. Morier also painted a number of equestrian portraits of the Duke himself, and a fine group showing the Royal Artillery in Holland during the campaign of 1748. For military historians the Morier paintings have especial significance, as it was under Cumberland that dress regulations were first brought in for the army, but there is little artistic merit in most of the pictures; the figures look more like tailor's dummies.

Thomas Sandby, as well as making a fascinating record of the landscapes and improvements in Windsor Great Park, also made many charming sketches of the Duke and his stud staff with the horses. Later Cumberland had the great good taste to employ Sawrey Gilpin as his own sporting artist, and Marlow the landscape artist. Gilpin, who had a room at Cumberland Lodge, executed one lovely oil painting now in the Royal Collection showing the Duke and his stud in the Long Walk below the castle, besides a number of other equine portraits such as 'Cypron and her brood' which records Cumberland's great success with the mare. In his early days, Stubbs himself seems to have worked at Windsor; in particular his 'Mares by a Lake' now at Ascott, near Aylesbury, once hung at Cumberland Lodge and was almost certainly done near Virginia Water for the Duke.

In the applied arts, too, Cumberland was showing a new and active interest. The French carpet-makers who produced Cumberland's gift to the Princess Dowager that year had formerly been with the Savonnerie factory in Paris; they had set up a small factory in Paddington but run into financial difficulties. When Cumberland was shown a sample of their work he was so impressed that he paid off their debts and commissioned several pieces. They also created a knotted-pile portrait of the Duke in the Garter robe over a scarlet uniform. But though their workshops immediately attracted fashionable interest, the Frenchmen produced little that was saleable. The man whom they had hired as their agent, a defrocked French priest, then dismissed them and engaged some English workers to set up a new workshop in Fulham. But the Savonnerie style proved too expensive for the English taste. The Fulham workshop closed and many of the artisans moved to the West Country town of Axminster, to set up a more profitable and lasting enterprise.

Another manufacture that Cumberland encouraged was the china produced at Chelsea under Sprimont, a goldsmith from Liège whom Fawkener had brought to the Duke's attention. He purchased a considerable quantity of the Chelsea china during the raised and red anchor periods, including a great dinner service; and the factory's wide range of products included a portrait bust of him.

But despite all his social and domestic interests at Windsor the Duke continued his efforts to improve the army, whether reviewing manoeuvres and equipment with a critical eye or working behind the scenes to change outdated attitudes and practices. He repeated his orders, first made in 1743, that regiments should no longer be named after their colonels but adopt numbers instead. It was a sensible change in that the previous system not only gave undue eminence to the colonels but could also be very confusing when a regiment acquired a new colonel; but the move naturally met some resistance. He also supervised the first issue of Army Dress Regulations in 1751, which gathered together all the dress distinctions and regimental colours then in use. He developed a system to monitor the whole range of regimental administration, to ensure that company commanders kept proper accounts with no illegal stoppages and that complaints were heard and investigated. The earlier regulations governing drill and tactics, initially compiled by Napier for the Guards in 1747, had now been approved by the King for issue to all regiments, including the details of trooping the colour, first laid down in the regimental orders of the 1st Guards in 1749. To check that these regulations were heeded he introduced a system of annual inspections to be conducted by reviewing generals, who then had to make a detailed report to the Duke, via Napier. He strongly disapproved of the tendency in some units to devise new and unofficial drills, although occasionally he accepted suggestions for improvement, as when General Blakeney's regiment demonstrated a new manoeuvre in Hyde Park.

Despite the ridicule he met for what seemed petty changes, Cumberland's persistence was gradually producing the desired results. Much less satisfactory were the political intrigues that now began to affect him.

In June, 1751, Pelham and Newcastle devised a method by which to rid themselves of both Sandwich and Bedford. They would dismiss Sandwich, whom the King particularly disliked, and hope thus to force Bedford to resign. But Sandwich got wind of the threat and invited himself to stay at Windsor with Cumberland; he rightly assumed that his being sacked while under the Duke's roof would make for real éclat. Cumberland was well aware that his princely status was being exploited, but he was always loyal to his friends. Sandwich wrote to Bedford from Windsor:

The master of this house has received a confirmation this morning of the intelligence I gave you yesterday. As I think it will have a good appearance in the world I am determined to stay here today in the hopes of receiving my dismission under his roof.[14]

It was not the action of a gentleman.

Newcastle's plan worked: Bedford resigned the next day. In his place the Earl of Holderness was appointed Secretary of State (South) and Anson was now promoted the Admiralty chief. Anson was applying new standards to the navy, to match Cumberland's efforts in the army, and he and Holderness, once ambassador at The Hague, both met with the King's approval. But George II had humour enough to tell Pelham that Newcastle would soon grow jealous of the new Secretary 'if Holderness continues to be of my parties at Richmond on Saturdays and goes to those of Cumberland and Princess Amelia.'[15]

A further change was the arrival of Granville (formerly Carteret) as Lord President of the Council, where he was expected to support Newcastle's diplomatic policies in Europe. Despite Pelham's attempts to rein in the national budget, Newcastle was trying to buy support for Britain against future French aggression by paying subsidies to half the leaders of Europe; like the King himself, he continued to view Frederick of Prussia as an enemy and failed to see that old alliances were breaking down and new ones formed.

That Fox was now the only one of Cumberland's friends still in power was of much less concern to the Duke than to Fox himself. Cumberland was only too glad to be free of the niggling aspersions that he was setting up a rival political party with Bedford and Sandwich; he preferred to concentrate on his army and his affairs at Windsor.

But that autumn, in November, Cumberland had a bad fall while out hunting. He was knocked unconscious. On coming round he refused the normal treatment of blooding, but three days later he suffered complications, complaining of violent pains in the side, probably from internal bruising. He was now blooded five times and deprived of 100oz of blood altogether. At one time the doctors thought him near to death. Hearing of the accident, Parisian wits remarked that the Duke's horse must have collapsed under 'the weight of his virtues and his great abilities.'[16] The King, however, was beside himself with worry. Fox visited the patient with reports on how everyone had reacted. Both Pelham and Newcastle cried, he said. 'The Duke of Newcastle overacted but Mr Pelham seemed really in lament.'[17] One imagines that such news raised at least a smile on the invalid's chubby countenance.

# 19

# New Dimensions

PARTLY AS A RESULT OF HIS ACCIDENT, Cumberland spent much of the next two or three years out of the public eye. The King himself was eager for the company of his sole surviving son, and no doubt was beginning to feel his age. The year of 1751 had seen the death not only of his elder son but of his daughter Louisa, Cumberland's youngest sister, who had become Queen of Denmark, and also of his son-in-law, William of Orange. But in 1752 George II again took himself off to Hanover, accompanied by Lady Yarmouth and Newcastle.

Although pursuing a quieter life, however, Cumberland kept in touch with events not only in Europe but in North America. From the new settlement in Nova Scotia, Halifax, named after the chief of the Board of Trade and Plantations, Governor Cornwallis had written to Napier complaining that he needed more troops. 'The Governor of Canada is making encroachments in the most unwarrantable manner,' he wrote in December, 1749; he needed a regiment in Halifax itself and 'a good strength regiment in the Isthmus', the point opposite the French stronghold of Beauséjour.[1] In June, 1751, there had been an angry exchange of letters between Governor Clinton of New York and La Jonquière of the province of Canada concerning French encroachments into Iroquois country, and in 1752 a fort erected by the French at Crown Point, beside Lake Champlain, was held to be on British territory and 'very obnoxious to British subjects'. But George II and the Pelhams were less interested in developments across the Atlantic than those in Europe, and paid scant attention to the colonies.

It was a mistake. France took advantage of British neglect, sending the Marquis Duquesne out to Canada in 1753. He, with an expedition of French Canadians and Indians, was to seize control of the headwaters of the River Ohio, so as to open communications with the Mississippi basin and their Louisiana settlements, and in the process create an obstacle to

British expansion to the west. From a document obtained from a deserter and passed to him via the Board of Trade in 1753, Cumberland realized just how strong the French were in 'New France' with sixteen fortified posts in the province of Canada alone, and apparently 10,000 soldiers. Although more populous, the British colonies were too widely scattered to be defended by the hopelessly undermanned and ill-equipped independent companies; only in Nova Scotia was there the semblance of a reliable defence.

Robert Dinwiddie, Lieutenant-Governor of Virginia, received orders from London, dated 23 August, 1753, to send a party of militiamen to Fort Le Boeuf and to enquire of the French commander 'by whose authority he had invaded British territory with an armed body from Canada.' The man to whom Dinwiddie entrusted this mission was a young adjutant of militia by the name of George Washington. However, gaining no satisfaction, Dinwiddie then had to apply urgently for military support from Britain, in the meantime sending Washington back to remonstrate with the French with all the available force at his command: three regular independent companies of the Crown from New York and South Carolina and some provincial levies from Virginia and North Carolina.

From India, by contrast, there was at last some good news. The French governor of Pondicherry, Joseph Dupleix, and his military lieutenant, Charles de Bussy, had been attempting to extend French dominion over southern India, but had run into stiff opposition from the British East India Company troops led by Major Stringer Lawrence and a young man called Robert Clive. Indeed, by 1753 Clive and Lawrence together had made the French rethink their plans, and Dupleix was soon called back to Paris. Now was clearly the time for the British to consolidate their position. In January, 1754, Cumberland was asked to nominate a regiment from the Irish establishment to send to India, and on the recommendation of General Lord Rothes, the Commander-in-Chief Ireland, he chose the 39th. It would be the first battalion of the regular army to serve in the east. The 39th was commanded by Colonel John Adlercron (sometimes Aldercron), who was now summoned to a series of interviews in London and at Windsor to discuss plans with Cumberland, Fox and Holderness.

Adlercron would be facing a completely unprecedented situation, Cumberland warned him, and thus would receive unprecedented powers. He would be appointed Commander-in-Chief in India, with authority over the East India Company troops as well as his own; all would be obliged to fight according to the Articles of War, with a single code of discipline. In the words of the King's commission, Adlercron was to

> consider the honour of our forces, the good of the service and the interest of the East India Company whose territories and commerce you are sent

to protect and establish, whether on the coast of Coromandel [*south-east*] or Malabar [*south-west*].³

He and his 800-strong regiment, along with a detachment of seventy from the Royal Artillery and twelve short six-pounders, would sail out from Cork with four ships of the line and a convoy of supply ships under Admiral Watson.

It would be nearly a year before the first news of Adlercron's progress filtered back home.

In 1752-53, albeit fleetingly, Cumberland must have wondered if he would be called away from horse-breeding, racing and army reviews to organize a new campaign against the Jacobites. It was known that Jacobite sympathies persisted, albeit on a very subdued level, and also that in 1750 the Young Pretender had been buying quantities of arms in Antwerp. What was not known, however, was that in September, 1750, Charles Edward Stuart had paid a clandestine visit to London; he wanted to see whether his former friends would still support him, but it seems he was quickly disabused of the notion. Nevertheless, definite stirrings of discontent were identified. In March, 1753, Archibald Cameron was captured: an unrepentant anti-Hanoverian, he was trying to organize a new rebellion in Scotland, and later that year he was hanged. His execution marked the end of the Jacobite unrest.

However, if turbulence on a far wider scale was looming, as Cumberland felt sure it was, there was no active part he could play until the administration decided on a policy. Newcastle's subsidies to the Electors of Bavaria and Saxony were causing resentment in Britain over the expense, as well as in Europe. Frederick of Prussia and his uncle George II remained on bad terms, but it began to look as though Prussia was the only ally Britain now had in Europe. Maria Theresa, advised by Chancellor Kaunitz, the former Austrian Ambassador in France, had reverted to her insistence on recovering Silesia and was edging towards alliance with the French. In Holland Cumberland's poor sister Anne, the widowed Princess of Orange, was somewhat overwhelmed by the diplomatic game; it seemed likely that she would be forced by the pacific and trading instincts of the States General to yield to French pressure against the English connection.

Cumberland resumed his routine affairs. One of his great delights now was to show friends around Virginia Water. The lake was complete and stocked with fish and, although the plantations were still somewhat immature, the landscaping and many ornamental features made it a place of beauty and charm. On an island not far from the shore Sandby had built a small Chinese-style temple, which contained two rooms: 'the great room and H.R.H's closet.'[4] The great room, in scarlet and green with touches of gold and mirrored panels on the doors, was dominated by an elaborate glass chandelier, and on the chimney piece was displayed a fine set of china from the Chelsea factory. Another pleasing feature of the lake was a single-span wooden bridge, designed by Flitcroft, again in the Chinese style; although it could bear a carriage it was a thing of extraordinary delicacy − but alas, some decades later it was replaced by a stone one.

As if the lake and its surroundings were not captivating enough, Cumberland entertained his guests with a 'Mandarin' junk'. The 50-ton Thames-built hull had been sailed up river to the Bells of Ouseley Inn at Old Windsor, then manoeuvred onto rollers and towed overland to the lake by teams of horses. The saloon was suitably decorated with japanning and lacquer, furnished with ten banister-back chairs upholstered with painted taffeta, and lit with four Chinese candlesticks. According to Lady Jane Coke, who visited Virginia Water in October, 1753, the junk was 'by far the prettiest thing I ever saw with one very good room in it and no expense spared in the finishing.'[5] Lady Jane, a sister of the last Duke of Wharton and a connoisseur of country estates, was unstinting in her praise of Cumberland's achievements: they were, she said, 'magnificent beyond description.' By comparison, Blenheim Palace 'did not answer my expectation.'

Thanks to his own efforts at nearby Ascot, Cumberland enjoyed horse racing more and more. He had introduced races on the Newmarket pattern, such as the match of May, 1753, run over a new course, the best of three two-mile heats for a purse of £30. The same race was run in the following year, along with a four-mile race for four-year-olds for a purse of £90, won by a bay colt, Stock, owned by the Duke himself.

He had become an addict of the sport. Come hell or high water, he would attend every meeting at Newmarket, two in the spring, two in the autumn, every year for the rest of his life, except in 1757 when he was overseas. Ironically, it was in that very year that the Jockey Club Stakes appear as the first entry in the Betting and Stake book, on 5 February:

> We whose names are underwritten engage ourselves to stake 100 guineas yearly for five years from 1757 to 1761 to be run for yearly at Newmarket.[6]

The first signature, of twelve, is 'William'.

On 6 March, 1754, Henry Pelham died. He had long been in poor health but his death in office nevertheless came as a shock to the King and the other ministers, especially his brother Newcastle. The King turned to

Hardwicke for advice, and surprised the Lord Chancellor by insisting that the choice of new premier was a matter for the cabinet to decide.

Cumberland took no part in the decision. Newcastle, supported by Hardwicke, managed to control his grief sufficiently to take over his brother's role as First Commissioner of the Treasury, but Pelham's other duties as Chancellor of the Exchequer went to Henry Bilson Legge. This was a slight surprise, as Legge had been with the Leicester House opposition. Another new face in the cabinet was to be Sir Thomas Robinson, brought in as Secretary of State (South), while his predecessor, Holderness, took over Newcastle's former post in the northern department.

The King was disappointed that Fox was excluded from promotion, as was Cumberland, though perhaps he was less surprised than his father. Fox was in fact offered a position as Secretary of State, but on terms that he had to refuse; it was almost certainly a deliberate move on the part of Hardwicke, with whom Fox had violently disagreed earlier that Parliamentary session over the Marriage Act. The two men had long disliked each other, but when Hardwicke introduced his marriage reforms, including the need to publish the banns on three consecutive Sundays, Fox, the one-time eloper, felt they were a direct personal insult.

Just as disappointed was Pitt who had obviously hoped for advancement, even though the King could not abide him. So Pitt, still Paymaster General, and Fox, still Secretary at War, now formed a strange alliance against Sir Thomas Robinson.

For Cumberland, Fox and Pitt were both ministers of great ability and both well versed in military affairs. Fox he knew of old, but Pitt was something of an unknown quantity. Over the past few years Pitt had been suffering constant illness and had become something of a recluse, though this was about to change: in the summer of 1754 he was wooing Hester, a daughter of the rich and powerful Grenville family, and in November, at the age of forty-six, he was finally married. He had broadly supported the Pelham administration, but failing to receive promotion after Pelham's death he began to re-establish relations with Leicester House as a way of insuring his political future.

Despite the King's abiding dislike of the man, Cumberland knew that Pitt's political skills had been sadly wasted in the Paymaster General's office, and that his patriotic fervour and sheer power of oratory made him exactly what the country needed at this time: a great potential leader. It was thus Cumberland's wish to unite the two men, Fox and Pitt, in the service of his father.

In June, 1754, Fox stayed several days with Cumberland at Windsor. In August he and Pitt both visited Cumberland at Windsor. They no doubt discussed the nonentity, Robinson, who had acquired high office without serving any political apprenticeship or possessing any political skills whatsoever, and perhaps the worsening situation in North America; but the object of the meeting was to solve a long-standing problem concerning the Chelsea out-pensioners.

Cumberland had been interested in the welfare of old soldiers and soldiers' families since before Culloden, but one of the scandals of the day was that the Chelsea out-pensioners were paid their pensions in arrears, and as a result, most of them were in terrible debt to the loan sharks of the day. Cumberland had repeatedly urged the Treasury to act, but in vain. Now he brought together the two men he considered the ablest in the House of Commons to draw up a bill for pensioners to be paid six months in advance on first appointment. Pitt introduced the bill that November and it was passed a month later. Humanity and persistence had triumphed, though the credit would always go to Pitt.

Newcastle, meanwhile, had begun to realize that his ministry was drifting like a rudderless ship. Robinson, in particular, as the man with colonial responsibility, was in need of advice over a suitable response to the French threat across the Atlantic. Newcastle himself could not advise him, so when the King suggested he turn to Cumberland, Newcastle was happy to agree. At first Cumberland was merely asked to nominate a general and some half-pay officers to serve in North America; he replied that perhaps he should be told what the officers were supposed to do. Before he could advise on military matters he needed to know the extent of the country to be defended and 'the particular places properest for operations'; how many forces were to be employed and 'what was to be the particular service of the half-pay officers'; and 'whether to discipline only American troops or to be Regimented.'[7]

The upshot was a very important meeting held in Cumberland's rooms at St James's Palace in September, with Newcastle, Hardwicke, Anson (First Lord of the Admiralty but also the Lord Chancellor's son-in-law) and Sir Thomas Robinson. By this time news had reached London that Washington had been defeated by the French, adding fresh urgency to the talks. It seems likely that Cumberland was as well informed as any man at the meeting. Certainly, if one may judge by the letter Newcastle wrote to Albemarle just afterwards, the Prime Minister was well satisfied with the result:

> This consultation has put the Duke in a very high light as an officer. I must do his R. H. the justice to say that he behaved with great ability, decency and moderation and particularly upon the article of expense.[8]

But Newcastle did not say whether he shared the King's surprise that

'H.R.H. had made himself so entirely master of his subject in so short a time.'[9]

As we know, Cumberland had kept himself well informed of the French threat and the colonies' response to it, and now he heard from Governor Sharpe of Maryland that the George Washington débâcle had been caused partly by his very bad French interpreter, who had so mishandled negotiations that fighting broke out unnecessarily. Sharpe assured Cumberland that he was prepared to lead an expedition himself, to recover the area around the headwaters of the Ohio River where the French had built a new Fort, Fort Duquesne. But piecemeal solutions were not the answer. Until men such as Benjamin Franklin could persuade the separate colonies to unite in their own defence, Cumberland thought they needed a viceroy, on the Spanish pattern, to impose unity. He suggested that a British military commander-in-chief be appointed, to report to himself as Captain-General. He further suggested that regular regiments be sent from Britain as well as a cadre of NCOs from the Foot Guards to help train the colonial levies. He would revive the regiments of Shirley and Pepperell that had won the magnificent prize of Louisburg in 1745 and put them into British uniforms. And with this whole force he would order an advance on a broad front, to hold a clearly agreed territorial frontier. In his opinion, the last point was an essential prerequisite to peace in North America:

> None of your preparations, none of your military measures are of any effect till the government has fixed the bounds of the French in America. How far they should come and no further, which being once done and laid down as a permanent measure, whether of war or peace, the most express and distinct instructions should be drawn for the Commander-in-Chief that he may not be liable to future reproaches from one or the other colony, to be sacrificed to the clamour of the merchants at home, or their correspondents abroad. The operations should be conducted in several sectors: Nova Scotia, Crown Point, on Lake Champlain, and the Ohio.[10]

For viceroy Cumberland proposed Albemarle, currently Ambassador in Paris, but also nominally Governor of Virginia.

Cumberland's incisive suggestions were gratefully endorsed by Newcastle and Robinson and laid before the King for approval. Although the King vetoed his son's idea of a viceroy on constitutional grounds and refused to let the NCOs from the Guards go, he agreed to the general concept of his troops being sent out to North America.

Cumberland immediately set to work, considering which officers and regiments were best suited to the purpose. But Newcastle, worried about the expense, again began to dither. It was Fox who forced his hand, by making the proposals public. This was contrary to Cumberland's plans; he had hoped to take the advantage over the French with a new and far stronger force than they had so far encountered in North America, and he felt that discretion was essential. He had told Napier to alert the commanding officer at Bristol to take up the necessary transports 'as privately as he could'. Naturally, Fox's action made Newcastle furious. Apart from weightier considerations, the Duchess of Newcastle was in correspondence with Madame de Pompadour over her wish to import the French chef, Monsieur Fontenelle.

The regiments for America were to come from the Irish establishment, the 44th (Dunbar's) and 48th (Halkett's). To overcome the disadvantage of their low strength, Cumberland directed that they be brought up to 580 rank and file before they left Cork, with drafts from the 11th and 20th Regiments (Borland's and Bury's). Further recruitment would be carried out in North America. Together with the regular battalions of the Nova Scotia garrison, the independent companies of regulars in America, Shirley's and Pepperell's regiments, and other provincials including the friendly Indians led by an American Ulsterman by the name of Johnson, the whole force would be commanded by Major-General Edward Braddock of the 2nd Foot Guards.

Cumberland has often been criticized for his choice of commander. Braddock was sixty years old but still quite junior; he had only been promoted to major-general that year, when serving in Gibraltar with his regiment, the 14th Foot. He had seen service at Ostend and with Cumberland at Lichfield in '45 and in '47 he had been involved in the abortive attempt to raise the siege at Bergen op Zoom. He had a reputation as a coarse, loud-mouthed martinet with a fondness for women and gambling, but so did many officers of the day. To those who knew him better, such as the actress Ann Bellamy with whom he lived for a time, he seemed a genial enough character with a hearty manner that especially appealed to children.

Clearly Cumberland thought Braddock had the experience and character for the difficult assignment ahead. The Duke took considerable trouble to brief him personally. After agreeing operational instructions with Robinson, he summoned Braddock to Windsor on 16 November and explained his orders in detail. The object of the expedition was to recover Fort Duquesne and other territory that the French had seized from the King's colonial subjects and their allies, the Indians of the Six Nations, working northwards with the ultimate goal of securing the isthmus in Nova Scotia. Because Braddock would be commanding a very mixed column, he must make it clear to everyone that all embodied troops were to fight under the terms of the British Articles of War. Care should be taken to adopt and adhere to strict regulations concerning relations between the constituent parts of the army. Although Shirley, Pepperell and Johnson were all to receive the King's commission as major-generals, British regular officers were to take precedence over provincial officers of equal rank, and there was to be no field officer status for provincials unless given the King's commission.

That Braddock later chose to ignore many of these instructions cannot be held against his Captain-General. Nor can Cumberland be blamed, as many with hindsight have tried to do, for sending such a relatively small force out from Britain and so late. Newcastle, if anyone, was to blame for the mean, muted and slow response to problems in America; but Newcastle did his best to offload responsibility: 'The measures for conducting [the campaign] and for the execution of it are entirely H.R.H.'s'[11]

After reviewing his troops at Cork in November, Braddock returned to Windsor again. Cumberland's instructions were clear enough in scope, though he was wise enough not to tie Braddock down to exact dispositions and timings. The plan was for Braddock and his regiments to sail with Commodore Keppel to Hampton Roads in Virginia, then march west through the Allegheny Mountains at the Cumberland Gap — discovered only ten years earlier, and named in honour of William Augustus — to attack Fort Duquesne. The Duke even went so far as to warn Braddock:

> You should be careful to prevent any panick in the troops from Indians to whom the soldiers being not yet accustomed, the French will not fail to make all attempts towards. Visit your posts and outposts often and make all officers do so as well, making all the troops sure that there can be no excuse whatever for a surprise.[12]

There was not much more that Cumberland could do, beyond approve the artillery train and ordnance and bid farewell to Braddock in December.

# 20

# Universal War

CUMBERLAND FACED AN ANXIOUS few months before news would come from Braddock. In fact the first news from across the Atlantic came from Braddock's QMG, Sir John St Clair, who had sailed a month earlier, and his initial impression of the provincials was not good. 'Their sloth and ignorance is not to be described,' he wrote. 'I wish General Braddock will make them shake it off.'[1]

Cumberland's apprehensions of the winter of 1754-5 were not eased by the stubborn designs of his friend Fox who, like Pitt, still craved promotion. By pleading his case with Lady Yarmouth, Fox ensured that the King would do what he could to persuade Newcastle. Cumberland desired to retain for the King's ministry the services of both Fox and Pitt, and he feared that Pitt would take it amiss if Fox were promoted and he were not. He urged Fox to curb his ambition, at least until the impending crisis was resolved. Recklessly Fox followed his own course, badgering Newcastle in whatever way he could, and in the process earning the King's disapproval as well as Cumberland's exasperation Finally, in March, 1755, Newcastle agreed to give Fox a seat in the Cabinet, on condition that Fox backed his policies in the Commons. Just as Cumberland had thought, Pitt was bitterly angry; Fox and he were now antagonists for life.

Cumberland was fully convinced that France was resolved on war. The King tended to underrate the threat to Britain but he was growing anxious for his Electorate; besides, he wanted to pay his customary biennial visit to Hanover. Newcastle was terrified of war breaking out, particularly while the King was abroad, but, to Cumberland's dismay, not even Newcastle's pleas could persuade the King to stay. However, the King's speech to Parliament on 25 March contained a few phrases that were certainly prompted by Cumberland: his ministers, he said, would augment the forces by sea and land and 'take such measures as may best tend to preserve the general peace of Europe and... secure the just rights and possessions of the Crown in

America.'[2] Then at the end of April he set off for Hanover, leaving the country in the hands of the Lords Justice, with, for the first time, Cumberland as their appointed chairman.

As chairman Cumberland had the power to initiate meetings of the Lords Justice 'if matters should require anything additional to their formal Tuesday meetings.'[3] At this time they included not only Newcastle himself and the two secretaries of state (Robinson and Holderness), the Lord Chancellor (Hardwicke), the Lord Privy Seal (Duke of Marlborough) and the Duke of Argyll with responsibility for Scottish matters, but also the Archbishop of Canterbury and various great officers of the Court such as the Lord Chamberlain, Lord Steward, even the Master of the Horse, and, another new departure, the Secretary at War, much to the satisfaction of Henry Fox. Such a body was unsuitably large for much detailed business and sometimes Cumberland merely assembled the inner cabinet in his rooms. It had also been agreed that Newcastle and a chosen few should meet less formally, for preliminary discussion of certain more complicated issues, in advance of the Tuesday meetings. This, unfortunately, gave Newcastle a chance to organize concerted opposition to Cumberland's policies whenever he felt so inclined.

The additional manpower mentioned in the King's speech referred mainly to 5,000 marines, to be raised in fifty companies, which at Cumberland's suggestion would be put under Admiralty control to save army regiments being called to serve aboard ship. The seven Guards battalions in London were brought up to a higher strength. The even lower-strength regiments in Ireland — at thirty men to a company — were also to be fully recruited. But ministers refused to authorize new regiments; Newcastle, it was said, did not wish to increase Cumberland's powers of patronage. However, even before the first meeting of the Lords Justice on 9 May, Admiral Boscawen and his squadron were sent off to sea with orders to fall upon any French ships that might be transporting reinforcements to North America, the anticipated riposte of Versailles to Braddock's expedition.

Braddock's reports from America were at last beginning to reach the Captain-General, and they did not make good reading. The colonists were far from unanimous in their support for the King's army from England, the roads were either non-existent or appalling, and progress was slow. Half the problem was that the instructions he had received from Cumberland, although based on the best available information in London, were totally unrealistic. The climate, the geography and most of all the political situation of North America were not understood in London. From Alexandria, Virginia, he wrote on 19 April:

I have met with infinite difficulties providing carriages — the men of

Maryland refuse to cross the Potomac — there is a total want of dry forage and we must carry all provisions.[4]

At Alexandria he had met the governors in conference, along with Shirley and the Indian expert William Johnson, but he confessed himself greatly disappointed by the colonial assemblies, 'who promised great matters but have done nothing'. Prophetically he concluded that the only solution would be to levy a defence tax. His main support initially came from Commodore Augustus Keppel, who provided manpower and materials to build boats for crossing rivers and lakes and also bolstered his supplies. Later he received valuable help from Benjamin Franklin, who managed to conjure up some horses and wagons — for a fee — when Braddock despaired of finding any in the whole of Pennsylvania. But by midsummer he was months behind schedule, and he still had mile upon mile of dense roadless forest to traverse before his column of 2,000-odd reached Fort Duquesne.

Other news of Braddock filtered back home. James Wolfe's friends in the force sent back favourable accounts of the general's efforts and relations with those under his command. Dinwiddie reported: 'He is I think a very fine officer, and a sensible considerate gentleman.'[5]

Further north, Colonel Monckton's force in Nova Scotia had much more success. In mid-June Monckton turned the French out of Beauséjour and promptly renamed it Fort Cumberland (which made two in North America). William Johnson and his 4,500 provincials managed to retake Crown Point and struggled as far as Lake Champlain, but late in the summer they were beaten back by a strong French force. Shirley, after a long delay caused by supply problems, set off with the two provincial regiments to cross Lake Ontario to Niagara, but far outran his supplies, hung about on half rations and then found the way barred by reinforced French garrisons. Unable to reach his objective, he withdrew in some disorder, leaving a garrison at Oswego on the shores of Lake Ontario.

Cumberland spent most of that summer in a state of mounting apprehension. Then, on 23 August, Commodore Keppel arrived home with terrible news. Braddock was dead, caught in an ambush seven miles from Fort Duquesne.

There are several separate accounts in Cumberland's papers of how Braddock met his fate. It seems that, impatient with the lack of progress, he divided his column into two and led the forward column himself. For twenty days he and his men made good progress. Expecting an ambush on the Monongahela River he took extra precautions, but having encountered no one there he seems to have concluded that the next bound would be the fort itself, which he expected to reduce by the use of his artillery. He had, in fact, let his guard slip at the last minute. The leading platoon ran into the

French. There was a brisk exchange of fire. Meanwhile, some 600 Indians had slipped around the flanks and surrounded the column. For three hours a bitter firefight ensued. Braddock was remarkably cool; he had four horses shot from under him. Then he himself was hit. His troops turned and fled, a human torrent, fighting their way back east; not even George Washington was able to stop them.

'We shall know better what to do next time,' Braddock was heard to mutter just before he died a few days later.[6]

When Cumberland first heard the news he thought the fault must lie with the troops. 'I fear we have beat ourselves,' he wrote to Robinson, 'as I see no account of enemies or of any prisoners being taken.'[7] Newcastle, for his part, wrote to Holderness, currently visiting the King in Hanover, drawing the lesson that in future Americans must fight Americans: 'Our regular troops must not be puffed up. I hope the King will see things in this light. P.S. You know who recommended Braddock and picked out the two Regiments.'[8]

A few days later, on 2 September, Newcastle was against writing 'entre nous' to Holderness: 'The Duke is violent for sending a Regiment of 1,000 from Glasgow to North America'[9] 'Violent' was not perhaps the mot juste, but Cumberland was indeed in favour of sending reinforcements across the Atlantic as fast as possible. Even before news of Braddock's death reached England, on 11 August a plan of operations for the coming year in America had been agreed by the Lords Justice. Cumberland was dissatisfied with this plan, and now he had Napier draw up some suggested alterations.

By raising 1,000 Highlanders from Glasgow, a town noted for its loyalty in the '45, Cumberland intended to bolster the surviving 44th and 48th Regiments (Dunbar's and Halkett's). He also considered it safe now to release 1,500 regulars from Nova Scotia. With the Shirley and Pepperell regiments and other provincial and regular formations brought up to strength, he proposed a massed attack on Quebec. The navy would offer support by blockading the mouth of the St Lawrence. As to Fort Duquesne, to avoid 'the tediousness, expense and difficulties' that Braddock had encountered, Cumberland envisaged a second assault from Niagara via the headwaters of the Ohio. The Commander-in-Chief's headquarters were, he indicated firmly, to be at the long-established settlement and inland port of Albany, on the River Hudson.

Broadly, Cumberland's aim was to protect the American colonies, in default of an agreed frontier, by seizing Canada and launching a maritime colonial campaign without actually declaring war. As Wraxall, the town clerk of Albany, wrote to Fox that September, 'A more favourable period of destroying the ambitious schemes of the French in North America cannot be hoped for than the present.'[10]

Unfortunately for Cumberland, the King's ministers did not share Wraxall's sense of the moment. In June that year Boscawen had intercepted a convoy of French ships making for Canada, but caught only two. Timidly, Newcastle had agreed that the navy should step up its operations and Admiral Hawke had sailed with seventeen ships of the line that July. But Newcastle delayed giving him the order to take the offensive, and so Hawke and his squadron spent the rest of the year loitering to no purpose in Atlantic waters, to the detriment of both ships and crews.

Newcastle's anxiety to avoid war with France was partly a reflection of the King's own fears. So far, Versailles had merely broken diplomatic relations with Britain, but, as Frederick the Great once advised the French, the way to hit the King of England was to strike at Hanover. The King had an extreme reluctance to ally himself with his loathsome nephew of Prussia, however logical this began to seem, and chose instead, as Elector of Hanover, to seek an alliance with the Tsaritsa Elizabeth of Russia, promising her an annual subsidy in exchange for a guarantee of support in time of war. In September, confident that he had arranged security for his beloved Hanover, he returned to England.

In London, however, a political storm was brewing, caused partly by the King's arrangements for Hanover, and Pitt was at the centre.

That summer Pitt had found a welcome at Leicester House. Prince George was seventeen, a year off his majority, but still very much under the influence of his mother and thus of the Earl of Bute. Although relations between Kensington and Leicester House had improved since the death of the Prince of Wales, the appointment of Cumberland as head of the Lords Justice had been seen by Bute as a confirmation of those old rumours; Bute apparently suspected that the Duke might use the threat of war as an excuse to seize power. In fact, advised by Bute, Augusta had administered a clumsy snub to her brother-in-law, refusing to let her sons join him on his inspection of the fleet at Portsmouth. Cumberland had issued the invitation at Prince George's birthday party on 4 June, which he had attended with avuncular pride, and the snub undoubtedly hurt the young princes more than their uncle.

At Leicester House Pitt began to unfold his opposition to the Newcastle ministry. Some of his views were shared by Henry Bilson Legge, who as Chancellor of the Exchequer was very perturbed at the extravagant subsidies to foreign powers. Legge, formerly ambassador in Berlin, was in favour of an alliance with Prussia; he also regarded as senseless the treaty, signed that year, whereby Newcastle could summon Hessian troops to England's defence in case of war.

Pitt's connection with Leicester House only added to Cumberland's despondency, as did the querulous series of communications now coming in from India. Adlercron had met a less than enthusiastic welcome from the officers of the East India Company and Stringer Lawrence had openly challenged not only his authority but the validity of the Articles of War in India. Moreover, since the two East India companies had agreed a cessation of hostilities by the time Adlercron arrived, there seemed to be very little for him and his men to do except pay their ceremonial respects to the local nawabs. For what purpose had he been stranded in this strange, far-off land in stupefying heat?

Exasperated at the man's lack of imagination and flexbility, Cumberland sent back soothing words encouraging Aldercron to make his peace with Stringer Lawrence and be patient. Earlier in '55 he had secured the King's approval to send three companies of the Royal Artillery out to India. The plan in London had been for an assault on Bussy and the Northern Circars, with Robert Clive being awarded a hurried commission under Caroline Scott, by now the senior officer in Bengal. But the plan had gone awry; not only had peace broken out but Scott had died of cholera in Madras in June, 1754. Clive, however, was to find other opportunities to display his military talents in the sub-continent.

In July, 1755, in a confidential letter delivered with instructions that it be burnt, Fox told the Lord Lieutenant of Ireland, the Marquess of Hartington, that Cumberland was in very low spirits, that in particular he despaired of being able to unite the country:

> He is more anxious and less sanguine about the affairs of this nation than I ever knew him about anything – and indeed, we never till now were fighting for our all without the assistance of one ally.[11]

And, although he never expressed disloyalty to his father, Cumberland was not happy about the subsidy treaties; he took the view that at the very least they made the King unpopular. Moreover, Newcastle annoyed him by trying to keep him in the dark over Irish politics – another sign of his jealousy. Because of its traditional importance as a military reservoir of regiments, Cumberland naturally took a good deal of interest in Ireland. He corresponded with Hartington as a friend and from time to time offered practical help, such as the services of Colonel Skinner, the Chief Engineer, who was sent over to Dublin to advise on coastal defences. In any case, Cumberland heard all about Irish affairs from his former aide, Henry Seymour Conway, who was Hartington's secretary and who often visited Windsor.

What is unclear, however, is whether Cumberland had any advance knowledge of the storm that was about to break in domestic politics. On 25 September Legge refused to countersign the warrants for the Hessian subsidy, and with the King's full approval Newcastle dismissed him, then took the opportunity to make a few other changes to his ministry. Legge would be replaced by Sir George Lyttelton, a former Leicester House man. More sensationally, Robinson was persuaded to accept a position at court, leaving the way free to appoint Fox the new Secretary of State (South). And even more dramatic: Pitt was dismissed as Paymaster General.

Fox, of course, was thoroughly pleased with himself, particularly as he was also made leader of the House. Cumberland wrote him a warm letter of congratulations, adding: 'As to your successor, it is a flea bite.'[12] He was referring to the fact that he, as Captain-General, had not even been consulted over the appointment of the new Secretary at War, Lord Barrington, a man with no experience whatever of army administration. It was another deliberate slight by Newcastle. What concerned Cumberland more was how Pitt would react, free as he now was from the restraints of government at a time when the nation was sliding into war.

The King opened Parliament on 13 November and Pitt immediately went in to the attack. He denounced the subsidy treaties, berated Newcastle and Fox and in effect criticized the King himself. In December he backed a motion by George Townshend to reinstate the English militias to defend the country instead of the imported Hessian mercenaries. But Pitt had only limited support in the Commons; thanks to Fox's leadership of the House, Newcastle was able to weather the storm. The treaties with Russia and Hesse were both signed, and, better still, on 16 January 1756 the Convention of Westminster was signed between Britain, Hanover and Prussia. Frederick the Great had guaranteed that Hanover would be safe from Prussia, and so the King was content.

However, the prospect of war had by no means been averted, and, while the diplomatic manoeuvring went on, Cumberland struggled to persuade the King's ministers that the American war required a fresh impetus from Britain, and urgently.

On 20 January Cumberland held a meeting for senior ministers at St James's Palace. Back in October, 1755, he had secured the King's agreement to several measures aimed at strengthening the army. Twelve more independent companies were being raised from the Chelsea out-pensioners for static garrison duties at home. Each of the nineteen regiments of Foot stationed in England, Ireland and Scotland were recruiting two new companies of eight NCOs and a hundred men. A Guards Brigade of three battalions from the London garrison had been ordered to encamp. Altogether, including the results of Cumberland's earlier efforts, the total peacetime establishment had risen at the end of 1755 to 34,263 men (of whom 3,360 all ranks were on the garrisons of Gibraltar and Minorca) with another 6,705 in America and the

West Indies. Furthermore, Parliament had now voted £120,000 for the colonies' defence.

At last Cumberland found that the ministers were listening to him; he was even able to expand his plans made the previous summer. Two battalions from Ireland, to be replaced from England, would be shipped to America. Nearly 2,000 Highlanders would be sent to Nova Scotia, to release the bulk of the regular garrison for mobile operations. And an idea had formed in Cumberland's mind for an entirely new regiment of four battalions, to be called the Royal Americans. The idea won parliamentary approval in February, 1756. It was to be a rifle regiment (forerunner of the 60th Rifles), raised from among European and Protestant colonists. Altogether a total of 13,400 troops would be in action against the French in North America.

Cumberland originally proposed that the new commander-in-chief should be the Earl of Rothes, Lieutenant-General in Ireland; however, to his annoyance, Rothes declined the posting. His second choice was John Campbell, Lord Loudoun, who had served him well during the '45, and indeed in Flanders. He was in his early fifties, a competent soldier, a capable administrator and endowed with a good deal more political sophistication than the plain soldier of the Braddock type. If he was surprised that the ministers should take him aside and brief him out of Cumberland's hearing — probably another attempt by Newcastle to undermine the Duke's influence — he took it in his stride, and continued to look to the Captain-General for orders.

After hearing all the various accounts of the problems and obstacles that Braddock had met, Cumberland had a rather better idea of the conditions that Loudoun would have to face, particularly the wild virgin territory and the men who had made it theirs, the Indians and the long-time settlers. What was needed was a force of men with the discipline of the trained soldier but also the qualities of the scout. As he wrote to Loudoun:

> I hope that you will in time teach your troops to go upon scouting parties; for till Regular officers with men that they can trust learn to beat the woods and to act as irregulars, you never will gain any certain intelligence of the enemy.[13]

But Loudoun did not reach New York until July and the difficulties he would encounter were not the sort to be overcome by scouting parties.

As yet an uneasy peace reigned in Europe. French aggression had been confined to a few infringements of the Treaty of Aix-la-Chapelle, such as the reinforcement of Dunkirk. But the Anglo-Prussian rapprochement had provoked a new mood of defiance in Versailles, which now turned a more receptive ear to Maria Theresa and Chancellor Kaunitz.

Furthermore, news began to reach London that France was preparing an invasion force of 60,000 men on the Channel coast.

# 21

# First Blood

CUMBERLAND HAD LONG CONSIDERED the possibility of invasion. During 1755 he had personally made two reconnaissances of the coast of Sussex, on one occasion staying at Newcastle's house at Bishopstone, although his host was absent at the time. He also issued quiet instructions to one or two senior officers, when visiting coastal areas, to consider what if anything could be done to improve coastal defences. But some officers were less than discreet. When the good people of Essex heard that Guy Carleton of the 1st Guards was having a look at the beaches there, they became so alarmed that Cumberland was obliged to apologize to Sir Thomas Robinson.

He had his own source of intelligence in Jeffrey Amherst, who had built up a network of agents throughout Europe, including the French ports. Mason and Fawkener were also instrumental in collecting intelligence reports for the Duke, primarily of a military nature but spiced from time to time with other scraps of information. In fact Cumberland had recruited at least one mole in a Paris ministry, whose irregular but useful reports had helped him form a fair assessment of the ambitious plans of Maréchal le Duc de Belleisle, the French Minister for War.

Newcastle, with his own network of agents, was equally well aware of French plans, but he was thrown into a lather of doubt and indecision. When further news arrived from southern France in late February, 1756, indicating another ominous massing of troops at Toulon on the Mediterranean coast, he could scarcely assimilate his own options let alone those of the French.

Cumberland took the view that the navy should send a squadron to the Mediterranean at once, to protect the British garrisons in Minorca and Gibraltar. General Blakeney, the octogenarian governor of Minorca, would be in particular need of assistance if the French decided to attack. However, as Anson pointed out, Hawke and his ships of the line had spent most of the second half of 1755 at sea; the fleet had returned to port in desperate need of maintenance and repairs, and Boscawen alone had lost 2,000 men sick. Besides, the threat of invasion in southern Britain seemed the more urgent. For the time being, the navy would stay at home.

In March Parliament voted to continue the Hessian subsidy; at a time of war, with so many of her troops abroad, Britain was in need of all the help she could get. Now Fox proposed, at Cumberland's prompting, that the King be asked for Hanoverian troops as well. Again the motion was carried, despite a scathing denunciation by Pitt on the use of foreign mercenaries to defend England. Pitt and George Townshend had been working on their ideas for a national militia 60,000-strong and knew that they had considerable support even among Newcastle's followers. In May Pitt introduced the militia bill to the Commons — and it was passed. The Lords, however, defeated the bill, partly because it would create recruitment difficulties for the army and the navy.

Cumberland was not in favour of a militia. He doubted whether such a force could effectively defend the country, and feared that the ad hoc regiments that would result would be difficult to discipline and train and virtually impossible to co-ordinate. Newcastle remarked sarcastically: 'We love nothing but regular troops.'[1] Townshend hit back at his former chief by posting bills all over London featuring his own satirical sketches of Cumberland, caricatured as 'a lump of fat.' But Pitt was not finished; he would revert to his militia theme soon enough.

Newcastle, meanwhile, had conceded that the French seemed to be planning to attack Minorca, so in mid-March Admiral John Byng was appointed to lead ten ships of the line to the defence. But it was not until 7 April that Byng sailed from Portsmouth, carrying a regiment. By the time they arrived in the Mediterranean, the French had already declared war, landed on Minorca and laid siege to Fort St Philip.

Cumberland was confident that Fort St Philip would hold out for several weeks at least. Of formidable construction and sited on a rocky promontory overlooking the entrance to Port Mahon, it was also within easy reach of resupply ships. As soon as it was learnt that the French had landed under the Duc de Richelieu, a further four ships were ordered to sail from Plymouth under Thomas Brodrick. At Gibraltar General Fowke had already received orders (via Byng) from Barrington, the new Secretary at War, to send reinforcements to Minorca; but Barrington's orders were unclear and Fowke misunderstood the urgency of the situation at Fort St Philip. Indeed, when Brodrick arrived at Gibraltar with a second battalion from England, Fowke wrote to Barrington explaining that as the French had already landed in Minorca his council of war had agreed to keep all the reinforcements in Gibraltar.

No succour was ever sent to the besieged garrison. Moreover, Fort St Philip was short of supplies and under-manned: some men were simply away on leave, others had fallen sick. Cumberland's rotation of battalions had been interrupted by preparations for war at home. As long ago as February, officers on leave in England and the newly drafted recruits had been ordered to report for departure. But the transports that ought to have been delivering them to Minorca, along with the replacement battalions and fresh stores, had been diverted to fetch the Hessian troops from up Channel. Old General Blakeney did his gallant best, but without help he could not keep the French at bay for long.

On 20 May, after an inexplicable six-day delay at Gibraltar, Byng encountered the French warships off Minorca, tried unsuccessfully to engage them, then committed his fatal error: he allowed them to escape. Instead of pursuing the French fleet he simply returned to Gibraltar. He never made contact with Blakeney's hard-pressed garrison.

On 31 May Cumberland learned, via Fox, that Fowke had retained the reinforcements intended for Minorca. Fox's reaction was defeatist: 'We are undone and I see no help for it,' he remarked.[2] Cumberland, on the other hand, was furiously angry. He went at once to see the King and raged about 'an infamous council of war infected with terror and void of obedience.'[3] But he thought there was yet time to retrieve the situation. His audience with the King turned on finding someone immediately to relieve Fowke, and General Tyrawley was appointed. On 1 June Tyrawley received orders at his home at Blackheath to report to the Duke of Cumberland in London. By the 2nd Tyrawley was at Portsmouth, aboard HMS *Antelope*, with Cumberland's firm orders to take over from Fowke, embark the reinforcements at Gibraltar and sail at once to Minorca with Admiral Hawke, who himself was appointed to relieve Byng. Bad weather, however, kept *Antelope* at anchor in Spithead for a week; she finally set sail on 10 June. On 2 July she arrived in Gibraltar and one week later turned back for England with a cargo of sacked admirals and generals.

But Hawke, Tyrawley and all the reinforcements were too late. After holding out for seventy days, General Blakeney had signed an honourable capitulation on 28 June, 1756. He would return home a hero, to be ennobled by the King and received with warmth by Cumberland. Byng and Fowke both faced courts martial, the former sentenced to be shot, the latter dismissed the service by the King.

The British nation was aghast at the loss of Minorca, a strategic toehold in the Mediterranean. Ultimately Newcastle was the man responsible. His hesitation, his weakness, his miscalculations had produced this catastrophe. But Minorca was just the first in a series of setbacks to affect his ministry that summer of 1756, and Newcastle faced a desperate struggle to remain in power.

Britain and France were at war, and France had drawn first blood. Furthermore, at Versailles in May a treaty had been negotiated by which France and Austria forged an alliance which Russia then joined, the treaty with Britain having lapsed. The combination of a tripartite army of aggression squeezing Prussia prompted Frederick the Great to attack first. At the end of August he marched into Saxony. Just as he had provoked the War of the Austrian Succession by invading Silesia, so he now provoked the Seven Years War.

That this was to be a world-wide struggle was very evident in London in the autumn of 1756. Apart from Minorca, bad news was on its way from North America and India. Fort Oswego, supposed by London to be securely held by Shirley, had been under siege half the summer and was finally overrun by the new French leader, the Marquis de Montcalm, during August. The French had thus acquired control over Lake Ontario, and indeed the whole of the Great Lakes including the St Lawrence seaway. It was a disaster for Anglo-American interests for which Shirley would be held to blame. Loudoun, the new Commander-in-Chief, had arrived at New York in July, 1756 and moved up to Albany as Cumberland wanted, but he was meeting the usual lack of co-operation in the colonies. By October Cumberland was receiving letters of complaint from Loudoun, whose execrable handwriting and long-winded circumlocutions tested his patience as much as the constant delays. In India the friction between Adlercron and the East India Company had persisted — but far worse, up in Bengal in May there had occurred the atrocity known to history as the Black Hole of Calcutta. The local nawab, with a force of many thousands, had fallen upon the East India Company garrison at Fort William and captured it, then packed 146 of the survivors into the punishment cell; only 23 were still alive the following morning, the rest having suffocated. To avenge this outrage the Company authorities wanted further help from the regular army, but Britain could not spare the troops. In the event it would be Clive who led the Company's revenge the following year, with only three companies from Adlercron's 39th Regiment among the victorious Europeans and sepoys.

Naturally, however, Cumberland was mainly concerned with the state of Britain's own defences. The nation had spent the summer in the grip of invasion fever, which, though he did not share it, had obliged him to take public measures to strengthen fortifications at Chatham, Portsmouth, Dover, Plymouth and elsewhere. The master gunner at each fort was ordered to call in all his gunners and prepare all guns. Additional coastal batteries were erected along the east coast from Sheerness to Tynemouth. An artillery train was assembled at Byfleet. Colonel David Watson, Chief Engineer, was recalled from Scotland to reconnoitre invasion routes and recommend camp sites for the field force reserves.

A review of the army strength at home that spring had revealed that including the Guards there were 11,000 infantry fit to take the field and 4,500 cavalry. A further 7,000 invalids, mainly Chelsea out-pensioners, were in static garrisons at the main fleet bases and in London. Even with the 7,000 Hessians and 10,000 Hanoverians, it was perceived that the threat to southern England warranted the raising of more troops, even though they would obviously not be trained before the end of the summer. In September Cumberland was authorized to raise 612 further cavalry for the new light troops for each regiment, as well as more than 7,000 infantry for nine new battalions, and two additional companies for every existing regiment in Ireland. The latter move was a significant concession in that the Irish establishment had long been held at a maximum strength of 12,000 men, and now would rise to 15,000. This was partly a result of Cumberland's efforts to help his friend Hartington, now the (fourth) Duke of Devonshire. But as Conway explained to Cumberland, apprehensive Irishmen wanted the northern Irish recruits − being mostly 'industrious Protestants' and seen as a stablizing influence in an otherwise Catholic nation − to be retained at home, not sent to Nova Scotia. Napier's drafting plans were altered accordingly.

In London, encamped in Hyde Park, the Guards diverted anxious crowds with busy firing practice and demonstrations of their drills. General Tyrawley, who had been given command of the London District before the summons to Minorca, had organized the arrest of all suspicious aliens, particularly priests belonging to the foreign embassies and anyone of French nationality. He issued orders to the city train bands concerning guards to be mounted on London bridges, and even recommended special arrangements about street lighting.

Public enthusiasm for the Hessians and Hanoverians had rapidly diminished over the summer. Cumberland had deployed them in a reserve role well back from the coast, encamped at Maidstone, Winchester and Blandford, where their foreign ways were regarded with increasing nervousness by the local populace. After a few petty incidents of looting and misbehaviour among the mercenaries, the surge of outright hostility was unmistakeable.

Needless to say, both Fox and Pitt endeavoured to use the crisis to their own advantage. Suspecting that Newcastle planned to use him as scapegoat for Minorca, and feeling excluded from any real power, Fox resigned as Secretary of State in mid-October. The King was furious, rightly assuming that Fox merely intended to topple Newcastle's administration; in his eyes Fox was no better than a deserter on the field of battle. But all along

Cumberland had advised his friend to try to work with Pitt, and now Fox approached Lady Yarmouth with a suggestion to put to the King: that Pitt be appointed the new Secretary of State. Fox declared that he was prepared to serve under Pitt 'in a subaltern capacity', the phrase itself reflecting the language of the Captain-General.[4] 'The Duke likes this as very honourable,' he wrote at the time; 'I hope Pitt will come and then my path is plain.'[5] But Pitt intended to achieve power on his own terms. When approached by Hardwicke on Newcastle's behalf, Pitt made it clear he had no intention of ever serving under Newcastle again. On 11 November, 1756, Newcastle resigned.

That a Fox-Pitt partnership very nearly came off is clear from a letter to Fox from a hunting friend of Cumberland's, Lord Bateman:

> I think I may wish you joy now the grand obstruction of every good is removed. I heartily wish Pitt may join you, but if he won't and nothing will satisfy him but being sole dictator, surely his arrogance must detach many of his adherents and establish you.[6]

However, Pitt now had all the cards. With extreme reluctance the King asked him to form the new administration, in partnership with the Duke of Devonshire. At the King's request, Devonshire became First Lord of the Treasury; Legge reoccupied the Exchequer, Barrington remained Secretary at War and Holderness Secretary for the north, while Pitt came in for the south and his brother-in-law, Richard Grenville, now Earl Temple, was made First Lord of the Admiralty. Fox was excluded.

Almost the first act of the new government was to order the Hessians and Hanoverians home, though in the Lords a vote of thanks to the King was proposed for the loan of his troops — a move that upset Temple, Pitt's brother-in-law, who, wrongly seeing Cumberland's hand in it, declared him to be a 'malignant influence'. Secondly, an amended militia bill was tabled for a force of 30,000 men to replace the departing mercenaries. And thirdly, reinforcements were to be sent to North America.

In December, 1756, Cumberland wrote to Loudoun that 'all was at first confusion on Pitt's arrival.' He went on:

> Nothing can be worse than the situation here at home, without any plan or even a desire to have one. Great numbers talked of to be sent you but without any consideration of how and from whence, without considering what they should carry with them. I write in my own hand trusting that you will burn this as soon as read.[7]

Despite his respect for Pitt, Cumberland felt that the new Secretary of State needed to be apprised of certain practicalities, such as the time and money it would cost to raise new troops and send them to America. Over the next two or three months there was a series of fierce arguments between the two men. Eventually, however, Cumberland managed to cut the suggested 8,000 regular troops to 6,000, and also persuaded Pitt to allow the commanders in the field a certain degree of flexibility. Pitt wanted to issue precise orders, so there could be no excuse for miscalculations or disobedience, but Cumberland, having been at the receiving end, believed such a system to be quite impracticable. It often took two or three months for orders to cross the Atlantic and find their destination, by which time the conditions pertaining at the time the orders were issued might very well have changed.

And Pitt, despite his suspicions of Cumberland, had to admit that the Captain-General's advice was worth heeding.

In his December letter Cumberland had also told Loudoun:

The King will spare you five old battalions from Europe and 2,000 new raised Highlanders which will make 6,000. I will send a proper train of artillery with them. Prepare your plan for one army up the St Lawrence River and for the other to keep the enemy in check from where your army now is. I will send you my thoughts more fully with a plan of mine for your operations, which you shall be left at liberty either to adopt in part, or not at all, as you shall find it proper from your better information.[8]

As we have seen, those new raised Highlanders were not the first to be sent to America, and, although historians have tended to credit Pitt, the idea can more fairly be attributed to Cumberland. He first considered making use of Highlanders in America as early as 1754, and it was only the time factor that led to the plans being set aside. A year later he revived the idea, and soon found support from the Newcastle government; Loudoun mentions their low strength in a routine letter to the Captain-General. But it was not until 1757 that the Highlanders were first regimented, apparently after discussions between Cumberland and the Duke of Argyll, who supervised recommendations for officers' commissions.

It is evident from Cumberland's continuing authority in American military affairs that George II took little or no part in colonial business. But it was precisely the fact of the Duke's authority that so irked Pitt. Cumberland, in contrast, was irritated more by Pitt's manner, a mixture of overweening deference and outrageous conceit. In typical fashion, Pitt one day announced that he 'could not acquiesce to a negative upon sending another battalion' to America: 'The ruin of the Kingdom should not lie at my door.'[9] The King himself regarded Pitt as intolerable, even though Pitt now found it expedient to embrace what he had once opposed — the subsidies to Hanover and the King of Prussia. Quite apart from George II's personal dislike of the man, there was a fundamental difference in outlook between them: Pitt's eye turned always to maritime adventure, especially across the Atlantic, whereas the King instinctively thought of Europe.

In January, 1757, the Convention of Westminster was confirmed, declaring that Britain, Hanover and Prussia would provide mutual support in time of war. The King was under severe pressure from his nephew to adopt specific plans for the European theatre. Frederick urged him, through the British Ambassador in Berlin, Andrew Mitchell, to protect Hanover by deploying a so-called Army of Observation along the River Weser, which would also help to protect the Prussians' western flank. According to Frederick, the French planned to assemble an army of 60,000 on the Lower Rhine in the spring, so if Hanover was to be safe George II would have to act fast. By late January Frederick had his uncle's agreement, and by the middle of February Pitt had been so far converted that he personally proposed the concept of the Army of Observation in Parliament.

Such matters, however, were of less immediate concern to the average Briton than the fate of Admiral Byng. On 27 January Byng was found guilty of negligence under Article 12 of the Navy Discipline Act and sentenced to death. The court martial had no option; there was but one sentence for such a crime. Never mind that the legal profession was deeply uneasy at the severity of the sentence; never mind that there was a growing agreement that the loss of Minorca was not, in fact, such a catastophe as had first been thought. The nation had clamoured for a scapegoat for the loss of Minorca and Byng was to take that role.

The King believed that the law should be upheld and supported the court martial verdict, though he did delay confirming the sentence for a fortnight so that certain legal objections might be explored. Cumberland personally was in favour of clemency, but felt that he could not interfere in a legal and naval affair. Pitt was equally reluctant to interfere, knowing that in any case the King would never listen to advice from him or his brother-in-law, the pompous Temple, now the admiralty chief. And above all, public opinion was with the King. Byng was shot at Portsmouth on 14 March.

A parliamentary enquiry agreed that Newcastle and Fox could be exonerated for their parts in the Minorca fiasco; with luck or a fighting admiral, Fort St Philip might have been held. But it was too much for any politician to admit that, had Cumberland's counsel for earlier preparations been acted upon, the result would certainly have been very different.

On 21 February Parliament agreed to contribute the sum of £200,000 'for the just and necessary defence and preservation of His Majesty's electoral dominions and towards the discharge of his obligation towards Prussia.'[10] However, the composition of the Army of Observation and the appointment of its commander were primarily matters for the King to decide as Elector of Hanover.

There had always been an element of conflict in the interests of Britain and Hanover, and now it would come to a head: an acute illustration of the perennial British dilemma — whether to yield to the pull of the continent or whether to pursue a maritime strategy. It was never more difficult to resolve than in the reign of George II, an English king of Hanoverian birth. And Cumberland, the first of the Hanoverian princes to be born in Britain, would be torn apart in the attempt.

Frederick of Prussia was demanding urgent action of the King. He himself suggested a commander: Prince Louis of Brunswick, the new Dutch Commander-in-Chief. But the Dutch as usual were reluctant to become involved and Louis refused point-blank. The King proposed the senior Hanoverian general, Zastrow, aged seventy-seven. Frederick rejected him, and now proposed Cumberland.

At first the King could not bear the idea of sending his son off to Europe; he felt himself beleaguered by hostile policitians and wanted Cumberland at his side. Besides, Cumberland was not in good health. During the previous summer he had suffered very badly from pains and stiffness in his wounded knee and, although he made light of it, he was never entirely free of discomfort. He had also developed asthma, and one asthmatic attack early in 1757 was so bad that Ranby ordered him to bed. Undoubtedly his problems were compounded by obesity, though it may be unfair to link this with the fact that his bedroom floor collapsed that February at Cumberland Lodge.

On 16 March Frederick again pressed for Cumberland's nomination. The King countered by objecting to Frederick's choice of subordinate commander for the 20,000 Prussian troops joining the army of observation: Frederick of Hesse-Cassel. The Prince of Hesse was the King's own son-in-law, but George II had good reason to dislike him. Not only had he converted to the Roman Catholic religion but he was cruel to his wife, Mary; in fact the two were now separated, Mary having taken their three sons and gone to live with her father-in-law the Landgrave of Hesse. Cumberland had other reasons to dislike the Prince; he thought poorly of his military performance at Perth in 1746, and there had been jealousy between them when Hesse had once laid rival claims to the favours of Lady Rochford.

Frederick was adamant, however. Cumberland it had to be.

Cumberland himself was reluctant to go. He would be leading another motley army, which was technically raised for purely defensive purposes; he would be taking orders from the King's Hanoverian ministers, whose interests did not coincide with those of Britain, and he would be dealing with a Prussian cousin he did not trust. Even more to the point, as

Captain-General he felt that he was required at home, to co-ordinate the fight against French aggression not merely in Europe but in North America and India too. In addition, his father was approaching a crisis in his relations with Pitt.

Fox now returned to the fray, suggesting that if Cumberland were absent for several months, as seemed likely, it would give Leicester House undue leverage over the country's affairs. Bute still affected to believe that Cumberland was plotting to seize power with Fox, Devonshire, Bedford and others — and he may have found support from Lord George Sackville, now a major-general and prominent at Leicester House, who seemed to think that if Cumberland went abroad then he stood a chance of taking over military affairs at home. It is also possible that Bute got wind of surreptitious intrigues involving Cumberland and simply chose to misinterpret them.

The King had made up his mind to get rid of Pitt. He was arrogant, demanding and pedantic, he lacked a clear body of support in Parliament and he had lost public confidence over his sympathy towards Byng. In mid-March the King asked Cumberland to approach Newcastle with a view to creating a new administration. Cumberland was ill again and delegated the job to the Earl Waldegrave; personally he did not favour Newcastle's resuming office and made no attempt to persuade him to change his mind when he made a negative reply.

By the end of March news of Cumberland's likely departure had become public, and it was rumoured by his enemies, notably Bute, that he planned to take English troops with him, including a personal bodyguard comprising his own Guards regiment. Fox stood up in the Commons and denied the rumours on the Duke's behalf, then asked Legge, as Chancellor of the Exchequer, to confirm that no proposal had even been mooted to send English troops to Germany. Legge duly obliged.

By this time Cumberland's health was evidently better and he was busily making preparations for his departure. He found time, however, to attend an elaborate party at W: ndsor after the Garter installation ceremony, a ball that went on until four in the morning and a feast that included a saddle of beef weighing 186lb, and desserts marvellously fashioned in the shape of fountains, terraces and colonnades, all decorated with flowers and evergreens. A few days later he held a great levee in his rooms at St James's, and among the many guests who afterwards took formal leave of him were his sister-in-law the Princess Dowager and his niece, nineteen-year-old Princess Augusta.

By the end of March Cumberland's travel plans were made and all arrangements settled. After discussions with his father, he had received his instructions on 30 March, written in German and signed by Münchhausen, the King's Hanoverian minister in London. But these orders were apparently not seen by any of the English ministers, a fact that would lead to serious trouble later for the Duke. He had issued his orders to the army at home, disposing troops in five summer camps across southern England, including one under Sackville, with the Guards encamped in Hyde Park. He had organized, with Fawkener, a private and confidential courier service to keep him in constant touch with political friends at home, and he had chosen the men whom he wanted to accompany him. Apart from Edward Mason, his private secretary, they included Albemarle (formerly Bury: he had inherited the title when his father died in 1754) who had been with Cumberland at Fontenoy and Culloden; Colonel Guy Carleton, the future Lord Dorchester; Colonel Lord Frederick Cavendish, brother of the Duke of Devonshire; and young Lord George Lennox, brother of the Duke of Richmond. In addition Cumberland could rely on the services of the ever faithful Jeffrey Amherst who had travelled on ahead.

But on 4 April the crisis finally arrived: George II dismissed the obnoxious Temple. The King was hoping that this would prompt Pitt to resign, to show solidarity with his wife's brother, but Pitt did no such thing. So two days later the King dismissed Pitt too, evidently thinking that Waldegrave would soon form a new administration with the support of Fox and perhaps Newcastle, if he could be persuaded. Cumberland undoubtedly made some suggestions as to people who might be brought in to replace Temple at the Admiralty, but there is no evidence to suggest, as Walpole did, that the Duke refused to accept command in Germany until his father had sacked Pitt. What is certain is that the King wanted to change his ministry long before Cumberland was given the command, and merely enlisted his son's help in achieving his own ends.

In fact, on 10 April when Cumberland left Harwich to sail for Germany, he clearly felt thoroughly depressed; Cavendish has recorded that he stayed below decks throughout the voyage. While his young staff made merry, eating and drinking to the success of their expedition, the Duke was unusually unsociable and in poor spirits. It is little wonder. He was not only leaving his elderly father in a political vacuum, but embarking on a military endeavour of which he did not wholly approve.

# 22

# Sacrifice of Hanover

CUMBERLAND'S TEMPER CANNOT HAVE IMPROVED during the journey to Hanover. He had originally intended to take the short crossing to Holland, where Joseph Yorke, now Ambassador at The Hague, had procured a suitable closed travelling carriage. With the growing danger of French military action, however, he had to change his plans and sail instead to the mouth of the Elbe, then travel roughly a hundred miles south to Hanover on atrocious roads. Reaching Hanover on 18 April, he found affairs in considerable chaos. For one thing, he had been assured that the King's Master of the Horse at Herrenhausen would mount them all, but the stables were bare. Out of his own pocket he had to buy horses for himself and his staff.

Far more worrying was the fact that the King's ministers in Hanover proved to be more fearful of Prussia than of Austria and France combined; rather than fight they wanted to negotiate neutrality. In consequence their preparations for war had been something less than whole-hearted. Cumberland had to be his own 'general, quartermaster and commissary' he wrote to Fox, adding:

> I am forced to change and alter most things, for they were in a thorough state of confusion and as much hatred and party here as amongst us in England. But a little resolution and one may knock their heads together for the service of their master – this is the most difficult campaign that ever man was engaged in.[1]

In another letter to Fox he wrote:

> I hope by this time the King's affairs are got into some consistency... But I can't allow myself time to reflect on such trifling politics as ours are in comparison with the present state of Europe. I fear neither pain nor spirit

will get the better of our misfortune. Nothing prepared for the campaign and hardly bread and forage in the country. How all will end God knows.[2]

And he saw no point in hiding the truth from his father. The King wrote back on 5 May:

Knowing your affection for me I shall never impute to you the negligence of those old fools by whose stupidity you find yourselves distressed. How I depend upon your capacity and application.[3]

But it was not just the Hanoverians that caused problems for the Duke.

On paper the army of observation comprised 27,000 Hanoverian troops, 12,000 Hessians and 6,000 Brunswickers with further small contingents from Schaumburg-Lippe and Saxe-Gotha: something under 50,000 men in total. In addition, the six Prussian battalions, presently garrisoned at Wesel in Westphalia and under the nominal command of the Prince of Hesse, were supposed to act in association with Cumberland's army. But Hesse's brief from Frederick tended to limit their immediate role to the defence of other Prussian possessions in Westphalia, such as Lippstadt and Rietberg, and to all intents and purposes the Prussian battalions never formed part of Cumberland's army. Yet he was expected to defend Hanover against a French army that was roughly 100,000 strong.

According to the King's instructions, Cumberland was not to act offensively against Austria or any other power, but should merely 'protect our territory and that of our allies from hostile invasions of foreign troops, repelling force with force.' The instructions went on:

If a much superior French army march against us, we depend upon the presence of our son and on the bravery of the troops that all that is humanly possible will be done. Foresight will be needed, however, that in any position taken up, the protection of our dominions will be the chief aim, and to keep a retreat towards Stade open and free, that in the case of the utmost extremity our army may maintain itself there: to wait the issue of what the times may bring forth.[4]

They were hardly instructions to cheer Cumberland's heart when he heard that the French had begun to move.

The new French commander on the Rhine was Maréchal le Comte D'Estrées, only recently appointed Marshal of France but an experienced soldier who had been fighting since before Cumberland was born. As a cavalry commander he had served under Saxe and had played an important part at Fontenoy and at Laffeldt. He had spent the previous autumn in

Vienna, co-ordinating plans with the Austrians, and some Austrian troops would deploy with his army on the Rhine as a token of unity. At the end of April he was preparing to advance into Westphalia. Should Hanover not remain neutral, he had orders to continue his advance eastwards, to cross the River Weser and seize Hanover before moving against Prussia, while a detached corps crossed the middle Rhine and marched through Hesse towards Magdeburg, to support an Austrian counterattack against Frederick in Bohemia.

On 1 May the second Treaty of Versailles was signed, confirming the Franco-Austrian alliance, and D'Estrées set off east across the Rhine.

Meanwhile in Hanover Cumberland had met General von Schmettau, who was Frederick's liaison officer, and the meeting gave the Duke some encouragement. He now had both verbal and written assurances that if he could weather the storm alone for five or six weeks west of the Weser, he could expect sufficient reinforcements from Frederick to protect Hanover from the French. He ordered the troops to start assembling along a ridge of hills near Bielefeld, some sixty miles from Hanover, but himself remained behind until some clarification was forthcoming on the question of neutrality.

His frustration was intensified by the news from home, where Leicester House and the Tories had whipped up a national fury over the King's dismissal of Pitt, but no new ministry had been formed. The Minorca enquiry had just ended with no blame laid on any specific minister, and Cumberland did not miss a joke at Pitt's expense:

Does the man mountain bellow much? I hear not, but that like Mount Etna he groans out, Minorca, Minorca, and that old England is lost because he, the only man that could save it, is out of power.[5]

But the Duke's mounting sense of isolation is clear from the rest of that letter: 'I shall not trouble my friends with my problems; you neither understand them or heed them.'

Suddenly his problems multiplied. The French marched a corps into Münster and so scared Frederick of Hesse that, without orders, he abandoned Wesel and yielded up Lippstadt and Rietberg; the Prussians now joined forces temporarily with the Army of Observation. Cumberland instructed General Zastrow to detach twelve of the twenty-five battalions at Bielefeld, and ten of the twenty squadrons, and to hold Paderborn. His intention was to narrow the field of action for the French and deny supplies to their foraging parties. But the outlook was dismal. He had received a letter from D'Estrées saying that it was up to him what sort of campaign he made it, and the letter was addressed to the commander of '*L'Armée Britannique*' rather than of the Hanoverian army. The French were under no mistake; they were simply exploiting the ambivalence of Cumberland's position.

Indeed, Cumberland himself was unsure of his position. He was still Captain-General of the army at home, but in Germany he was commander of the Army of Observation; and he was not at all clear how far the King as Elector was being financed by the British government. He corresponded throughout the whole campaign with Ligonier and Barrington, who remained Secretary at War despite the empty ministerial benches around him, and was delighted to hear through Fawkener, who had good connections in the City, that the Duke of Devonshire was having less trouble than anticipated in raising credit for the war effort.

Nevertheless his immediate concern was to confront the French at Bielefeld and Paderborn. He left Hanover for the front on 2 May.

As it happened the French were hardly to be seen. D'Estrées was still hoping that Hanover would acquire neutrality at Vienna, where the Elector of Hanover's ministers were talking to the Austrians. Moreover, the French army was in a shambles, huge and unwieldy, and D'Estrées himself was no Marshal Saxe. He lacked the confidence of both Madame de Pompadour and his own subordinates. He had an embarrassment of high-born, even royal generals under his command, who insisted on taking all their personal impedimenta into battle, while the men under them were forced to scour the countryside for basic supplies.

Cumberland's aide, Frederick Cavendish, was of the opinion that the French were so lacking in spirit they might even retire over the Rhine. They were known to be losing many deserters. All seemed calm at the headquarters at Bielefeld and Cumberland was using the time well, creating a regiment of scouts or 'Jägers' from the gamekeepers and foresters of Hanover. He had asked Frederick the Great for a squadron of hussars, but when they were not forthcoming he raised the four companies of Jägers, two mounted and two on foot, all wearing green for camouflage. Cavendish had mixed feelings about the German troops. 'The Prussians beat us all for discipline,' he noted, 'but they are the scum of all parts of the earth and middlingly commanded.'[6]

Throughout May Cumberland remained at Bielefeld, drilling the Hanoverians and Hessians and waiting for the French to make a move. He even wondered whether he should try and recapture Lippstadt. It was six weeks since von Schmettau had assured him that help would come from Frederick of Prussia, but nothing was happening. Then at the beginning of June the French lurched into action once more, this time on two fronts: one column turning Cumberland's right flank as though to cut him off from his main supply base at Nienburg, and one column advancing towards Hesse.

Taken by surprise, Cumberland felt obliged to withdraw his whole force north-west, while he established a new headquarters at Holzhausen, near Minden. It was a hasty and nervous retreat, however, and bad march discipline led to confusion developing among the rearguard troops who started firing at each other. Taking advantage of the confusion, a party of French hussars supported by a couple of Swiss regiments were able to inflict considerable casualties on the Prussian rearguard, who also lost at least 200 deserters overnight. The only success of the manoeuvre was achieved by the Jägers, led by General von Schulenburg, who were thrown into action to good effect near Herford. But the Hanoverian general who had been ordered to hold the town, General Block, decided without orders from Cumberland to evacuate Herford, and the whole body had to continue the retreat east towards Rinteln and Hameln.

Clearly Cumberland had not yet got a firm grip on his disparate army. Although his sources of intelligence were poor and local people's loyalties were uncertain, he knew he had to accept responsibility for the muddle. But, as he wrote to Devonshire, the French had achieved very little and paid a heavy cost: he estimated that they had lost 200 killed, while he had lost just twenty. His argument seems justified, for at The Hague the French Ambassador told Joseph Yorke that Cumberland had done well and they had lost 600 men.

Devonshire, meanwhile, had written two newsy letters dated 7 and 10 June, which evidently worried Cumberland more than his own predicament, for his reply was suffused with emotion: 'Never did letters give me more concern for the true situation I see the King in.'[7] He had earlier written to Devonshire expressing the wish that the King would soon be supported by a 'general inclusive administration' by which he meant Devonshire, Newcastle, Pitt and Fox, uniting all the men he regarded as most able in the service of their King and country, even though he acknowledged the difficulties:

> Can I flatter myself that the Duke of Newcastle and Mr Pitt, the two most different men in themselves and agreeing solely in being the most impracticable, can be brought to any reasonable firm plan?... I can't as yet believe it possible: as to Mr Fox I know him so well that whatever part is best for the King he will act it.[8]

Even more specifically, he had expressed the wish that Newcastle and Pitt would agree to Fox's being made paymaster, for 'these three would be a stop to the silly lies about my dangerous ambitions that have been so industriously propagated.' But as Devonshire had explained in detail, all three politicians were creating difficulties, making impossible demands of each other and the

King. Cumberland wrote furiously about the 'intolerable' position they put the King into and expressed particular contempt for Newcastle: 'His treachery to the best of masters cannot be excused even by irresolution or cowardice.'[9] Devonshire showed this letter to the King, who was much moved and remarked that Cumberland was 'the best son ever man had.'[10]

Devonshire himself had found life too hot in the politicians' kitchen; in late June he accepted the post of Lord Chamberlain. By then, however, a new ministry had been created, very much along the lines that Cumberland had wanted, including the two 'negotiating powers' as he called them, Pitt and Newcastle. Cumberland heard the news at the end of June. Pitt, Newcastle, Holderness and Legge were in; Temple was the new Lord Privy Seal; Anson returned to the Admiralty and Fox was Paymaster General. Barrington, at the King's insistence, was retained as Secretary at War: the alternative was Sackville who would have been no more popular with Cumberland than he was with the King.

Despite the fact that he himself had promoted the combination of Pitt and Newcastle, Cumberland was thoroughly disillusioned with politics and politicians. He wrote to his friend the Earl of Sandwich expressing a desire to retreat to Windsor and pursue the private life. His weariness and depression were almost palpable. His physical health was bad, too. In fact, shortly before this he had suffered so badly from his asthma that a special plea was made, via Yorke and the French Ambassador at The Hague, Monsieur D'Affrey, to Louis XV for a supply of Eau de Luce to ease his breathing problems. D'Affrey, sympathetic to Cumberland's plight, wrote a vividly descriptive letter to the French Foreign Minister, Cardinal de Bernis, to underline the urgency of his need: apparently Cumberland slept on a leather-covered chaise longue, being too heavy for a soft camp bed, with two valets by his side all night in order to help him turn from time to time and prop him up when he was unable to breathe. 'He can lean out so little from the couch that he is in danger of smothering himself,' D'Affrey wrote, and concluded that: 'From the quantity of Eau requested it seems he must need it continuously.'[11] Louis XV duly authorized the gift for the enemy commander, and D'Estrées sent a courier across the lines to deliver it. Cumberland paid the man a hundred *louis d'or* but made light of the whole episode, describing it as a 'ridiculous affair' in a letter of thanks to Yorke. It seems he was a little ashamed of his illness.

He was still depressed and ailing when bad news arrived from his cousin Frederick towards the end of June, and he reacted with uncharacteristic listlessness. On 18 June at Kolin, some forty miles east of Prague, the Austrians under Marshal Daun had inflicted a resounding defeat on Frederick the Great, capturing 10,000 of his men and eleven generals. Urgently Frederick called for the Prussian troops in Hanover; he needed them to hold the area around Magdeburg and Halberstadt. Now Cumberland really was on his own.

D'Estrées was advancing on such a wide front that Cumberland hardly knew where to focus his defence. By 1 July he had shifted to Dankersen, to the rear of Minden, and held a strong line between Minden and Hameln, but the French had already taken Rinteln. They had also taken the port of Emden, which the Prussian garrison had yielded without a struggle. Even now they were about to cross the upper Weser to advance through Hesse and threaten Hanover from the south. At all costs he must protect his line of communication running back to Stade; yet it began to seem that this would mean abandoning Hanover to its fate. He shifted his force south towards Hameln and Afferde — but too late. By the 18th D'Estrées had two parties across the shallow Weser near Holzminden. Cumberland, protected by a covering force of grenadiers, reconnoitred up river but concluded that the country was so broken and hilly that he could easily be caught out, straddling one approach from the south while the enemy passed unseen through hills to the east. He therefore withdrew down-river, and deployed his army in a defensive position south-east of Hameln. D'Estrées marched down slowly behind him, while his subordinate, Maréchal le Duc de Broglie, moved in parallel to the west of the river.   The consequence of Frederick's defeat at Kolin now became dramatically obvious. Frederick was not merely unable to help Cumberland, but was himself in need of help. In fact, through Andrew Mitchell he was calling for 9,000 British troops to be sent out as reinforcements for his own army. Hearing of Frederick's demands, Cumberland made it clear to London that he had given Frederick no encouragement in this proposal, and he briefed Fox not to press for the demand to be met. Whatever his own needs and whatever he thought of Frederick's position, he was well aware of political realities in London — yet even now Chesterfield suggested that he wanted such reinforcements himself in order to launch a military *coup d'état*! Perhaps a hint of Cumberland's real feelings emerged when he commented adversely on Pitt's new plan to send a further 2,000 men to America. Being asked to advise by Barrington and Ligonier on how they should be raised, he could not refrain from stating that in his view Britain had greater need to reinforce Germany than America. If men were sent to America, however, they should be recruits and not trained soldiers.

But reinforcements would have been too late in any case to turn the scale for Cumberland. He was about to fight and lose the only battle of the campaign.

The Battle of Hastenbeck is remarkable in mid eighteenth-century warfare for two main reasons. Because of the terrain, a mixture of wooded heights

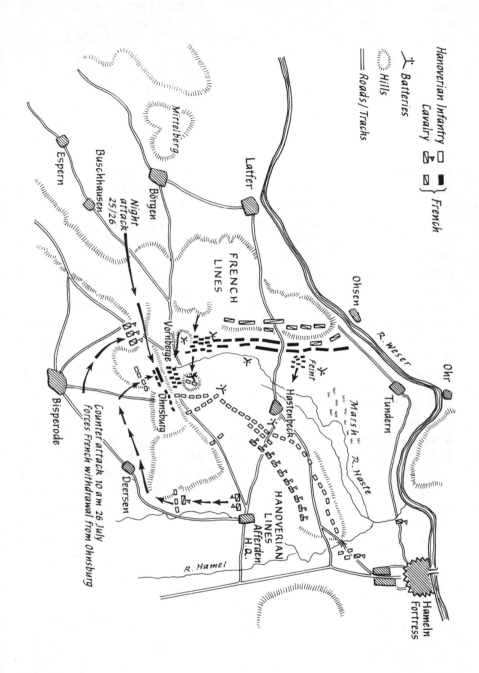

Hanoverian Infantry ☐ ☐ } French
Cavalry ⛿ ▮ }
⚒ Batteries ⚒ ⚒ French
◎ Hills
══ Roads/Tracks

Mittelberg

Espern

Börgen

Buschhausen

Laffer

Night attack 25/26

FRENCH LINES

Ohsen

R. Weser

Ohr

Vornberge

Feint

Tundern

Bisperode

Ohrsburg

Hastenbeck

Marsh

R. Haste

Counter attack 10 am 26 July forces French withdrawal from Ohrsburg

Deersen

HANOVERIAN LINES

Afferden H.Q.

R. Hamel

Hameln Fortress

Sketch Map of Hastenbeck based on the plan by Du Plat (Cumberland Maps 816.818) and marshy plains, the combatants — 60,000 French against 35,000 Germans — were not drawn up in line but disposed tactically as the ground required; this was therefore no set-piece battle. And, partly because of the terrain, which made it impossible for commanders to see what was happening on every side, at one point both sides believed they were beaten and simultaneously gave orders to withdraw.

The battle began on 24 July with an exchange of fire between French and German patrols. Bearing in mind his father's instructions not to risk the Hanoverian army unduly, and seeing how numerous was the French army, Cumberland initially prepared to retreat. However, he was persuaded by the Hanoverian generals against his better judgement to stand and fight a delaying action. The decision made, he wasted no time on doubts but swiftly ordered changes to his dispositions. The fortified town of Hameln lay to his right rear, the village of Hastenbeck to his front, in a semicircle of hills that stretched round to his left. Although his artillery was very inferior to that of the enemy, he deployed it with considerable skill, barring a direct approach to his centre through Hastenbeck with one 12-pounder and one 6-pounder battery. A further battery was placed higher up the hill to his left, where his composite grenadier battalions and the Jägers under von Schulenburg occupied the wooded summit. As he appreciated, the French would make every effort to seize this key feature which dominated the whole line. To increase his fire power he brought forward extra guns from Hameln, and warned General Behr with three battalions of Brunswickers to be ready to move to von Schulenburg's support.

Undoubtedly D'Estrées was surprised at his stand. Apart from some intermittent artillery exchanges, the rest of the day was uneventful. D'Estrées was reconsidering tactics; he was also waiting for Broglie and his infantry to cross the Weser to join him. On the 25th there was plenty of cannonading and skirmishing but not much progress on either side. Broglie and his infantry had arrived, but there was still no obvious means of throwing the Germans back. However, on the night of the 25th a French corps under General Chevert set off to make a night march through the close and hilly country. This in itself was a most unusual tactic, prompted as Cumberland had expected by the need to seize the high ground to his left.

Tuesday, 26 July, 1757, dawned amid grey mists. At 5.30 am the French artillery opened up. Cumberland had been in the saddle almost continuously for three days. According to Cavendish, the wound in his knee had enlarged to the size of a man's palm, and he admitted to his anxious staff that sometimes the wound reopened for weeks on end. But he was grimly determined to see this battle through. While the French artillery thundered on, he suspected a covert move on the key hill feature and sent off a mobile reserve column of three battalions and six squadrons, under Colonels Breidenbach and Dachenhausen, to support his grenadiers and Jaegers.

Chevert and his corps had captured Cumberland's battery and taken the hill during the night – but were themselves surprised by the German effort to recapture the hill. By a brilliant tactical march the two Hanoverian colonels and their three battalions managed to send Chevert reeling back down the steep slope of the hill, together with two reinforcing French brigades sent to help him by the Duc d'Orléans. By Amherst's subsequent account, three German battalions had beaten sixteen French ones and captured fourteen guns. D'Orléans cantered his cavalry across to stiffen his men's resistance, but was interrupted by D'Estrées who, thinking the day lost, gave the order to withdraw.

Meanwhile in the centre Cumberland had ridden to and fro, beneath the hail of cannonfire, issuing his orders and encouraging the men to stand firm. In Amherst's judgement the French fire was heavier than he had ever experienced but Cumberland paid it little heed. Only when his elderly Hanoverian ADC, Colonel Oberg, begged him to retire out of range did he turn back to his headquarters. His worry was that his main battery in the centre would be lost – as indeed it was, though a brilliant counterattack by the Prince of Brunswick at the head of two battalions had retaken it at the point of the bayonet. But the Hanoverian gunners could never re-establish this vital battery and Brunswick was driven out by enemy infantry advancing against the left centre; this, together with superior enemy artillery fire, led Cumberland to conclude that his delaying action could not be sustained. His troops had stood long enough. Even as Chevert's men were appearing on the hill to his left, and not realizing that over the hill the French had been thrown back, at 11 am he gave the order to break contact.

The battle was over. 'We are returning to Nienburg,' Cavendish wrote to his brother, 'so that Hanover and Brunswick are left to their mercy.'[12] Indeed, George II's Electorate now lay wide open to the French while Cumberland withdrew northwards. As always, he was conscious of his father's instructions, and now his chief thought was to 'keep a retreat towards Stade open and free' – for this, in his father's words, was a 'case of the utmost extremity.'[13]

# 23

# Kloster Zeven

ALTHOUGH D'ESTRÉES QUICKLY REALIZED that Cumberland was retreating, his own force was too disorganized to press the pursuit. Cumberland's men, by contrast, made a most orderly withdrawal. Cavendish wrote home to his brother:

> I believe there never yet was so brave and so determined a body of men as our army was composed: the Brunswickers and Hessians were most exposed and bore for six hours the severest cannonade that all the generals say they have ever heard and worse than Fontenoy. There was no confusion or break in squadrons or battalions. Their retreat was as astonishing as their behaviour in the field. Troops never marched from a parade in better order.[1]

And Cumberland himself was proud of the way his men had fought. The French had received a stern rebuff, and he had managed to save the greater part of the King's army. As Cavendish wrote, 'We were not beat, our loss was not great and the Duke is well and unhurt otherwise than in mind where he suffers much.'[2]

Cumberland's low spirits may be imagined, as he retreated slowly north along the line of his communications to the mouth of the Elbe. Halting for a few days at Nienburg until 7 August, it was there that he wrote a somewhat depressed letter to his father. On 9 August the King wrote back in sorrow more than anger, and with no sign of wanting to blame his son for what he called 'the distracted situation of my affairs in Germany.' In fact his letter is a mixture of firm practicalities and fatherly concern:

> I am convinced of your sense, capacity and zeal. Therefore you will receive powers to get me and my country out of these difficulties at the best rate you can by a separate peace as Elector including my allies. Nobody

attributes your bad success either to you or the troops under your command, to any cowardice or want of precaution, but it seems fate is everywhere against us. I trust my affairs entirely to your conduct. You will talk with my ministers and choose those you think proper for the negotiation. I now depend on your affection, zeal and capacity to extricate yourself, me, my brave army and my dearly beloved subjects out of the misery and slavery they groan under.[3]

And in a postscript he added:

I hear with great concern your leg is not well and your health not of the best. Pray take care of a life that is both so dear and so necessary for me; and when you have settled everything, come to a father that esteems and loves you dearly. Take care in your negotiations that there are no cavils and no tricks played either to my army or the troops of my allies.[4]

So now the King expected his son to play the diplomat at peace talks for Hanover while Britain continued at war.

The Pitt—Newcastle partnership, which had so far proved remarkably harmonious, was naturally against such a move but agreed that the British cabinet could offer no formal advice to the King on the matter and that sending troops would be 'hazardous and useless.'[5] When Lady Yarmouth criticized Cumberland's conduct at Hastenbeck and suggested that he should be ordered to take a few risks, Newcastle tried to calm her down and explained that this 'might be represented as an order from the English ministry to sacrifice the army.'[6] However, Pitt was in favour of doing everything possible to keep Prussia in the field, and to that end pressed for a strong diversionary raid on France. Despite opposition on this subject from Newcastle and others, Pitt's enthusiasm prevailed: the 9,000 troops that could otherwise have been sent to Germany would now form part of an amphibious assault on Rochefort, a port on the Bay of Biscay.

D'Estrées had been removed as commander of the French army. He had never been popular at Versailles and his failure to press home his victory at Hastenbeck was excuse enough to his enemies to be rid of him. He was replaced by the Duc de Richelieu, who had led the assault on Minorca. But Richelieu had apparently lost his fighting spirit and now was less interested in pursuing Cumberland than in seizing whatever plunder and riches he could lay his hands on, and wreaking vengeance on the wretched subjects of the Elector of Hanover for not having had the sense to remain neutral.

It was with Richelieu, therefore, that Cumberland would have to negotiate for peace. After leaving Nienburg Cumberland crossed the River Aller at Verden and continued north towards Stade. For several days Richelieu was too busy plundering Hanover and Brunswick to follow him. He had by now received a whole sheaf of papers from the King, signed on 11 August without the knowledge of his British ministers, giving more detailed instructions to his son for the negotiations.

The King praised Cumberland warmly for his conduct at Hastenbeck: 'It rebounds therefore to your immortal honour thus to have disputed the field inch by inch with an enemy so superior in numbers.'[7] But now Cumberland was to undertake a difficult diplomatic mission. There would be no reinforcements from Britain, Prussia could not help, Hesse-Cassel and Brunswick would probably pull out of the negotiations. The best Cumberland could do was save his army from destruction, and to help him the King enclosed a copy of Münchhausen's letter to Bernstorff, the Danish minister:

> H.M. has resolved to empower H.R.H. the Duke of Cumberland to propose to the French commander-in-chief a separate peace and preliminary agreement for his Majesty as Elector and his allies and to manage and conclude this agreement in the best manner possible.[8]

The object of any such agreement, the King was at pains to emphasize, was to free his Electorate from further devastation and to save his army, sending the artillery into Denmark if necessary. Finally, in a postscript again, the King specifically authorized his son to make decisions in consultation with the Hanoverian ministers:

> Such events might happen which require speedy measures and resolution for the saving my dominions and my army without there being time to obtain my intentions and approbation, in this perplexity I know of no other means than leaving it in your power to call together my ministers to consult with them on the best course to be taken, but likewise to put them in execution.[9]

And with the letter came a document to be given to Richelieu, signed by the King, formally granting full powers to Cumberland. It concluded with a sentence promising that the King, as Elector of Hanover, would agree to and carry out everything as agreed by Cumberland under the authority granted.

Armed with such powers Cumberland was soon deep in consultation with the Hanoverian ministers and Count Lynar for the Danes. Richelieu, during the interim, had conveyed a message to Cumberland to the effect that a suspension of arms did not for the moment suit the French court. Their Russian allies were making good progress against the Prussians further east

— indeed, on 30 August, the Prussians were defeated at Gross Jägersdorf. Berlin itself appeared threatened.

Besides, Richelieu was still eager to exercise the victor's rights of plunder, and by now was moving north, occupying Bremen on the 29th and Harburg on 3 September. Harburg was on the Elbe, opposite Hamburg, and a mere twenty-five miles from Cumberland's position at Stade.

By now Cumberland had been joined not only by most of the Hanoverian cabinet but by his sister Mary and her father-in-law, the Landgrave of Hesse, who had been forced to flee when the French invaded Hesse-Cassel. Although he seemed clear enough about his task, privately he was not hopeful. 'I am heartily sick of pulling like a draught horse at Smithfield against the post,' he wrote to Fox on 29 August.[10]

The negotiations began on 3 September, between Cumberland at Stade and Richelieu at his headquarters at Kloster Zeven, some twenty miles to the south, with Count Lynar acting as go-between. Richelieu had come round to the belief that the sooner he could neutralize Cumberland and the Germans, the sooner he would be free to proceed to Magdeburg and Prussia, where he expected even richer pickings.

On 8 September Cumberland signed the Convention of Kloster Zeven. As far as he was concerned, he had achieved peace on the best terms possible under the circumstances. He had saved the men and equipment of the Army of Observation, albeit by breaking it up, for he obtained Richelieu's agreement to letting the Hessians, Brunswickers and all except the Hanoverians return to winter quarters in their home lands. What he had not obtained was any measure of protection for the main Hanoverian territory from the march of armies against Prussia; but Richelieu had been insistent that apart from a garrison at Stade, the Hanoverian contingent should withdraw across the Elbe into Denmark, and Cumberland had been in no position to argue.

A week later Richelieu duly set off to plunder, as he thought, the Prussian lands to the east.

In London the King's mood had changed. Prompted perhaps by the fretful Lady Yarmouth, he began to speak critically of his son's performance at Hastenbeck. He was heard to say that Cumberland had lost his courage. Newcastle found him in tears, begging his ministers to help, and Princess Amelia made equally emotional pleas. The ministers offered to send a naval squadron to the Elbe, but the 9,000 troops that Frederick of Prussia had asked for were even now sailing for Pitt's raid on Rochefort.

On 16 September the King sent an urgent message to his son that nothing should be concluded; he even enquired whether Cumberland could not join up with the Prussian force by marching east to Magdeburg — a course that

Cumberland had carefully avoided, since the King's original instructions had been to maintain a line of retreat to the sea via Stade.

Of course the King's letter had crossed with the news that his son had already signed the Convention of Kloster Zeven. When word reached him at last, he exploded with rage. He told Newcastle that he had been given up tied hand and foot to France, that he did not know how to look anybody in the face and that he thought the Duke's head was turned. 'If any other man in the world had done it, he should conclude that he had been bought by France.'[11] To make matters worse, the King believed that he had to apologize to his loathsome nephew, Frederick the Great, for what he saw as Cumberland's betrayal: what the King did not know was that Frederick was even then attempting to bribe Madame de Pompadour and opening his own peace negotiations with France.

On 20 September the King wrote personally to Cumberland to express his displeasure. In his view Cumberland had virtually signed away his Electorate to the French: 'It is now totally in the power of France to keep possession and ruin my dominion as long as they please.' It was a 'shameful and ruinous' convention. He went on:

> Since clearly you must have some grounds and reasons unknown to me and which you were too scrupulous to put in writing, I wish to hear from you in person and the sooner the better for my tranquillity and your justification. Since you can achieve nothing further where you are I willingly give my consent to your request of coming back.[12]

And to emphasize his disgrace, Cumberland received in the same mail a formal letter from Holderness — not Münchhausen, the King's Hanoverian minister in London who had signed the original orders, but the British Secretary of State.

> I obey with the utmost grief and reluctance the positive orders I have received from the King which are to acquaint your R.H. with H.M.'s disapprobation of the convention your R.H. has signed and the King's surprise that you did it without his ratification.[13]

Cumberland reacted with a mixture of indignation and bewilderment. Replying to Holderness he asserted that he believed his actions at Kloster Zeven had in no way increased the King's difficulties, that he welcomed the intervention of the King's ministers and hoped they would be able to help. He would return as soon as a ship arrived to take him home.

He was back in London on 11 October. By the time he left Europe, Prussia's fortunes had suddenly improved. Not only had the Russians inexplicably withdrawn after their victory at Gross Jägersdorf, but Frederick the Great had pushed south to Erfurt, advancing against the French under the Prince of Soubise, a favourite of Madame de Pompadour. Richelieu had also received a setback at Halberstadt from a force of 7,000 Prussians fighting under Ferdinand of Brunswick. The war was now on the upturn but the Elector of Hanover's troops were as good as prisoners-of-war.

Cumberland evidently felt no sense of disgrace, however. Despite his own inclinations, he had obeyed the King's instructions to the best of his ability. He went straight to Kensington Palace, where Napier, Fawkener and Fox were awaiting him. To them he appeared to be in good health and excellent spirits. He showed none of the anxiety that Fox had expected. Brushing aside Fox's warning of the King's bad temper, he dressed for the audience in his best uniform and went through to this father's private apartments.

The King was in the cupola room playing cards with Amelia and Lady Yarmouth. 'Here is my son who has ruined me and disgraced himself,' he announced.[14] Cumberland's dignified attempts to reason with him only made the King angrier. He stamped out of the room, fuming.

Cumberland himself was furious but, clinging to his temper, asked Lady Yarmouth to give the King a message. Since he no longer had it in his power to serve the King, he had no favour left to ask but leave to quit. Lady Yarmouth suggested that he take time over his decision, but he replied that he had had plenty of time to reflect upon his conduct and it was irreproachable. He could not show due regard to his own honour by any other step than he was now taking — resignation from all his appointments.

# 24

# A Private Man

CUMBERLAND COULD NOT DISGUISE the hurt he felt at his treatment by the King. His father had publicly disowned him to 'all the courts of Europe' and had sent orders to the Hanoverian ministers to ignore the Convention, if possible, and renegotiate better terms at Versailles and Vienna. As soon as he could, on 15 October, he left London for Windsor to tend his wounded self-esteem in peace and privacy.

The politicians rejoiced at Cumberland's fall. 'Pitt had thought he would resign and is pleased,' Newcastle confided to his wife.[1] Newcastle himself was delighted; he had always been jealous of Cumberland's influence. Before the King could relent, the ministers succeeded in having Ligonier named Commander-in-Chief and made an Irish peer; he would give advice, yes, but he would take orders. And yet Lord Hardwicke had advised Newcastle as early as 19 September, on the eve of the fateful letter of recall: 'Don't take things too strongly against the Duke. Don't you remember that H.M. said to your grace, "I will order him to make a convention at the head of two armies"?'[2] Pitt, too, considered that Cumberland had by no means exceeded his authority at Kloster Zeven; in fact on 20 September, on Holderness's draft of the letter of recall, he had minuted: 'He had a full power.'[3]

Cumberland for his part held no animus towards the politicians although he ignored Holderness and was positively hostile to the creeping Münchhausen. Hearing that the King had gone so far as to canvass opinion of his leadership among the subordinate generals, Cumberland had returned from Germany with statements of support from the Hessian commanders. These he thrust into Munchausen's hands and told him with all the considerable anger he could command to mind his own snivelling business as a Hanoverian councillor. For Horace Walpole, the King's behaviour was simply 'treachery to the best son that ever lived.'[4]

Indeed, the King very soon repented of his anger. Within two days of Cumberland's resignation, he was trying to coax his son into changing his mind by inviting him to the royal breakfast table and pressing him to take back his regiment. Britain still faced war with France and his services were more than ever required. But as Cumberland told Fox, in the case of an invasion he would be happy to come up from Windsor and do his duty, otherwise in honour he could not continue to serve.

So passed from history the fine-sounding title of Captain-General of the British land forces (although the Honourable Artillery Company and Royal Marines, not being regiments, still have a royal Captain-General rather than a Colonel-in-Chief). Like the title of Lord High Admiral, it now has a faintly Ruritanian flavour.

Cumberland's disgrace coincided almost exactly with the fiasco of Pitt's first great combined operation at Rochefort: the force of 9,000 men had returned empty-handed to Portsmouth on 3 October. A court martial exonerated General Mordaunt, who had led the expedition, to the fury of both the King and Pitt. 'The honestest man in the world,' quipped Walpole, 'is so enraged at Mordaunt that he has almost forgot to sacrifice his son for obeying.'[5] But Pitt would make the same mistake again of launching a combined raid against the French coast.

The news from North America was no better. As we have seen, at the beginning of 1757 Cumberland and Pitt had argued over reinforcements for Loudoun and as late as 13 March Cumberland had conferred with Pitt over the nature of the instructions Loudoun should be given, Pitt wanting to give orders that Cumberland regarded as too specific. They had agreed, however, that Loudoun should attack first Louisburg, the French stronghold on Cape Breton Island, and then Quebec, with support from the navy under Rear-Admiral Holburne. But Holburne had made a very delayed departure and did not reach Loudoun at Halifax until July, by which time the French Admiral de la Motte had assembled his fleet to defend Louisburg and the St Lawrence. Moreover, the Marquis de Montcalm had led a successful assault on Fort William Henry and thus was poised to move either north up Lake Champlain or south down the Hudson River to New York. Loudoun decided that his attack on Louisburg must be postponed.

Pitt was furious at this news and held Loudoun responsible. But Cumberland informed Barrington that from his reading of Loudoun's despatches he could not find him blameworthy. 'No man should be condemned unheard,' he wrote. 'You will think I say that, not forgetting myself, who am, as I suppose, the object and topick of every coffee house politician.' And tellingly he added, 'If the King is satisfied I mind not in the least.'[6] To Loudoun himself he wrote on 26 November to express regret that he was unable to help. 'The unfortunate circumstances of the campaign in Germany and some other particular reasons have induced me to lay down entirely all military command,' he wrote, signing off as 'your affectionate tho' useless friend.'[7] He never did enlarge upon the other particular reasons; one is left to wonder whether he was referring to his poor health or the fact that, having lost the King's trust, he no longer wanted to fight the constant battles with ministers who regarded a royal Captain-General as a constitutional anachronism.

What is certain is that during this time at Windsor he was going through all the papers on the campaign in Germany, along with his secretary Mason and his military staff, so that by December he had drawn up a short but dignified defence of his conduct should it ever be called for (which it never was). He made it clear that it was by the King's orders that he had gone to Stade, and that he had believed he had full authority from the King to treat with Richelieu and to bring an end to local hostilities. And by signing the Convention he had also saved the King's Hanoverian army, if not his Electorate. He did not point out, as he might have, that only an overriding sense of loyalty to his father had induced him to accept command in Germany in the first place, without British troops, without even the approval of the King's British ministers. And hindsight allows us to see the curious irony that it was Cumberland's sacrifice in 1757 that ushered in the final phase of Pitt's conversion to a continental commitment for Britain.

Another irony is that across the Channel Richelieu too was in disgrace. Cardinal de Bernis, the French Foreign Minister, claimed that Richelieu had had no authority to sign the Convention and in any case had agreed terms that were far too favourable to Hanover. Furthermore, Richelieu had broken the terms of the agreement: he had tried to disarm the Hessian troops on their way back to Cassel. It was this lucky circumstance that allowed George II and his Hanoverian ministers to repudiate the Convention and fight on.

Thanks to the excellent state in which Cumberland had left the Electoral army, it was well able to respond to the new demands placed upon it by George II and his British ministers — for Pitt and Newcastle agreed to take it wholly into British pay as soon as operations could be restarted. The new commander-in-chief would be, at Frederick's behest, his brother-in-law Ferdinand of Brunswick. Ferdinand arrived at Stade on 23 November and by 28 November the Hessian and Brunswickian contingents had been persuaded to resume the fight, on British pay.

Richelieu had no stomach for the fight. Having gorged himself on booty, he asked leave to return to Paris and arrived there before his successor, Comte Louis de Clermont, had taken over. While Clermont endeavoured vainly to restore order to the ill-disciplined troops — 'quite naked, without tents and with companies less than twelve strong... in short, we are in an inconceivable mess'[8] — Richelieu was reverting to his dazzling career of amorous conquests and using his booty to build a palace for himself, the

Pavillon d'Hanovre. Like his opponent at Hastenbeck, he was never again employed on the field of battle.

Cumberland, at the age of thirty-six, had effectively retired. Although he retained his rooms at St James's and Kensington, he appeared at court only very infrequently and seldom held levees of his own. His disillusion with politics and public life ran very deep, but even deeper was the hurt he felt at the King's disfavour. He took comfort in the company of friends and his private staff at Windsor, and found release in cynical, sometimes bitter comments on the affairs of the world. To Sandwich he even expressed an 'absurd notion' that Britain might be better off for the loss of Hanover, that 'we are the greater people because the King has lost a considerable country.'[9] But it was just a fleeting thought. 'God knows,' he went on, 'how these motley politicians will ever get themselves or the great vessel they steer out of the black storm they have led us into.'[10]

The threat of invasion by France was still exercising the country, yet Pitt was sending every available regiment to North America and relying on the new militias to defend England. Cumberland regarded this as absurd. To Fox he confided his own 'humble opinion for the raising of more troops', although he suspected that Pitt would resent any suggestion coming from him:

> I don't know whether the dauntless man mountain will think it proper, or perhaps he intends to meet the enemy at their landing in person at the head of his new valiant militia. If so, what has England to fear?[11]

At the end of the year the man mountain wrote to Loudoun, dismissing him. The new commander-in-chief in North America would be General James Abercromby: it would be his task now to retake Louisbourg, with naval support led by Admiral Boscawen. But Cumberland played no part in these decisions. Although it was he, and the men he had appointed, who had created the new and stronger British army, it was Pitt who would wield that army to its greatest effect.

Even at the time there were many in the army who, like James Wolfe, regretted Cumberland's resignation. During 1757 an anonymous pamphlet was published with the title of 'A Letter to the Gentlemen of the Army.' One passage read:

> I must confess our army is greatly improved in points of discipline, for which we are obliged to the Duke, and indeed nothing less than a person of H.R.H.'s authority could ever have removed our prejudice in favour of our licentiousness which we erroneously called liberty.[12]

But it was not until later that Cumberland's firm hand and guiding spirit were really missed, when administration and training reverted to the former shambles and the officer corps again fell into jobbery and wayward practices.

And so, while Pitt concentrated his energies on foreign affairs and Newcastle co-ordinated the support he needed at home, Cumberland was in retreat at Windsor. At the end of 1757 his sorrows were increased by the death of his sister Caroline at the age of forty-four. She had never married nor did she possess the energies of Amelia and the Duke had never been particularly close to her, but her death remained a blow. Mary of Hesse was still in exile with her father-in-law in Hamburg, existing on subsidies from the British government, and in Holland Anne was now firmly under the thumb of the States General, who had forced her to surrender to French pressure against the English connection, at a very vital time for her brother's military career in Westphalia in 1757. With the King himself now ageing fast, it seemed the whole family's fortunes were ill-starred.

The nation's fortunes, on the other hand, were about to rise at last.

# 25

# Turn of the Tide

ALREADY BY THE END OF 1757 the nation was celebrating the success of Robert Clive in India. He had not only retaken Calcutta a year before, in January, 1757, but in June he had avenged the Black Hole by defeating the despicable Nawab at Plassey. And now, in early 1758, came news of success in Germany. With the army that Cumberland had saved, Ferdinand of Brunswick recrossed the Elbe and began to push the French back south. By mid-April Clermont's troops — half the strength that Cumberland had faced — had been reduced to a rabble and were retreating across the Rhine. Perhaps the most active and successful element of Ferdinand's force was the unit of Jägers that Cumberland had formed. By the end of June Clermont was beaten, shortly to be replaced by Contades; only Broglie's force now retained any cohesion.

Pitt, having reversed his views on British troops in Europe and finally committed himself to the continental campaign, now sent 8,000 men to Westphalia, including a garrison, the 51st Regiment, to hold Emden at the mouth of the River Ems. Frederick the Great was delighted — regular British troops on German soil! But Leicester House was not so happy. To the Earl of Bute, Pitt now seemed to be acquiring a dangerous prevalence over foreign affairs, and young Prince George, still under Bute's tutelage, came out strongly against Pitt's new involvement in Germany. 'We shall be drawn deeper in a continent war than ever,' he wrote to Bute, and in the following year he referred to 'that horrid Electorate which has always lived upon the very vitals of this poor country.'[1]

The coolness between Pitt and Bute increased that summer when another of Pitt's diversionary raids failed, and he blamed the officers recommended through his Leicester House connections. Originally one of the commanders on this expedition, to attack St Malo, was to have been Cumberland's friend, Albemarle, but on the Duke's advice Albemarle had turned the offer down. Neither Cumberland nor the King approved of Pitt's policy to help Prussia in this way; diversionary tactics were in Cumberland's opinion a waste of effort and men. Sadly, it was his old regiment, the 1st Guards, that suffered the greatest casualties at St Cast when they failed to get back to their boats in Cancale Bay; their commanding officer General Dury was killed and Lord Frederick Cavendish taken prisoner.

But Pitt's prime hope that summer was for success in North America. In February Boscawen had sailed to support Loudoun's replacement, General James Abercromby, in the assault on Louisbourg. Not only would it be a fillip to the nation's morale to recover the fortress that had been regretfully returned to the French under the treaty of Aix-la-Chapelle, it would also give the British control of the waters at the entrance to the St Lawrence seaway. In effect, Louisbourg was the key to success in Canada.

In mid-August the news came at last: Louisbourg had been taken. But it was too late in the year to move on to Quebec, and a simultaneous attack on Ticonderoga had been rebuffed with heavy casualties. Abercromby went the same way as Loudoun: the new commander-in-chief was to be Jeffrey Amherst. Another of Cumberland's most trusted friends was appointed to command an attack on the French-held island of Martinique in the West Indies, but again Albemarle refused the appointment. Undoubtedly both men consulted the Duke before making their respective decisions.

Cumberland was also consulted, indirectly through Ligonier, on the selection of many subordinate officers and troops to serve abroad, and the King was still wont to ask his son's advice on matters of military policy. But he resisted all attempts to lure him back into public life. He had found solace and contentment at Windsor, and although his excessive weight, asthma attacks and chronic pain from his knee wound prevented him from hunting on horseback, he took particular pleasure in his horses: breeding them and racing them, both at Ascot and increasingly at Newmarket.

Among the Cumberland Papers there is a series of notebooks — many annotated in his own hand — that testify to the personal interest he took in his horses and the mating plans for them, particularly after his resignation from the army. He noted special recognition marks for each horse and, beginning with the October '58 meeting at Newmarket, kept a careful record of matches made, races run and their results.

Although in previous years he had been too busy to pay such close personal attention to detail, Cumberland was already one of the dominant figures of British racing. His enthusiasm, his administrative skills, his involvement in the Jockey Club, all helped to raise the standards of courses and races. As a modern historian of racing has written: 'No man before or since has exerted so profound or so lasting an influence on British racing.'[2] And by his eye for a horse he improved the quality of the English thoroughbred out of all recognition. In fact, it was he who bred two of the three predominant stallions in British bloodstock, King Herod and Eclipse. King Herod he bred early enough in his racing career to have some pleasure with, as also with Marske, the sire of Eclipse, whom he acquired by a swap with a Mr Hutton who lived in Marske, a little village near Richmond in Yorkshire. In fact it was Marske who brought Cumberland his first racing triumph at Newmarket, in 1754, when he won three thousand guineas for the Duke in a match over four miles against Lord Gower's colt by Shock.

At Newmarket, where he introduced extra spring and autumn meetings as well as the July meeting, Cumberland stayed in the hunting lodge built by James I (on the site of the present Rutland Arms hotel) and made it very much the centre of events during meetings, as noted in the *Daily Advertiser* of 27 April, 1753: 'We hear that H.R.H. has ordered four tables to be kept open during his residence at Newmarket for the entertainment of the nobility and gentry.' And not just the nobility and gentry, one feels; according to Horace Walpole he 'received everybody at his table with the greatest good humour and permitted the familiarities of the place with ease and sense.'[3]

Apart from the horses, however, and the routine of his duties at Windsor, Cumberland had spent an entire year away from public affairs, and clearly he felt the better for it. Gradually he began to appear more often at Court, particularly after November, 1758, when the King caught a severe cold and was for a time considered to be dying. Although he recovered, the King was lonely and increasingly irritable these days, plagued by the pettiness of Newcastle and the mixed arrogance and flowery deference of Pitt. Fox, as Paymaster-General, was no longer in the cabinet and was quietly devoting his time to amassing a sizeable private fortune. Only Lady Yarmouth and Princess Amelia could be counted on for company. And the new year brought further sadness when Anne, his eldest daughter, the Princess of Orange, died at The Hague on 12 January, 1759. His grandson and heir was, the King felt, too much under the spell of the Earl of Bute, whom he instinctively disliked and mistrusted, and during the coming year, when the Prince of Wales applied for a commission in the army, the King curtly refused his request.

But Cumberland and Fox apparently made an attempt, during 1759, to re-establish good relations with the Princess Dowager through Amelia's good offices — or so it would seem from the gossip of that strange figure on the London political scene, Count Viry, the Sardinian Ambassador to the Court of St James, who had found favour with Bute. It is at least possible that Cumberland had suggested to Augusta that her son should ask for a military appointment.

However, the old King still had enough life left in him to enjoy the military victories of the coming year — Pitt's *annus mirabilis*.

By the end of 1758 Hanover had been entirely freed from French control, and Ferdinand of Brunswick won the credit together with an annuity from the grateful Elector of £2,000 for life. In India, too, Clive had taken control of Bengal for Britain, though the French continued the fight further south under a new general, the Comte de Lally-Tollendal. Pitt now arranged for reinforcements to be sent out to India; Eyre Coote, who had fought at Plassey, was appointed their commander. As always, though, Pitt's attention was focused on North America and, cheered by the news that in November Fort Duquesne had finally been taken − and renamed Fort Pitt (subsequently Pittsburg) − he spent the winter of 1758-9 planning the assault on Quebec.

At first the new year brought less welcome tidings. In Germany Ferdinand found his progress blocked by a newly strengthened French army. Even worse, France had decided to make a direct attack on the flow of men and supplies reaching Ferdinand from Britain by invading southern England. Once again invasion fever seized the nation, which must now depend on the 30,000-strong militia for lack of adequate troops at home. It was rumoured that Cumberland might be recalled to command the defences, but when the rumours were repeated to him by the Duchess of Bedford, he replied, 'I do not believe, Madam, that the command will be offered to me but when no wise man could accept it and no honest man would refuse it.'[4] But midsummer saw the tide turning. First came word from the West Indies, where the expedition against Martinique had swerved and taken Guadeloupe instead. In August, under Ferdinand, six British battalions led the Anglo-German force against the French at Minden and won the day: this was to prove the decisive battle in the continental campaign. That same month Boscawen scored a naval victory too, off the Algarve. And in Canada at last the great expedition against Quebec had begun. While Amherst moved north via Ticonderoga towards Montreal, Wolfe laid siege to Quebec. Finally, on 12 September, scaling the Heights of Abraham which the French had thought unscaleable, Wolfe led the attack on Montcalm's defences. Quebec was won, but in the attempt both the gallant attacker and the gallant defender were killed.

The news reached London on 16 October and was greeted with great rejoicing; now surely the French would sue for peace. Indeed, in late November the Royal Navy sealed the matter when Admiral Hawke followed the French fleet into Quiberon Bay, Britanny, and virtually destroyed it. Without her warships France could no longer guarantee protection to the invasion fleet, still less supplies to North America, the West Indies or India.

Yet the struggle lingered on in North America for another year. Such was French strength in Canada that even with Quebec in British hands, Amherst had to launch a new attack from the south before the French caved in. At last, on 8 September, 1760, the Marquis de Vaudreuil signed the document of surrender.

Seven weeks later, secure in the knowledge that the enemy was beaten, George II died.

The death of his father was as sudden as the stroke that Cumberland had suffered in August. It had been only a mild stroke, affecting his speech for a time and drawing his face down on one side, though Thomas Gray held that his physical dilapidation included the dropsy in a certain rather private part. Cumberland in characteristic fashion made light of his ailments but he was by no means fully recovered when the news reached him on the morning of 25 October that his father had just died of a heart attack.

*The King is dead! Long live the King!* The official proclamation was accompanied by the usual inefficiencies attending mid-eighteenth-century ceremonial. Cumberland was summoned from Windsor to attend a Privy Council meeting at Kensington Palace, but on arrival found that his nephew, the new King, George III, had gone to Savile House for the meeting. Finding no one there Cumberland hung about for two hours, unable to make sense of the conflicting excuses offered him by confused officials, then finally was sent to Carlton House. Here at last the new King's first council was held and the formalities were observed. Cumberland sat on his left hand, taking precedence after George III's younger brother, Edward, the Duke of York.

It was immediately clear that the new King intended to rule by guidance from his 'dearest friend' and mentor, Bute. At twenty-two, George III remained dependent on his mother and her friend Bute, whose hand was behind the King's first address to his Privy Council which concluded by calling the war with France 'bloody and expensive'. Cumberland was just as shocked as Pitt. However, the King was persuaded to alter the wording so that by the time of publication the war had become 'just and necessary'. When the King proclaimed to the world that he 'gloried in the name of Briton' it was taken as a subtle way of comprehending the Scots and excluding the Hanoverians. However tentatively, the young monarch had already made his mark upon the nation.

The funeral service for the old King was held in Henry VII's chapel at Westminster, late on a November night, in the flickering blaze of a myriad flambeaux and candles which searched out with unequal illumination the intricate traceries of the vaulting overhead. Cumberland was the chief mourner. He stood, massive and motionless as a guardsman, on his weak leg for nigh two hours. He was wrapped about in a black cloak with five yards of train. His face looked bloated and queerly distorted, the mouth sagging and one eye dragged down at the side. The only disturber of his silent reverie was the Duke of Newcastle, visibly moved to tears, who had shifted his stance onto the train of Cumberland's cloak the better to warm his feet.

stance onto the train of Cumberland's cloak the better to warm his feet. Horace Walpole felt an unaccustomed sympathy for the man at whom he had so often poked fun: 'A hero reduced by injustice to crowd all his fame into the supporting of bodily ills and to looking upon the approach of a lingering death with fortitude is a real object of compassion.'[5]

Towards his uncle the new King felt no particular animosity. His mother's priggish notions about racing and gaming and the company that Cumberland kept were outweighed by Bute's assurance that Cumberland no longer constituted a threat; indeed, that he could prove to be useful. There was, however, a difficult episode between nephew and uncle caused by the late King's will. George II had left his Electoral monies to his three surviving children, Cumberland, Amelia and Mary, but as this amounted to very little — the King having spent so much on the campaign to save Hanover — Cumberland promptly surrendered his share to his sisters. He had also been left, in a personal bequest by the King, some jewellery that had been his mother's. The new King apparently believed that these items belonged to the Crown, but magnanimously offered to purchase them from his uncle. Negotiations were opened through Bute, the Duke of Devonshire as Lord Chamberlain and various other officers of the Crown. Cumberland was not happy with either the inventory or the valuation; he could not reconcile the King's list of jewels with the list made by his father's former mistress, Lady Suffolk, who reported that the sixteen items included one stomacher which on its own was worth £29,000. However, in the end he felt obliged to accept £53,950, the figure offered him by the King, and moreover to take payment in instalments.

His financial position was now somewhat uncomfortable. He had of course lost all his military salaries and perquisites on his resignation from the army three years before, and though he retained the annual £25,000 grant dating from Culloden, his income from the reorganized Civil List remained at just £15,000. His expenses were huge. He had spent many thousands on the work at Windsor and Virginia Water, on buying, breeding and training horses and maintaining the stables, and on a large household staff and costly entertaining — not only at Windsor but at Newmarket too, and of course the formal levees held in his rooms at St James's or Kensington. He had also acquired the habit of playing for high stakes both at the race course and at the card table. In 1761 he was even obliged to borrow £1,000 from his friend Fox, who kindly refrained from charging interest (but charged him four per cent interest on a further £8,000 loaned to the Duke early in 1762[6]: this Cumberland returned pretty sharply, after the two finally fell out). Fox not only had all the monies available to the Paymaster-General of the Forces, but, unlike Pitt, made use of his position to line his own pocket; he had also had the astounding good luck to win £10,000 in a national lottery.

apartments in the royal palaces. The Princess took a house in Cavendish Square and acquired Gunnersbury Park, having given up the rangership of Richmond Park where her attempts to restrict public access had made her most unpopular. Cumberland at first leased Schomberg House in Pall Mall, by arrangement with his friend Sandwich, though in 1762 he would move again, this time to a house that had once belonged to the Jacobite Duke of Beaufort, on the corner of Grosvenor Street and Park Lane. The lease cost him £15,685, but Cumberland House as it was now called had a fine set of reception rooms at ground and first-floor levels, with a double staircase rising from the hall, as well as a garden and adequate stabling.

The King, however, showed a particular respect for his uncle by laying down that Cumberland's name should still be included in prayers for the royal family, and he and Bute made every effort to stay on friendly terms with the Duke. In any case, Bute's sights were set on Pitt and Newcastle. Shrewdly, he encouraged the inherent jealousies between them, and soon the war-winning ministry was riven with mistrust and doubt. Biding his time, Bute achieved a measure of power when in March, 1761, Holderness was dismissed and Bute appointed as Secretary of State (North). Pitt, though, was not a man to yield without a fight.

While Bute urged peace, Pitt continued his crusade against the French. During the winter of 1760-61 he had conceived the idea of an expedition to take Belle Ile, the island off Quiberon Bay. This Cumberland approved of, and he was delighted when his former ADC, Studholme Hodgson – now a major-general and Colonel of the 5th Foot – was appointed to command the expedition; not only that, but his friend Commodore Augustus Keppel, the younger brother of Albemarle, was to take charge of the escorting fleet. Despite the strong French defences, Hodgson, Keppel and 9,000 troops captured the island after a two-month siege on 8 June, 1761.

This timely victory encouraged France, or so it seemed, to sue for peace; but the new French Foreign Minister, the Duc de Choiseul, was only playing for time. He knew that Spain might now be brought into the war. The Spanish king Ferdinand VI had died in 1759, to be succeeded by his half-brother, Charles III, and in August, 1761, Charles promptly signed a third 'Family Compact' with France.

Pitt was well aware, through his intelligence sources, of the new Franco-Spanish alliance. He was all for taking on Spain as well. But the cabinet lacked his confidence and, besides, the nation was tired of war. Newcastle in particular was horrified at the thought of war with Spain. When Pitt in his usual high-handed way insisted on calling off the peace talks with France, otherwise he would resign, the rest of the cabinet called his bluff. On 5 October Pitt was out.

This political crisis occurred immediately after the marriage and coronation of George III. Before succeeding to the throne the King had conceived a passion for Lady Sarah Lennox, Fox's sister-in-law. However, he was persuaded to take a German princess as wife instead: Charlotte of Mecklenburg-Strelitz. By no means a beauty, Charlotte was a healthy and sensible girl, and a much more suitable match. Cumberland excused himself from the bedding ceremony; he was weary after the long day of celebrations and besides, as he told the Dowager Princess of Wales, 'Madam, of what use could I possibly be? If she were to cry out I could not be of any assistance.'[7] Charlotte proved to be a dutiful wife for a dutiful husband; scandalized by the frivolity and gaming of London society and encouraged by her priggish mother-in-law, she immediately set about improving standards. Cards were abolished and no courts were held on Sundays. Cumberland and Amelia were no doubt glad to escape from the monotony of St James's.

Ten days after the royal wedding, on 22 September George III was crowned. A year after his stroke, Cumberland was clearly in good spirits by now, roaring with laughter when Lord Talbot tried to back his recalcitrant horse away from the King's presence, the whole length of Westminster Hall, and succeeded only in making an exhibition of himself. That evening he sent for Fox and warned him that Pitt was going to resign. Fox did not believe him. Possibly he did not realize to what extent Cumberland had now been drawn back into public affairs. But ever since his father's death the Duke had found himself consulted, not only by the new King and his advisers, but by men such as Newcastle who had wondered whether to leave office upon the new reign. Cumberland, however, had stressed the value of continuity to the new King.

To Devonshire Bute confided that in his view Cumberland was one of the great props of the royal family and that he would like to see him back at the head of the army. But when this was relayed to Cumberland, he made it clear that he no longer wanted this position, though he would gladly offer all assistance to the King in his evident keenness to manage the army himself. Even so, Bute had politely kept Cumberland informed on military matters and, indeed, sent him a message of congratulation when Hodgson captured Belle Ile. Calcraft, a friend of Fox and the greatest of all the army agents, wrote frequently to Amherst of affairs at home, and did not fail to note in July, 1761, that 'The Duke and his friends meet with the greatest civility from His Majesty.'[8] In addition, Cumberland often saw details of military operations, sent either to Napier or direct to himself by those involved.

One such channel was Eyre Coote, who had remained in India after Adlercron was deemed a misfit and removed. Together with the remnants of the 39th Regiment he had fought at Plassey, whereupon Clive promoted him to lieutenant-colonel. Through his regular correspondence with Napier,

Cumberland was among the first to hear that Pondicherry, the last French stronghold in India, had been taken in January, 1761. When Coote heard the rumour that Cumberland might again be made Captain-General, he wrote, 'No circumstance or event can afford me more real happiness.'[9] But India without the challenge of the French held no charms for Coote, and he grew frustrated at the restrictions of peace. 'For God's sake, dear General,' he wrote to Napier for Cumberland's ear in 1761, 'contrive some way to get me home, for I'm quite tired of this country.'[10] He was indeed brought home in 1762, though he later returned to India to gain yet further glory as Commander-in-Chief, dying in the field near Madras in 1783.

Through Hodgson, too, Cumberland was well aware of the present low strength of the army; when Albemarle predicted a shortfall of 20,000 men for the coming year he was certainly speaking for the Duke. But Pitt had been undaunted by such worries. He wanted to launch another expedition against French holdings in the West Indies with troops from North America. In mid-October 6,000 troops were embarked by Captain Rodney and his fleet and sailed off down the eastern seaboard to attack Martinique. By the time they arrived, however, Pitt had resigned.

# 26

# The Peace of Paris

LIKE PITT, CUMBERLAND HAD SEEN the inevitability of war with Spain; he was unsurprised when Charles III declared war on Britain on 19 December, 1761. His chief concern was to help the King and country survive this new turn of events. To that end he urged Newcastle to remain in office despite the changes wrought in the wake of Pitt's resignation. Pitt, for all his belligerence, still had the nation's popular support and Bute could not hope to replace him overnight. Knowing of Cumberland's good will and continuing powers of influence, Bute now sought to enlist his help through Devonshire.

On 7 January, 1762, after a meeting with Bute the previous day, Devonshire approached Cumberland on the question of withdrawing British troops from Germany in order to meet the threat from Spain. Cumberland was vehemently against such a move. He told Devonshire to make it clear that

> though as a matter of principle he would never wish to disagree with the King's ministers upon this point, he thought his honour so much engaged to friends abroad and the point so detrimental to the true honour and interest of the country, that if he was the only man he would divide the House upon the question.[1]

Cumberland also advised against Bute's plan to invite Fox back into the cabinet, commenting to Devonshire that he was very dissatisfied with Fox 'who had gone over entirely to Lord Bute and was acting a very weak part.'[2] Evidently he had realized that Fox could not be relied upon to see this war through to its just conclusion.

Pitt by now had been replaced by the Earl of Egremont, a political nonentity whom Bute thought to control, and Newcastle found himself isolated within the cabinet. Matters came to a head in the spring of 1762, when Newcastle asked Cumberland's advice as to whether he should stay on at the Treasury 'under Bute's domination.' 'Every day I grow more insignificant,' he complained.[3] Increasingly he turned to Cumberland, even showing him diplomatic exchanges relating to the peace negotiations. Thus alerted, Cumberland repeated his opposition to any peace plan that was confined to Germany alone. But in May, Bute refused to renew the subsidy to Prussia. Although the war in Europe was virtually won, this could have produced problems for Frederick the Great if Russia had not now withdrawn from the conflict; the Tsaritsa Elizabeth had died in January and her nephew Peter III, who succeeded her, was eager to make peace with Frederick.

Bute's action, however, prompted Newcastle finally to resign. Cumberland's part in all this is summed up by a political cartoon of the time, entitled 'The State Ballance or Political See-Saw.' Cumberland is shown astride the pivot of a see-saw, crying out 'Oh D— —n that heavy Boot!' with Pitt and Newcastle being flung off one end and Bute with George III and his mother weighing down the other. The Duke of York, the King's younger brother, who was often in his uncle's company, is seen to be encouraging him: 'Preserve the Equilibrium Uncle if possible, or fall with your Country.' And the inevitable Scotsmen standing by exclaim, 'Gin the Fat Mon's shook off, we shall ha' nothing to fear.'[4]

Yet even though Bute was opposed to the war in Germany, he had been impressed enough by Pitt's victories across the Atlantic to want to carry on. Not only was the expedition to Martinique encouraged but another expedition was now launched, this one to the Spanish island of Cuba. This time Albemarle gladly accepted the command, with Guy Carleton as his chief of staff, and set sail in early March with Admiral Pocock and four full-strength regiments in one of the most complex amphibious operations ever mounted. And, as Albemarle's acceptance of the mission indicates, Cumberland was very closely involved in the arrangements, although he tried to disguise the fact. In February he had written to Albemarle:

Any bystander would think me the projector and fitter out of this expedition, but the truth is the subject is so tender that I cannot allow even suppositions which perhaps are not quite groundless.[5]

In the same letter he conveyed precise information about where Albemarle should land in Cuba, for he was taking advice from Admiral Knowles, whose knowledge of the Caribbean went back to his service with Admiral Vernon in 1740 and his subsequent years as Governor of Jamaica. Knowles was a self-made man, a good linguist and mathematician, and although regarded within the navy as difficult he was a welcome visitor at Windsor; in fact, on Cumberland's death the inventory shows Knowles as having a room allocated to him at Cumberland Lodge.

The expedition to Havana had set off before it was known that the Martinique expedition had been a resounding success. Not only Martinique but Grenada and St Lucia had been taken. French holdings in the West Indies had been reduced to one: Haiti. Bute, now with overall power, decided that the time was ripe to re-open peace talks with France.

Cumberland had no wish to go against the King in any way but he took the view that Bute was becoming too powerful for the best interests of the country. For his part, Bute suspected him of trying to co-ordinate opposition to the peace talks, and Fox took the same view: 'The two material things I really differ with him on are the German war and the Duke of Newcastle.'[6] In July, Devonshire charged Fox with disloyalty to Cumberland – a charge that Fox resented. He admitted he disagreed with Cumberland over the question of peace in Europe but insisted that the Duke did not hold this against him. But as Devonshire pointed out to Fox, even though he did not show it Cumberland was undoubtedly hurt by his friend's behaviour.

However, to Cumberland's delight the King asked him to stand godfather to his first-born son, George, and at the christening in early September Cumberland deduced from his conversation that the King was not wholly behind Bute. Later that month there was further opportunity for a quiet exchange with the King at the installation of Bute and Prince William – the King's second brother, later the Duke of Gloucester and Edinburgh – as Knights of the Garter at Windsor. Cumberland on his knees before the altar delivered up to the Bishop of Salisbury the sword, helm and crest of his late father, as well as his personal banner; then with the Duke of York he conducted Prince William to his stall. The Dukes of Newcastle and Rutland then led Bute to the stall made vacant by the death of the Duke of Portland. That afternoon Cumberland was further honoured by a visit by the King and Queen to Cumberland Lodge, and in the evening at the banquet in St George's Hall Cumberland sat on the King's right hand.

What Cumberland and the King discussed will never be known, but very shortly afterwards Cumberland invited Fox to Windsor and tried to find out whether there was any way Bute might be persuaded to step down from political responsibility, though still retaining his position at court. Fox agreed that Bute's team was not a strong one, and that the clamour against him in the country was great; but he also indicated that in his opinion Bute would not step down. Furthermore, he informed Cumberland that the peace negotiations with France were already well advanced.

Then, while Fox was still at Windsor, the news reached Cumberland on 29 September that Havana had been captured. It was a magnificent achievement and as soon as he could, on 2 October, Cumberland wrote expressing his pleasure to Albemarle:

> No joy can equal mine. I strut and plume myself as if it was I that had taken the Havannah — I take your siege to have been the most difficult since the invention of artillery: 68 days in that climate alone is prodigious.[7]

But he warned Albemarle that

> the ministry is not quite so much obliged to you for you have removed the peace... and great as you and the army have made us appear abroad, as little are we at home by unwarrantable divisions that increase daily. ...This is an improper subject for a letter.[8]

The unwarrantable divisions, of course, referred to the conflict of opinion over Bute's handling of the peace negotiations. Unfortunately, the news of Havana had arrived simultaneously with news from Paris: Bute's specially appointed ambassador to Paris, the Duke of Bedford, had agreed peace terms with France.

And even more unfortunately for Cumberland, Fox had gone to Bute after his visit to Windsor and relayed his own very imprecise version of what Cumberland had said to him — specifically, that Cumberland was in favour of peace but would rather see anyone but Bute sign the peace. Not surprisingly Bute now saw Cumberland as the foe.

The King invited Cumberland to a formal audience to go through the proposed peace terms, clause by clause. Cumberland was frankly critical, though he allowed that some of the terms were reasonable — the boundaries for Canada, for instance, which now became formally British. But with one exception, the King and Cumberland found themselves broadly in agreement over which terms to accept and which to repudiate: the exception being the separate peace for Germany. This Cumberland condemned as betrayal of an ally, Prussia, for there was no guarantee that Frederick would regain his territorial possessions on the Rhine. The King was somewhat taken aback, although the meeting remained perfectly good-tempered.

Bute now took the obvious step of ensuring the formal support of Fox, offering him the post of Secretary of State and also that of Leader of the Commons. The former Fox rejected as too burdensome, but the latter he accepted eagerly. This, at last, was the position he felt he deserved.

To Devonshire Cumberland admitted: 'I own I am hurt and therefore not fit to reason on Fox's action.'[9] Fox was oblivious to the hurt he had caused. 'I think I act on principles he taught me,' he announced. He had visited Cumberland immediately before seeing the King to accept his new post and 'the Duke was excessively good and kind and friendly':

> His goodness to me at a time my notions of duty carry me so contrary to his inclination is the greatest obligation I ever received. If I could love him more than I did before, I should upon this occasion.[10]

Fox was always able to convince himself of his own qualities even if others were sometimes harder to persuade.

Nor was Fox's the only betrayal that autumn. Sandwich, whom Cumberland had long treated as a friend, also accepted a position from the Bute ministry: as ambassador to Spain. Two of Cumberland's friends had now left him for lucre. Devonshire also fell from grace, having incurred the King's wrath for refusing an invitation to discuss the peace terms, and he resigned. 'I must pity the poor young King,' wrote Cumberland to Devonshire,

> that has bereft himself of the most useful and zealous subjects through the instigation of the most dangerous and wicked adviser ever a young King had. Whenever the vermin the court is now full of be swept away, we may see you there again at the head of our real friends, for our family must not be long without a Duke of Devonshire in the administration.[11]

As Cumberland had already admitted, 'I fear strong measures now that Fox is chief counsellor.'[12] His apprehension was correct. Fox intended to ensure a good strong majority for his new friend Bute in Parliament, so he set about aligning the votes with a vengeance. Aided by Calcraft, the army agent, he won over as many of the military as he could. He used bribery and threats, persuasion and force, as he thought fit. Lord Ancram was offered £4,000 to give up his seat to another.

Newcastle, meanwhile, was attempting to rally the opposition. He knew that Pitt disapproved of the preliminary peace terms, which were now on the point of being formally agreed in Paris, and sent emissaries to Pitt's home at Hayes, near Bromley. Pitt was ill with gout. Vitriolic about Bute and depressed at the state of the nation, he refused Newcastle's every blandishment. Cumberland, for his part, cautioned Newcastle that it would be foolish to take up a formal stance of opposition, particularly without Pitt, but cannot have been surprised when Newcastle then enlisted his own help in persuading Pitt to fight the Bute ministry.

Pitt agreed to meet Cumberland at Cumberland House on 17 November. The preliminaries to the peace treaty had already been signed in Paris, on 3

November, which Pitt regarded as a complete betrayal of British interests around the world. However, much to Newcastle's disgust the meeting ended inconclusively, although Pitt and Cumberland agreed to keep in touch through Wyndham, the Duke's treasurer at Windsor.

On 9 December Parliament was asked to approve the preliminary articles. Cumberland, in the House of Lords, listened to the debate with the closest attention. He judged Bute's speech commending the terms one of the finest he had ever heard. Newcastle and Hardwicke spoke against, but feebly. There was no division. In the Commons, Pitt made a dramatic appearance, swathed with flannel about the legs and obviously still unwell, and spoke for three hours against the peace — but his arguments were loose and rambling and he left before the vote was taken. The day ended with Fox and Bute victorious.

Now, as Cumberland had predicted, Fox rubbed salt in the wound. There was a thoroughgoing proscription of all who had ever opposed him. The Dukes of Grafton and Newcastle and the Marquess of Rockingham were all stripped of their lord lieutenancies. Lady Poyntz, the widow of Cumberland's old friend and governor, who had died in December, 1750, saw her pension snatched away. Mr Greening, the retired royal gardener who had overseen so much of the work at Windsor, was deprived of his annuity. Such petty cruelty so enraged Cumberland that he tackled Bute and managed to get Lady Poyntz's pension restored at least. But all he could do for the others was offer words of consolation. 'I fear we must still see worse before we get better times,' he had told Newcastle.[13] To Lord Waldegrave he expressed a sense that Fox had duped him,

> not as you think, by giving me up; he might be angry with me talking to Newcastle and Pitt; but he has deceived me because I thought him good-natured, but in all these transactions he has shown the bitterest revenge on humanity.[14]

But Fox's job was nearly done. He had won the peace debate for Bute; all he wanted now was to secure his own position.

Bute's position was even more precarious than Fox's. He might have won the parliamentary debate, but he was vilified throughout the country for accepting peace terms considered overly favourable to France. Whereas Pitt and Cumberland saw Bute's preliminary articles as a straightforward betrayal of Germany, the nation was more incensed over concessions to France such as fishing rights off the Newfoundland coast. In the West Indies, Guadeloupe and Martinique were returned to France and Cuba was returned to Spain in exchange for Florida. Another exchange resulted in Britain's recovery of

Minorca for the loss of Belle Ile, but Minorca no longer roused the British as it had in 1756. In India the French were allowed to continue trading. In fact the terms in themselves were less objectionable than the nation's outrage would indicate. Bute, the man not the measures, as Fox himself remarked, was the main object of the nation's hate.

As usual the scribblers and caricaturists were active, most notable among them an MP by the name of John Wilkes, who had set up a journal (with financial backing from Temple, Pitt's brother-in-law) called *The North Briton*: even the name itself was a jibe at Bute. That winter Wilkes and his like were in their element, using satire and innuendo to provoke opposition to the Bute ministry. Quite literally, Bute was subjected to considerable mud-flinging. Pitt, on the other hand, was still the country's hero, and as Cumberland's opposition to Bute emerged he too was hailed as a potential saviour. There was even a popular toast, in the inns and taverns of the day, to 'Will Pitt, Will Cumberland and the Will of the People!'

In February, 1763, the Peace of Paris was finally signed. The Seven Years War was over. Prussia and Austria came to a separate agreement by which Frederick managed to keep Silesia; but he would never forgive the British for having deserted him at the eleventh hour.

For Bute the sole problem now was financial, the war having drained the nation's coffers. In March, his Chancellor of the Exchequer introduced a new tax – on cider. This provoked an uproar, particularly in the West Country, and Pitt threw himself into the fray, attacking the tax as unjust and intrusive. Although Cumberland disapproved of Newcastle's plan to rally opposition on this point – in his view it was constitutionally wrong to oppose the Crown on a vote of supply – he cannot have been surprised when Bute then decided he had had enough, and resigned.

With Bute in retreat, fleeing to Scotland and claiming bad health, the poor young King was left without a chief minister. At twenty-five, George III was very much dependent on his advisers; although he had learnt many a useful lesson from the first two and a half years of his reign, he still required a steadying hand as he strove to find a way through all the pitfalls of Whig and Tory politics. But it would take another crisis before he found that steadying hand.

# 27

# Return to Duty

GEORGE GRENVILLE, ANOTHER OF PITT'S pompous brothers-in-law but a life-long Tory, was appointed the new prime minister in April, 1763. This had been Bute's parting advice to the King, but the King was soon dissatisfied with Grenville and vainly looked around for a replacement. For a time he even considered Fox, but Fox made his position clear: he had done his duty and now he wanted his reward — a seat in the House of Lords. On 16 April, much to his chagrin as he had hoped for an earldom, he became Baron Holland of Foxley, Wiltshire.

Newcastle, of course, saw this as his chance to return to power, and started agitating for Cumberland's support. But Cumberland was most reluctant to interfere with the due constitutional processes and disapproved of Newcastle's eager politicking; on one occasion he even had to ask Newcastle not to make use of his name as the leader of a party of opposition. Although frustrated by his royal friend's scruples, Newcastle was not deterred; after three decades in politics he knew how to be patient. Writing to Devonshire, he referred to 'the most unjust supposition that the Duke of Cumberland pushes on the opposition, the contrary of which your Grace as well as myself know to be true.'[1] But the Tory pamphleteers were doing their best to play up Cumberland's known hostility to Bute, and insinuating that he was equally hostile to the King.

Suddenly the King himself took centre stage. Wilkes's *North Briton* had overstepped the mark. In issue No.45 the journal attacked the King outright, and the King ordered Wilkes to be arrested for seditious libel. Halifax, the Secretary of State, promptly issued a general warrant, which allowed the arrest of anybody connected with the publication, and scores of printers and booksellers were among those rounded up and thrown into gaol. Wilkes himself was taken to the Tower to await the King's pleasure.

Even allowing for the insolence Wilkes had shown, his arrest was not the wisest move the King could have made. As an MP Wilkes could depend on support from the Commons, and as a journalist he could squeal very loudly to the public. Moreover, when brought before a court Wilkes was able to plead parliamentary immunity, and was freed a few days later — though this was by no means the end of the story.

Meanwhile Bute was planning to return to power, albeit at arm's length, through Grenville. Newcastle, who hoped to build on the outrage over the Wilkes affair, decided that Pitt should now become involved. Pitt shared the public outrage, and was a particular friend of Sir Charles Pratt, the Chief Justice responsible for Wilkes's release; but while he hankered after power, he was in no mood to be rushed. On 28 May, Newcastle called on Cumberland at Windsor for advice, and found him equally inclined to caution.

Besides, Cumberland was enjoying himself. It was an early summer, and Windsor and Virginia Water were at their most beautiful. He had undertaken several other projects devised by Thomas Sandby, one of which involved the rebuilding of Holbein Gate, which in 1759 had been removed stone by stone from Whitehall where it caused intolerable traffic blocks. Sandby had suggested widening the gateway by adding Tudor-style wings to the flanking towers, the whole thing to be erected as a great folly on Snow Hill; but the plans were eventually dropped. Another project had come to fruition, however: the building of a triangular belvedere on top of Shrubs Hill, overlooking the lake and with splendid views in all directions. It was intended to be a place of quiet refuge, with a library and a salon boasting a magnificent Chelsea china chandelier, which cost the Duke £700. Six years after Cumberland's death John Wesley visited the belvedere and wrote:

> We viewed the improvements of that active and useful man, the late Duke of C. The most remarkable work is the triangular tower, surrounded by shrubberies and woods — and commands a beautiful prospect three ways — one of the rooms a study. I was agreeably surprised to find many of the books not only religious but admirably well chosen. Perhaps the great man spent many hours there with only Him that seeth in secret; and who can tell how deep that change went which was so discernible in the latter part of his life.[2]

But a century and a half later, when the belvedere had been enlarged and renamed Fort Belvedere, it acquired a national notoriety as the private hideaway of the King who abdicated his throne — something that Cumberland would never have approved of.

By now Cumberland's household included Albemarle, who had returned from Cuba in February that year. His mistress Sally Stanley and their two small children had stayed with Cumberland during his absence. As victor of Havana Albemarle had garnered not only a wealth of stories to entertain the Duke but also a very considerable share of the spoils: £120,000. Now Albemarle became Cumberland's confidential secretary, handling his political correspondence much as Sir Everard Fawkener had done before his death in '58, with Mason continuing to deal with his official and military papers.

In addition, in June '63 Cumberland had a houseful of guests for Ascot races, including Devonshire and Rockingham, a young racing friend like the third Duke of Grafton who also shared vaguely Whiggish sentiments. There was undoubtedly some political talk, but the house party devoted most of their time to the serious business of the turf.

Newcastle, a frequent visitor at Cumberland Lodge but not during the races − he was sadly lacking in leisure interests − managed to repay the Duke by inviting him over to Claremont, some fifteen miles away. His fussy ways and Cumberland's tastes in food are equally revealed by the correspondence before the event. 'I know in the first place he would like not a crowd nor a show,' Newcastle wrote to Albemarle:

> In the second place I shall have very plain English dinner with beef roast, cold stakes and collops at 11 in the morning, and my servant will be at Dicker's bridge to conduct him from thence. You shall have no fuss of any kind, my intention is to please the Duke and not show for myself. I propose after the tea and the coffee is over to have the honour if I am permitted to carry H.R.H. in a most easy one-horse chaise all over the grounds before dinner. Do let me know if the Duke takes turtle, for otherwise I would not give H.R.H. the trouble of it.[3]

The turtle was turned down; the Duke did not like anything fishy, Albemarle declared. And he went on:

> The less ceremony you show my master the better. H.R.H. seems most uneasy lest he should be troublesome to the Duchess of N., begs her Grace not to put herself the least out of her way for him. The plainer the dinner the better.[4]

And, according to Albemarle, Cumberland's tipple was 'Rhenish cup toaste and water in the tee and claret.'[5]

Evidently the visit was a success. Cumberland wrote to Newcastle in his own hand:

> A thousand thanks for the agreeable day − tho' I was most agreeably surprised with the great improvements that I found, yet the manner of

spending my time and the hearty and sincere concurrence of opinion with my own that I met with surpassed the other pleasures. The only drawback can be fearing my having given a great deal of trouble.[6]

This letter of thanks Newcastle circulated proudly to his friends. Evidently an identity of view had been established and he must have thought he could now rely on Cumberland's whole-hearted support.

Indeed, Cumberland made a round of country house visits that summer, and it would appear that his intention was mainly to see how the wind was blowing. Between 25 July and 10 August he visited Chatsworth, Welbeck and Wentworth Woodhouse and later in August he also went to Woburn. As soon as he had returned south from seeing Rockingham at Wentworth Woodhouse, he wrote to Newcastle commenting on the encouraging signs he had found. One sign in particular pleased Cumberland: Pratt had convinced Pitt of the illegality of general warrants, and so Pitt now saw a worthy and justifiable cause on which to hang his cap.

Suddenly a new factor threw all political plans into turmoil. On 21 August, while Cumberland was at Woburn, word arrived that the Earl of Egremont had died in office; a new Secretary of State would have to be appointed. The King, on Bute's advice, sent for Pitt and asked him to form a new ministry. But Pitt refused to mention more than two names at this interview: Cumberland and Pratt. Pitt wanted Cumberland to replace Bute as general adviser to the King on politics and foreign affairs. The King was somewhat taken aback. 'Surely I have always been civil to him,' he remarked,[7] thinking perhaps of the special loo parties he and the Queen kept arranging, rather against their principles, for Uncle William and Aunt Amelia. Pitt then suggested that it would be for the benefit of the nation if Cumberland again had the power of recommendation in military appointments. Secondly, Pitt wanted a guarantee that Pratt would be advanced in place of Mansfield as the King's legal adviser. Beyond that, he requested that the Whig lords generally should be reinstated in their lieutenancies. The interview ended with Pitt assuming that the King had found nothing unreasonable in his requests and agreeing to return two days later with names for a new administration.

But at the second interview Pitt evidently overplayed his hand. The King took umbrage; the deal was called off.

On 8 September, having already heard Pitt's version of events, Cumberland was no doubt much intrigued, while attending the christening of his great-nephew Frederick, to hear the King's version from the Princess Dowager. While sympathizing with the King's predicament and acknowledging Pitt's perversity, Cumberland observed that he was amazed how many of Bute's creatures Pitt was prepared to allow to remain at court.

But some days later Cumberland was appalled to hear that Sandwich, his one-time friend, had been appointed the new Secretary of State under Grenville. Moreover, Sandwich planned to continue the persecution of Wilkes – and Bedford, too, had been enticed into the ministry as Lord President.

Newcastle was frantic; the new parliamentary session was about to start and he desperately needed Pitt's support. As Cumberland had told him, 'Nothing good can be brought about without Pitt.'[8] It was agreed that Cumberland would once more take on the task of trying to win Pitt over. The meeting was not a success, however. Pitt took the line that there was no need to oppose a set of ministers who were so incompetent they would soon fall anyway. But the particular sticking point was the question of parliamentary privilege. Although reluctant to support Wilkes himself, Pitt was vehemently against any move that might curtail the MP's right to avail himself of this defence and wanted to make an immediate issue of it. Cumberland advised caution; 'Privilege and prerogative should be very tenderly handled and well considered before either of them should be the subject of Parliamentary debate.'[9] Pitt was unmoved.

For the time being at least, Newcastle's hopes were dashed. When Parliament opened on 15 November, the opposition remained at odds with each other – and especially with Pitt.

The first business of the parliamentary session concerned Wilkes. Sandwich had known Wilkes personally, both having frolicked at the Hell Fire Club orgies at Medmenham, but now the man whose friendship Cumberland had once enjoyed showed himself to be a brazen hypocrite. Seeking to curry favour with the King, he had by devious methods obtained a copy of the 'Essay on Women', an obscene parody of Pope's 'Essay on Man' which had been printed on Wilkes's presses, and proceeded to read out long passages to illustrate the kind of filth Wilkes dealt in.

Disgusted more by Sandwich's behaviour than the dirty 'Essay', Cumberland agreed to vote against the government motion – that parliamentary privilege should not be an acceptable defence for seditious libel. Although Pitt, too, opposed the motion, the lack of concerted action meant that the opposition lost the day. Wilkes by now had fled the country, but issue No.45 of his journal was condemned to be burnt as seditious libel by the common hangman in the presence of the Sheriff of London.

Not surprisingly, Cumberland's action had been noted at court. Most of his friends and members of his household had also voted against the government, including his former ADC, now a general, Henry Seymour Conway, who thereby put his commission at risk – as did Albemarle himself. The King expected opposition from the likes of Pitt, but his uncle's attitude on this matter gave him serious cause for thought. But Cumberland was far from being out of favour. After Christmas he spent a few days at Woburn with Bedford, whose action in joining the government he had apparently forgiven, and then returned to London for the marriage of his niece Augusta. With much pleasure he had agreed to give her away at her wedding to Charles, Duke of Brunswick-Wolfenbüttel, at the Chapel Royal, St James's, on 16 January, 1764. After the ceremony, supper was taken at Leicester House and later there was a ball at St James's. Nor was that the end of the junketing, for on the 24th Cumberland arranged a grand entertainment for the happy couple and 300 guests at his London home. A few days later the Dukes of Grafton and Devonshire held another ball in their honour at Mrs Connolly's rooms in Soho Square – Mrs Connolly being notorious as one of Casanova's mistresses; it is quite possible that Casanova himself was presented to Cumberland that night.

Cumberland was in excellent form these days, attending every party and staying to the end even if that were not until six o'clock the morning after. He was also much amused by his new popularity with Londoners. The Wilkes affair had provoked much public attention and cries of 'Wilkes and Liberty!' were hurled angrily at government ministers as they drove through London. Then, on 5 January, the day appointed for the public burning of No.45 of *The North Briton*, the assembled mobs had created such a riot that the common hangman was unable to fulfil his task. And now the cry was: 'Wilkes, Temple and Cumberland!'

Early in February the opposition seemed to gain ground. Indeed, on the 17th, when a vote was held on the question of the legality of general warrants, the ministry scraped home in the Commons only by a dozen votes. Pitt, though ill again with gout, managed to speak in the five-day debate, but a number of military MPs who voted with the opposition, notably Conway, were now deprived of their commissions.

Suddenly Cumberland had another slight stroke and his sister Amelia found out from Windham that Ranby wanted to operate. It appears he was also suffering a glandular discharge into the throat. But when Amelia visited him, Cumberland was as alert as usual and within three days was fit enough to receive a visit from Newcastle. The King treated Cumberland's indisposition in an offhand way, telling Grenville that he did not feel much sympathy for someone who had behaved so unkindly towards him. However, the King himself had been unwell with a fever and perhaps his jaundiced attitude reflected his own ill health more than calculated hostility.

Grenville by now felt himself safe from interference from the King and Bute, who had learnt the lesson the previous summer that Pitt, Newcastle and the opposition could not provide a viable alternative ministry. He was exercising his undoubted administrative abilities in running down the war machine and attempting to redress the nation's finances. In an endeavour to lower the land tax and halve current expenditure, he ordered drastic cuts for the army and navy and imposed all kinds of indirect taxes. Furthermore, believing that the colonies ought to contribute more to their own upkeep, he was planning changes in the way North American and West Indian duties were collected, notably for sugar.

There was little oppositon to Grenville's plans. Pitt stayed at home in Hayes most of the summer, still plagued with gout. When Rockingham called on him to test the water for Newcastle he found him polite but intent on 'determined inactivity.' Newcastle was himself in low spirits. Not only had his co-ordinated oppositon evaporated but he had lost one of his oldest and wisest advisers in early March when the Earl of Hardwicke died.

Cumberland, by contrast, was once again enjoying life and trying to regain his health. Although scarcely able to walk he attended both spring meetings at Newmarket, and won a considerable sum on the races. But his winnings by no means covered his costs, for he continued to entertain on a lavish scale at the Newmarket lodge. Mrs. Gregory, the housekeeper, was paid over £800. The post horses alone, for himself and his staff to Newmarket, cost Cumberland £156 15s 6d that April, with an additional payment of £40 for mounts for the footmen, and Robert Hayden, responsible for keeping the horses at Newmarket, was paid £412 8s 1d for the quarter.

Early that summer, to his enormous delight, Cumberland's mare Spiletta dropped her long-planned foal by Marske in a paddock by Cranbourne Lodge. A chestnut colt, with a white blaze and one prominent white sock on the off hind leg, he was born at the very moment of a dramatic heavenly conjunction and Cumberland appropriately named him Eclipse. The foal had a great future ahead — in fact, he was never beaten: 'Eclipse first, the rest nowhere,' as the saying went. He died in 1789, but by 1906 no fewer than 82 of his progeny had won the Derby out of a possible 127, testifying to the breeding skills of the Duke of Cumberland. Alas, Cumberland was not to taste the fruit of his success. Within eighteen months, Eclipse was knocked down at Tattersalls for £75.

At the Ascot meeting in June, King Herod won another of his many races and Cumberland celebrated with his usual houseful of guests. On this occasion he also provided a most extraordinary entertainment; a fight between a stag and a tiger. Over the years he had acquired something of a menagerie at Windsor, thanks to gifts of exotic animals from military protégés around the world, and the tiger appears to have come from Bengal. The fight was staged on the Saturday of Ascot in a palisaded arena on the lawn by the racecourse. An old red deer stag was first led in, then the tiger, blindfolded and restrained by its Indian keepers. The blindfold removed, the tiger ignored the stag. But the stag wheeled round, lowered his antlers and rammed the tiger head on. Prodded by the keepers, the tiger still refused to attack – then whirled and leapt over the palisade and disappeared into nearby woods. The crowds of onlookers had melted away in terror, but gradually returned as the keepers tracked the tiger down to a clearing in the wood, where a herd of fallow deer were quietly grazing. The tiger seized one wretched doe and while thus distracted was recaptured by the keepers and led off to its cage. The stag was deemed by Cumberland to have triumphed and was adorned with an inscribed silver plate below the antlers, recounting his exploit and excusing him from being hunted ever again.

The event was later marked by a painting by Stubbs, entitled 'Cheetah and Stag with two Indians' and apparently done at Windsor. Evidently the tiger had either died by then or was otherwise considered an unsuitable subject; it is almost certain from all accounts of the event that the animal at Ascot was a tiger. Clive of India also sent Cumberland a tiger, but only after the encounter at Ascot.

That Cumberland had other things on his mind than racing, however, is made clear by the gossiping Lady Sarah Bunbury, née Lennox, a lady of fashion who regularly attended race meetings with her husband. The previous year at Newmarket she had remarked that Cumberland 'won everything on earth' and called him 'a fat wretch.' But in June '64 she noted that he paid little heed to the racing 'for whispering among his friends.'[10] Rockingham and Grafton were certainly there that Ascot, and at other times Cumberland saw Newcastle, Devonshire, even Pitt himself at Windsor. Other guests that summer included his niece Augusta and her new husband the Duke of Brunswick, who went on to visit Newcastle and also Pitt, thus earning the accusation from St James's that they were consorting too much with the opposition.

Most of the politicking went on at Claremont, Newcastle's home, but Cumberland was kept well informed. He was broadly in favour of the oppositon policies, where these touched on foreign affairs, but he disapproved strongly of the notion put forward by the erratic Charles Townshend, brother of George (now Viscount Townshend), that a new alliance should be forged with Fox and Bute. In Cumberland's view neither man had anything left to offer the country. He still hoped that Pitt might be persuaded to join forces with Newcastle. But, so long as Pitt held himself aloof, there was nothing Cumberland felt he could usefully contribute.

Late that summer there was a ferocious storm at Windsor. Cumberland called in all his staff, labourers and everyone he could find in the park and forest to shelter in the Lodge, while thunder burst and lightning flashed and hailstones up to six inches in diameter battered the surrounding area. Beans were torn from their stalks, fruit beaten off the trees, cornfields were flattened and as far away as Gunnersbury Princess Amelia had most of her windows broken. Cumberland Lodge alone took £150-worth of damage. For the superstitious it might have seemed a baleful omen.

That autumn, against the physicians' advice, Cumberland went to Newmarket as usual. Abscesses had developed on his wounded knee, causing him untold pain and making it all but impossible to walk. But King Herod had been entered in a four-mile match against another great stallion, Antinous, and Cumberland was determined to be there. Bets of £50,000 were laid, and the winnings would be tremendous. To the Duke's gratification, King Herod won, in a time of eight minutes, two seconds. His jockey, Mr South, was well rewarded.

But the abscessed knee could no longer be ignored. While the meeting was still in progress, Ranby had to operate. He would have to make several incisions to drain the pus, but Cumberland refused to be tied down for the operation and to Ranby's embarrassment insisted on holding the candle himself. Halfway through the operation, Cumberland shouted 'Hold!'

'For God's sake,' Ranby protested, 'let me proceed now; it will be worse to renew it.'

'I say hold,' the patient repeated, then instructed staff standing by to fetch Ranby a clean cap and waistcoat for 'the poor man has sweat through these.'[11] It is recorded that Cumberland never uttered so much as a groan, and before the end of the second meeting was out on the course in his carriage.

Throughout that winter Cumberland's health continued to give serious concern to those close to him. As well as his bad knee, intermittent asthma and the effects of stroke, his corpulence was far beyond healthy limits. According to Walpole he had been estimated at twenty stone some years earlier, and rather than shedding weight he had since added more. Some of his contemporaries claimed that he was also half blind, and it does appear that apart from the drooping eye resulting from his first stroke, he had suffered from some undefined ailment in that eye while in Holland fifteen years earlier; but to judge from his firm clear handwriting he had no trouble with the sight in his other eye.

Yet he refused to curtail his activities. In February, 1765, he was again taken ill, after being seen dancing cotillions at Almack's New Rooms, and this time it was serious: another stroke which convinced even the Duke that he must take to his bed. He was repeatedly blooded and, not surprisingly, became weaker and weaker. At one stage, asked whether he thought he would recover, he dryly observed that if he had been the son of a poor man he probably would but as he was a prince it was doubtful. Wintringham, the physician now attending him, was more in earnest; there seemed to be nothing he could do for the Duke.

Newcastle was in despair, especially as he had just lost another close friend and ally, the Duke of Devonshire, whose company Cumberland himself had much enjoyed. At forty-four Devonshire had been in failing health for some time and he died at Spa in Belgium while seeking a cure in the famous waters. From Cumberland's Irish valet, Peter Faddy, Newcastle learnt on 1 March that the Duke 'has not been so well these five months' but that he was recovering: 'sleeps well and quietly – out for 3-4 hours on fine days in the chaise and has a good appetite – not sleepy at all at dinner time.'[12] And on the 3rd Albemarle was astonished to find the patient much recovered: 'H.R.H. looks well, articulates much better, sleeps very little in the day and is in prodigious good spirits.'[13] On the 10th, Ranby and Wintringham agreed that the Duke would pull through.

And once again, the King too had been ill. It had begun with a bad cold in the middle of January, but from 25 February until 10 March the King was unable to receive even the Prime Minister. This was not the first such episode of mysterious illness, and the poor King would suffer many more attacks before finally, in his seventies, losing all contact with reality. As clinical historians now believe, he was suffering acute intermittent porphyria, a metabolic disease whose symptoms include abdominal pain and mental confusion of varying degrees of severity. But Cumberland was certainly unaware of the seriousness of his nephew's condition until 7 April, 1765, when the King invited him to Kew for an informal discussion.

# 28

---

# The Last Act

---

WHEN NEWCASTLE CALLED IN AT WINDSOR towards the end of March he was horrified to hear that Cumberland intended going to Newmarket races on Easter Monday. 'You must all insist with H.R.H. to take unusual care of himself,' he wrote to Rockingham on the 26th. And he added, 'I am afraid the King is not quite perfectly recovered.'[1] But as Cumberland found, the King was well enough to be aware of the constitutional difficulties his illness was causing. Grenville was apt to dismiss the King's fears but George III, while his heir was still a minor, had to consider the possible need for a regency. It was to discuss this matter that the King had invited Cumberland to Kew on 7 April.

After enquiring over his uncle's health and judging him to be as fit of mind as he had always been, the King made it clear that he had already instructed Grenville to start drawing up a new regency bill. Cumberland was doubly shaken: that his nephew had really been so ill, and that another regency crisis seemed to be looming. The King then began to expatiate on his dislike for his ministers, particularly Grenville and Bedford; they had no 'foreign system' and the new conquests were being neglected. Indeed, there was already a row brewing with France over the Newfoundland fisheries. Grenville was interested only in restoring the nation's finances and paid no heed to matters of policy and position in the international community.

It seemed that the King wanted Cumberland's help in removing the Grenville administration.

At Newmarket the following day Cumberland was given further food for thought when the Earl of Northumberland, whose son was married to Bute's daughter, approached him with more details of the King's dissatisfaction with his ministers. They agreed to talk again at court the following week. On 14 April they duly met and Cumberland mentioned that for legal reasons he did not want to interfere until the regency bill had been agreed; above all he wanted to avoid the ludicrous situation that had arisen during 1751.

Suddenly Northumberland seemed embarrassed, though it was not until Cumberland had returned to Windsor that he discovered why. His name had not been included in the list of members of the proposed regency council.

This was not the King's doing but Grenville's, and when Albemarle spoke to the King on Cumberland's behalf the King immediately ordered an amendment to include Cumberland's name on the council. Another mistake that Grenville made was to omit the Princess Dowager's name, on the grounds that she was not a British subject and would not be acceptable to the nation. The King was livid. Grenville was forced to back down when an enactment in Parliament raised hardly a murmur, but the King remained furiously hostile towards him.

Cumberland was kept in touch with the King's plans by Northumberland, and realized that he might at any moment be called upon to create the next administration. Newcastle had irritated him by standing up in the House of Lords and calling on the King to name a regent, which as Cumberland well knew the King was loath to do; duly rebuked, Newcastle had promised to meddle no further. Pitt was now the main name left for Cumberland to conjure with.

In May Cumberland received the call he was expecting. He summoned the Duke of Grafton and told him straight out: 'The King was totally dissatisfied with the present ministry.'[2] George III had already agreed to exclude Bute and to accept Pitt if Cumberland could get him. Now Cumberland planned to approach Pitt, Temple and Rockingham, and was offering Grafton the Board of Trade. But Grafton politely refused, claiming he preferred the idle country life. It was not a good start.

On 18 May Cumberland visited the King at Kew and won approval for a formal visit to Hayes, escorted by a troop of Household Cavalry. His plan was to enlist Temple's support in persuading Pitt to join the new ministry. Pitt, as always, was the central figure in Cumberland's thoughts, the one man who could control the Commons and help the King. The following day, with his fine escort and much brouhaha, Cumberland drove over to Hayes. Temple, as requested, joined him there and together they wrestled over terms for five hours. To no avail. Pitt was his usual proud, stubborn, unhelpful self. Furthermore, Temple was strangely restrained in his backing for Cumberland's plans.

Sadly Cumberland had to tell his nephew that he had failed. Meanwhile there had arisen another crisis in which the King required his assistance. A bill had come before Parliament to limit the importation of foreign silk, so as to protect the weavers of Spitalfields; but Bedford had caused the bill to be thrown out. Now the weavers had taken to the streets and riots were breaking out, threatening the royal family and particularly Bedford's house in Bloomsbury. The King effectively wanted his uncle to resume his position as Captain-General, and to call out the troops; but Cumberland demurred, saying he thought it was hardly necessary to make a campaign against 'such poor wretches.' A guard of Household Cavalry on Bedford House sufficed.

Still Cumberland worried away at the possible combinations for a new ministry for the King. Throughout the second half of May he was coming and going, exchanging letters and messages, fretting, losing sleep and generally doing his utmost to produce an alternative to the detested Grenville regime. He tried Lyttelton, another of Pitt's relations by marriage. He tried Newcastle. But even Newcastle turned him down; without Pitt, there was no hope that he could manage the Commons. Cumberland was forced eventually to conclude that the King would have to keep Grenville and Bedford.

It was a bitter moment for both the King and his uncle. Luckily there was a short interlude from the mad carousel of politics: on 24 May it was the King's birthday, and Cumberland was invited to dine with the King and Queen at St James's and to attend the celebration ball afterwards in their company. On the following Monday the King and Queen further honoured Cumberland by dining with him at Windsor, and for the first time they attended the Ascot races.

On 12 June the King asked Cumberland to press on with forming a new ministry. He had granted an audience that day to Bedford who, with an insolence born of knowing that his position was secure, gave the King a list of demands that he and Grenville wished to be met if they were to continue in office. Once again the Duke trailed down to Hayes to talk with Pitt. On the 18th they argued almost through the night. On the 19th they spent three hours in audience with the King. Pitt did most of the talking. He too had a list of men and measures for the King to swallow. He wanted a triple alliance with Prussia and Russia. He wanted sacked military officers reinstated — which would rescue Conway — and general warrants made illegal. Pratt was to be made Chancellor. Many of Bute's followers were to be removed. The King agreed and asked Cumberland to arrange another meeting with Pitt.

Cumberland felt that success was at last within his grasp. He urged Grafton to reconsider. Temple was alerted to await the call. On the 22nd Pitt returned to see the King, and proved that he had mellowed; he would allow the King to retain a whole posse of Tories in junior posts. But two days later Temple visited his brother-in-law at Hayes and suddenly the whole deal foundered. Temple refused to join the new administration.

Was this a convenient excuse for Pitt to pull out, or were his protestations of regret to Cumberland sincere? He wrote to the Duke 'to express how much it confounds me to occasion so much trouble to your Royal Highness.'[3] But on 25 June Pitt broke off the negotiations. Cumberland believed him to be genuinely mortified at Temple's fastidiousness. What Temple had been too cowardly to say outright was that he was prepared to serve in an administration formed by the Duke of Cumberland but only if the Duke subsequently faded out of the picture. He had, moreover, patched up the disagreement with his brother Grenville, and felt that by joining Pitt and Cumberland he would be in some way betraying the family.

After all his efforts, all the visits and talks, all the hopeful notes to Pitt signed 'your very affectionate friend William', Cumberland now became very despondent. Pitt would not reconsider his decision. Newcastle, knowing only that something was in the air and still believing Pitt to be considering terms, pressed Cumberland to continue his efforts. Evidently he had pressed too far; the following day he wrote to Albemarle to apologize: 'The Duke seemed vexed with me.'[4] Newcastle now summoned all his friends for a working dinner at Claremont. But he knew that it all still rested with Cumberland. As he had written in a letter to Rockingham, 'The Duke of Cumberland is and ought to be at our head.'[5]

Grimly Cumberland battled on. If Pitt would not come in, then he would have to form an administration without him. After talking to Newcastle, Rockingham, Grafton, Conway and others, he began to see a glimmer of new hope. On 5 July he went to the King and suggested Rockingham as the new prime minister. The King indicated that he would be agreeable, but how about the rest of the team? Cumberland went away and thought some more.

By 21 July it was settled. George III had a brand new administration – which Edward Gibbon described as 'unparalleled in our History' in that all four most senior posts had gone to men who 'were never in any public office before.'[6] Rockingham himself was only thirty-five, known to the public if at all for his love of horse racing, and so diffident that he could hardly bring himself to address the House of Lords. The new Chancellor of the Exchequer was to be William Dowdeswell, a Tory who had nevertheless found favour among the Whigs. Grafton, at the age of thirty, was made the new Secretary of State (North), while Conway, taking over the southern department, was the eldest of the leading ministers at forty-four. Newcastle was obliged to be content with the post of Lord Privy Seal.

To some the ministry was 'a thing of shreds and patches not likely to last a twelve-month.'[7] The ministers were said to be 'persons called from the Stud to the State and transformed miraculously out of jockeys into Ministers.'[8] Grenville, Bedford and Sandwich were incredulous. Sandwich wrote, 'I will never believe it till I see it with my own eyes – the most rash attempt that ever was made.'[9] They claimed to see Bute's hand in this as well as Cumberland's. But most pathetic of all is the reaction of the Baron Holland, Cumberland's erstwhile friend Fox, who on 18 July wrote a begging letter to Cumberland although addressed to Albemarle. It ended:

I can with the strictest truth affirm solemnly that my affection was never alienated one moment from H.R.H., my gratitude never lessened. H.M. (with whom H.R.H. has had lately much discourse I hear) could if he pleased give ample testimony of this. But it may be said why should the Duke forgive and see me?

I don't presume to have an answer soon — when it does come it's the whole difference between a cheerful and a discontented decline of life — to my dear Lord, yrs etc.

P.S. Nobody knows or will know that I have had the courage to write this letter.[10]

But H.R.H. was too weary and disinclined to play Fox's little games now. Although he had achieved a near miracle in forming a new administration, he still had to guide the tentative young ministers in their first halting steps in power. And by the end of July their first crisis was clamouring for attention.

# 29

# Death

Back at the beginning of 1765 when Cumberland was ill, a new act had been introduced by Grenville: the Stamp Act. The intention was to raise money by direct taxation on the colonies of North America and the West Indies by imposing a stamp duty on newspapers and legal documents, just as in Britain. At the time this measure had met very little opposition; the only notable MP to speak out against it was Conway. Now, however, the colonists themselves were up in arms over the Stamp Act and as summer turned to autumn it became clear that their resentment was not going to disappear.

Cumberland was not technically involved, but the new ministers were constantly in and out of his London house, asking advice and seeking support. Newcastle remained anxious about the Duke's health, although in August Peter Faddy assured him that his master was 'as well as your grace could wish though he did not eat so much as he did some time ago.'[1] Early in September Newcastle approached Cumberland with grumbles about the inexperienced young ministry, particularly Rockingham who lacked confidence, yet was disinclined to consult his colleagues over decisions. Newcastle wanted Cumberland to ask the King for a dissolution and new elections; he undoubtedly thought to strengthen his own position. In the middle of the month he followed this up with a long and reasoned letter to Albemarle, repeating his belief that the present administration could not survive and that it would be better to go to the country at a time to suit the King.

Cumberland sympathized with his old friend but knew that Newcastle's motives were not untainted with jealously. For the time being he believed that Rockingham could survive. Besides, at the very time that Newcastle was worrying him with his proposals, Faddy wrote from Cumberland House to say that his master had asked to see Wintringham:

H.R.H. told Sir C.W. that he was better in every part of his body but his legs are so very weak that he is not able to follow the birds a yard. He dines with Princess Amelia tonight and goes to Windsor after.[2]

Windsor always helped to restore Cumberland's health, and although he had to return to London for a couple of cabinet meetings – a round journey of two and a half hours by chaise – as Faddy reported to Newcastle, 'The journey did H.R.H. a lot of good. I have never seen him so lively.'[3]

One of the meetings was held at Cumberland House on 13 October to discuss the growing uproar in North America over the Stamp Act. The colonists' attitude was not fully understood in London. The troops in America were now costing the British taxpayer some £350,000 a year, to which the Stamp Act might contribute £100,000. But as the Virginia Resolution averred, there should be no taxation without representation; although the colonists still regarded themselves as British subjects, they had no representatives in Britain.

At the meeting of the 13th, the Earl of Northington, as Lord Chancellor, recommended the use of force to subdue the unrest in America. The use of force had been debated as early as 30 August, but was then regarded as unnecessary. Now a compromise solution was found, ordering 'lenient and persuasive measures to be adopted wherever possible with such a timely exertion of force as the occasion may require.'[4] This was very far from ordering out-and-out military repression as some of the Duke's enemies later suggested. On the contrary, Cumberland always tended to share the liberal views of his old friend and chaplain, Bishop Shipley, his former ADC Lord Frederick Cavendish, and the Duke of Richmond, all of whom later proved themselves staunch supporters of American independence. And it was his old friend Conway, with Rockingham, who would in due course move the repeal of the Stamp Act.

As usual, however, Cumberland escaped from the cares and responsibilities of London by attending the autumn meetings at Newmarket. He claimed that he felt much stronger on his legs. Indeed, in between meetings he went off to Norfolk to shoot partridges. Yet even now he was pursued by duties. Holland (Fox), having received no answer to his letter to Albemarle, had approached Rockingham for some sign of approval and Rockingham had requested Cumberland's advice. In his own hand, in a letter from Newmarket on 21 October, Cumberland wrote back, 'I am highly sensible of your delicacy towards me in not deciding on the propriety of this measure... without my opinion on the subject.' His advice was shrewd: 'Let the measure be his and acceptance only on your side.' In other words, Rockingham should see Holland and listen to whatever he said, but pay no real attention. 'Excuse the hurry of this letter and assure yourself that I am as jealous of your honour as you yourself can be, ever your most sincerely affectionate friend, William.'[5]

It is the last letter that Cumberland is known to have written personally. That night he had 'a prodigious good sleep', Faddy wrote to Newcastle, and he remained at Newmarket for a few days more, although 'keeping better hours than this last fortnight except one night up till 4 am.'[6] On 28 October he returned to London. He had had a slight cold, though Faddy assured Newcastle that it had cleared. After arranging a cabinet meeting for seven o'clock on Thursday the 31st, to be held at his house in London, he then returned to Windsor. Apart from catching up on sleep and playing dozy games of piquet with Studholme Hodgson, he did very little for the next day or two and arrived in London on the afternoon of the 31st.

At court Cumberland talked to the King and afterwards took tea with his niece, the Duchess of Brunswick, then dined with Albemarle in Arlington Street. No doubt their conversation centred on the business before the cabinet meeting that evening: chiefly North America. But on reaching Cumberland House the Duke complained of a pain in his shoulder. His breath was shallow and he felt cold and shivery. Although the cabinet ministers were already assembling, he let Albemarle lead him to another room to lie down. Suddenly he gasped, 'It is all over!' and collapsed to the floor.

Newcastle and Northumberland were called in to help carry the great motionless body to a couch while Wintringham was sent for. The physician arrived only minutes later and drew off blood, but to no avail. After twenty minutes he pronounced his patient dead.

Newcastle's grief was uncontrolled. Everyone was stunned. Rockingham at once sent word to the King and Princess Amelia. No one could believe that Cumberland was really gone. He was only forty-four. He had been a huge presence in their lives. He had been such a wise and calm influence – to the King himself, to the young Prime Minister, to old Newcastle, to everyone. He would be very sadly missed.

Cumberland had died intestate, but the King took the obvious and practical step of appointing Albemarle to administer his late employer's estate. When Albemarle offered the key of Cumberland's cabinet of private papers to the King, he returned it at once, asking Albemarle to 'destroy everything that his uncle, if living, might have desired to keep concealed.'[7] But the cabinet, which Cumberland kept in his bedroom, contained only a few letters. With his usual caution and efficiency, he had burnt all those he did not wish his librarian to keep just before leaving for Newmarket.

In fact Albemarle's main duty was to settle the Duke's outstanding bills, totalling more than £22,000. These included £682 10s owed to Sir Joshua

Reynolds, for some eighteen portraits that Cumberland had given to family and friends; £2,488 to Thomas Herring, the silversmith, for a service of plate; and £53 to Josiah Hancock for three pairs of Sheffield plate candlesticks. It seems that Cumberland's annual expenses, in the last year or two of his life, had reached roughly £50,000, hugely exceeding his regular annual income of £40,000; his winnings from the turf cannot be assessed, but obviously did not cover his costs for we know that as recently as October, just before Newmarket, he had borrowed £4,500 from Albemarle. His stud was broken up and most of it sold at Tattersalls that December for less than £1,200, including the unbroken colt, Eclipse, that would have surely brought him financial rewards to match a justified satisfaction.

The lease on the London house was sold, the lodge and rangership of Windsor reverted to the Crown, as did the racing lodge at Newmarket, and also the hundreds of maps bought and created to the Duke's instructions. For his forty-four years there seems to have been little to show; but what he had left behind was intangible. There is a cartoon entitled 'Lying in State' published at the time of his funeral, that sums up his achievements as victory over the Devil, Pope and Pretender,[8] and another entitled 'The Tombstone' which praises him for 'selecting a Ministry out of those virtuous few who gloriously withstood General Warrants, American Stamps, Extensions of Excise, etc, etc, etc.'[9] Yet there was so much more to applaud, most notably his army reforms. Although the officer corps continued to resist the changes he introduced, Cumberland was still held in affectionate memory by the rank-and-file. Indeed, even some of the officers saw the value of the reforms he had wrought, and more than thirty years later, in 1798, David Dundas was to deplore the falling professional standards: 'Our army had gradually suffered in some of these material respects from the death of the old Duke of Cumberland.'[10] Not until the appointment of Cumberland's great-nephew, Frederick Duke of York, did the British army gain a comparable commander-in-chief.

The political consequences of Cumberland's death were even more immediate. 'The poor, able and respectable Duke of Cumberland is no more,' Rockingham wrote quaintly to his wife, lamenting the loss of 'so respected and intimate a friend.'[11] But it was Rockingham's secretary, that marvellously gifted Irishman, Edmund Burke, writing in *The Annual Register*, who let his pen run to warmest effect:

> The loss of their illustrious friend and patron seemed at this period to be truly critical to the ministry; his influence, his authority, his good sense, his patriotism and the high regard the public held him in would have added greatly to their strength and security.[12]

As it was, the Rockingham ministry was swept away within a year. Pitt, although voicing strong support for Rockingham's policies, refused to join his ministry and only returned to office in July, 1766, when Rockingham was dismissed; however, incapacitated both by gout and by his constitutional inability to compromise, he remained a constant thorn in the flesh of government.

The King had ordered a private funeral for his uncle, but with the full honours due to a Captain-General. The nation went into general mourning, with tailors taking on extra labour to meet the demand for mourning bands. At last, on the morning of 9 November, to the sound of minute guns booming in the Tower of London, a farewell salute of 21 guns in the Park and a triple volley from three battalions of Guards lining the route, in the chapel of Henry VII in Westminster Abbey the Duke of Cumberland was laid to rest. Eight generals upheld a canopy over the bier: the Duke of Grafton was chief mourner.

# 30

# Epilogue

THE CUMBERLAND OBELISK in Windsor Great Park is still standing, despite the vicissitudes of time and opinion alike. Originally the shaft bore the word CULLODEN but this was erased on the orders of Queen Victoria, who considered it a tactless reminder of what a guidebook of 1864 called 'a victory which is gladly forgotten.' Two of Victoria's uncles, Cumberland's great-nephews, also left their mark on the obelisk. George IV, in a burst of self-glorification inscribed his own name; this was later erased, but William IV's inscription, half hidden now by ivy, still adorns one side of the base, informing the world that the monument stands not for Cumberland's immodesty but for George II's paternal benevolence.

Another monument comprised a handsome equestrian statue of the Duke, erected, five years after his death, in Cavendish Square at private expense; the lead statue was removed a century later by the Duke of Portland, who claimed that it represented a public hazard, but the stone base may still be seen with its triumphal inscription. And even today Cumberland is chiefly associated with Culloden. No less a Scotsman than James Boswell, who initially greeted news of Cumberland's death with malicious delight, later noted:

> My very honourable friend, General Sir George Howard, who served in the Duke of Cumberland's army, has assured me that the cruelties [of the Culloden campaign] were not imputable to His Royal Highness.[1]

But with the Jacobite threat contained and finally judged to be extinct, Culloden came to be regarded even by the English as an embarrassing episode and Cumberland's achievement as best forgotten.

The man who was defeated at Culloden outlived his opponent by more than twenty years. The Pretender himself died in January, 1766; and, after half a life spent in exile and heavy drinking, abusing his mistress, abandoned by his wife, ashamed of his illegitimate daughter, Charles Stuart died in Rome on 31 January, 1788. He was in fact a man to be pitied, yet somehow was transformed by myth into 'Bonnie Prince Charlie.' Such is the British propensity to exalt the loser.

Writing his memoirs in the late 1750s, shortly after the humiliation of Kloster Zeven, the Earl Waldegrave described Cumberland as 'too much guided by his passions, which are often violent and ungovernable' but stood up for his reputation over Scotland:

> All his good qualities were overlooked; all his faults were aggravated. False facts were advanced against him and false conclusions drawn from them.[2]

And Horace Walpole was very clear who was responsible: the Scotch, the Jacobites and others who were jealous of Cumberland, who 'never rested until they had propagated such stories of his tyranny and severity as entirely lost him the heart of the nation.'[3] But, while Cumberland was never a man to court popularity – he had too much personal dignity for that – he did win the warm affection and loyalty of those who knew him well. Only the self-seeking Fox and frivolous Sandwich ever betrayed his friendship, whereas Albemarle, who knew him all his life, remained devoted to him to the end. And it was Walpole, writing in his more mature years, who ranked the Duke as one of the five greatest Englishmen of his time. Furthermore, Walpole judged that Cumberland would have made a good king: 'You would have loved him, if you had not feared him.'[4]

As a prince, a soldier, a statesman, the Duke of Cumberland had reached both the heights of public acclaim and the depths of infamy: yet he was neither the conquering hero exalted by Handel nor the butcher condemned by the Jacobites. As Waldegrave further noted, Cumberland had his own standards of honour and generosity, 'worthy of a prince', and by these he abided. Often impatient, sometimes haughty, occasionally guilty of misjudgement, he nevertheless served Crown and country with indefatigable energy and sense. If he sometimes wished that he were not a king's son but an ordinary country gentleman able to indulge his passion for horses and racing, he could never be accused of neglecting his royal duty. It is useless to speculate what more he might have achieved if he had been spared for a few extra years, but what is undeniably true is that Cumberland had died at the height of his power and influence.[5] The man whom history has tagged 'the Butcher' deserves a nobler niche: perhaps he ought rather to be known, as he was known to his contemporaries, simply as 'the Duke.'

# Notes On Sources

1. For full book titles, see Bibliography.
2. *Abbreviations used below:*

Add. MSS    British Library Additional Manuscripts
BL          British Library
CP          Cumberland Papers
CRO         County Record Office
DNB         Dictionary of National Biography
EHR         English Historical Review
RA          Royal Archives, Windsor
HMC         Historical Manuscripts Commission
PRO         Public Record Office

*Chapter 1: The Early Years*

1. As William's governor, Poyntz regularly presented his household accounts to Queen Caroline for approval; they are preserved in the Spencer archives at Althorp (one of Poyntz's daughters married into the Spencer family).
2. Sedgwick, *Lord Hervey's Memoirs*, p.246.

*Chapter 2: By Land and Sea*

1. HMC Egmont, 3 vols, 1920; Diary II, 330
2. Diary of Lord Peter King, 24 June, 1725, quoted in Campbell, *Lives of the Chancellors*, vol. IV; King notes that Walpole told him this.
3. Bielfeld Letters Vol. IV, No. XXIX 1770.
4. Quoted in Charteris I, p.66.
5. HMC Egmont Diary III, 4, 1739.
6. Ibid.
7. Bielfeld Letters Vol. IV, No. XXIX 1770.
8. Bingley, *Correspondence of Lady Hartford*.
9. Ibid.
10. Ibid.
11. Norris's diary, Add. MSS 18, 133.
12. Poyntz to Newcastle (24 July, 1740), Add. MSS 32,694.

Chapter 3; The Battle of Dettingen

1. HMC Egmont Diary III, February, 1742.
2. Carteret to Newcastle (22 May, 1743), Add. MSS 32,700.
3. Willson, *Life and Letters of James Wolfe*.
4. Richmond to Newcastle (29 June, 1743), Add. MSS 32,700.
5. HMC, Frankland Russell Astley Papers (p.232 onwards for Cumberland's part in the campaign).
6. Ranby, *Treatment of Gunshot Wounds*, p.37.
7. Richmond to Newcastle (19 June, 1743), Add. MSS 32,700.
8. Cumberland to Newcastle (20 July, 1743), Add. MSS 32,700.

Chapter 4: Invasion Threat

1. Hay to Newcastle (20 July, 1743), Add. MSS 32,700.
2. State Archive, Hesse Darmstadt, Sign Abt D4Nr 502/2.
3. HMC, Frankland Russell Astley Papers p.299.
4. Lewis (ed), *Letters of Horace Walpole*, vol. I, p.391.

Chapter 5: Captain-General

1. Coxe, *Lord Walpole*, vol. II, p.225 (1798).
2. Poyntz to Trevor, quoted in Charteris I, p.163.

Chapter 6: Fontenoy

1. RA, Cumberland Papers 2/96.
2. RA, Cumberland Papers 2/147.
3. Add. MSS 35,363; and see Yorke, *Life of Hardwicke*.
4. See DNB. The Benedictine priest did come to England, as Father Alban Butler, chaplain to the Duke of Norfolk; and Cumberland did give him special protection. The Bishop of Norwich had confiscated certain papers that the priest was using for research into the lives of the saints, but Cumberland personally intervened, ordering the papers to be returned as necessary for the work of Catholic scholarship.
5. Richard Lyttelton to his father, quoted in Maud Wyndham, *Chronicles of the Eighteenth Century*.
6. *Reading Mercury*, 27 May, 1745.
7. RA, Cumberland Papers 3/36, 7 June 1745.
8. RA, Cumberland Papers 2/212, 21 May 1745.
9. H Walpole to Sir H Mann 24 May, Lewis.
10. Royal House-Archive The Hague. MS. A17, No. 430.
11. Quoted by Fawkener in a letter to Newcastle (14 June 1745), Add. MSS 32,704.
12. Undated letter (ends 'Burn this nonsense') in the Spencer Papers (with Poyntz Papers) at Althorp.

Chapter 7: The Rebellion of '45

1. Cumberland to Newcastle 28 July (N.S.) RA. C.P. 4/30.
2. Trevor to Cumberland (31 August, 1745), RA Cumberland Papers 4/209.
3. Cumberland to Ligonier (12 October, 1745), RA Cumberland Papers 4/220.
4. Cumberland to Harrington (14 October, 1745), RA Cumberland Papers 4/223.
5. Harrington to Cumberland and (19 October 1745) RA Cumberland Papers, 4/228.

6. Cumberland to Newcastle (6 September 1745), RA Cumberland Papers BL. Add. MSS. 32,705.
7. Quoted in Gordon Lennox, *A Duke and His Friends*.
8. Tyrawley to Newcastle (25 November, 1745), PRO State Papers, Scotland 36/75.
9. William Harris, quoted in Malmesbury's *Letters of the 1st Earl*.

*Chapter 8: Carlisle and Back*

1. Conway to Walpole (30 November, 1745) Lewis. Vol. 37.2. Thomas Anson to his brother George: see Anson Papers, Add. MSS 15,955.
3. Ibid.
4. Joseph Yorke, quoted in P. Yorke *Life of Hardwicke*.
5. Joseph Yorke to his father, Lord Hardwicke (15 December 1745), quoted in P. Yorke, op. cit.
6. *Transactions, Cumberland and Westmorland Archaeological Society*, 'Clifton Moor' Vol. X, pp.186-228.
7. Ibid.
8. Bateman to Duke of Devonshire (7 December, 1745), Chatsworth Papers, Chatsworth.
9. The run on the Bank was in September, after Prestonpans. By the time of Cumberland's return the financial markets had steadied. See Clapham, *The Bank of England*, p.233-4.
10. HMC Lothian MSS, 7 December 1745.
11. Add. MSS 32,700 (6 January 1746).

*Chapter 9: Pursuit in Scotland*

1. PRO, SP 36/78.
2. Hawley to Cumberland (17 January 1746), RA Cumberland Papers 9/99.
3. Burt, quoted in *Letters from a Gentleman*. Wade's report of 1725 is in RA Cumberland Papers 61/B2.
4. Blackwell report contained in RA Cumberland Papers 68/XI/137.
5. Letter written by a Captain Martin, quoted in Gordon Lennox, *A Duke and His Friends*.
6. Ibid.
7. Fletcher to Newcastle (1 February 1746), quoted in Charteris I, p.246.
8. Cumberland to Newcastle (30 January 1746), quoted in Charteris I, p.247-8.
9. Conway to H. Walpole, letter dated 7 February 1746, at Perth. Lewis Vol 37.
10. Ibid.
11. B.L. Add MSS 35,354 folio 191.
12. Quoted in P. Yorke, op. cit.
13. This is a paraphrase of the proclamation approved by the Lord Justice Clerk in Edinburgh. See *Gentleman's Magazine*, 1746, pp. 235-6.
14. Joseph Yorke's Order Book, Add. MSS 36,257.
15. Mrs Oliphant quoted in Charteris I, p.275.
16. R. Robertson to Duke of Atholl (7 February 1746), Atholl MSS, HMC.
17. Cumberland to Newcastle (14 march 1746), Aberdeen Add. MSS 32,706.
18. Hardwicke returns Cumberland's letter to Newcastle with sympathetic comment. Add MSS 32,707 folio 13.
19. Cumberland to Newcastle, Add. MSS 32,706, 4 April.

*Chapter 10: Culloden*

1. Conway to Walpole (6 April 1746). Lewis Vol. 37.
2. Alexander Taylor, quoted in Leask and McCance Regimental History, *The Royal Scots*, Thom & Co. Dublin, 1915, p.149.
3. *Journal of the Society for Army Historical Research*, Vol. XXIV, p.24.
4. Cumberland (18 April 1745), PRO SP 54/30.

*Chapter 11: Aftermath*

1. RA 52875, 24 April 1746.
2. B.L. Stowe MS 142 f. 113.
3. Quoted in Charteris I, p.281.
4. Collins, 'Ode on the Highland Superstitions.'
5. A postscript to Fawkener's letter of 29 April, Inverness. MS 3581 (viii) f.20-24, National Library of Scotland.
6. Northumberland CRO, Brackett Ord Papers, ZAN M12/C39 f.55; also RA CP 24 f. 385.
7. Quoted in Findlay, *Wolfe in Scotland*.
8. Add. MSS 32,707 f. 87.
9. Ibid.
10. Michael Hughes, cited in Speck, *The Butcher*, p.170.
11. Forbes, *Culloden Papers*, Vol. V, p.104.
12. Ibid, p. 110.
13. RA CP 15 f. 101.
14. RA CP 15 f. 271.
15. Ashe Lee to Fox, 31 May 1746, Holland House Papers.
16. George Sackville to Duke of Dorset, Fort Augustus, 24 June, Kent CRO, De La Warr MSS, U269 c142/8.
17. National Library of Scotland, Campbell of Mamore MS 374/74.

*Chapter 12: Conquering Hero*

1. Forbes, cited in C. L. Kingsford, 'Highland Forts 1745-6' EHR 1922.
2. Marchioness Grey to Mrs Gregory, letter of 26 July 1746, Bedford CRO, L. 30.
3. Forbes, *Culloden Papers*, Vol. V, p.134.
4. Fawkener to Poyntz, Inverness, 20 May 1746, Nottingham University Library, NEC 1,744.
5. Ibid.
6. Figures taken from Seton and Arnob, *Prisoners of the '45*, Scottish History Society. See also Murray, *Forbes of Culloden*.
7. Albemarle to Richmond, 17 June 1746, Albemarle Papers, East Suffolk CRO.
8. Sackville to Duke of Dorset, 23 August 1746, Kent CRO, Maidstone, V 269 C142/9.
9. HMC Polwarth. V.
10. Ibid.
11. Paget and Whitley, *Letters of Thomas Gray*.

*Chapter 13: Back to Europe*

1. Chatsworth MSS. 249/34.
2. RA CP 39 f.116 encl.

3. Add. MSS 32,709 f. 258.
4. Ibid, f. 367.
5. Ibid, f. 384.
6. Saxe, *Lettres et Memoires*.

*Chapter 14: The Affair of Laffeldt*

1. Royal Artillery Order Book, MS 53, Woolwich RA Institution Library.
2. Ibid.
3. See *Gunner at Large* ed. Rex Whitworth, Leo Cooper 1988. MS Wood's Diary, RA Institution Woolwich Library.
4. Townshend MSS, National Army Museum Library.
5. HMC Russell-Frankland Papers p.372, Yorke to Colonel Barrington, enclosed in Russell's letter of 10 July.
6. Lewis, op. cit. Walpole to Montagu, 2 July, 1747.
7. Lewis, op. cit. Walpole to Sir H. Mann, 3 July, 1747.
8. Chatsworth MSS, Pelham's letter to Hartington, dated 29 June (OS).
9. Ibid, letter dated 28 July.
10. Ibid.
11. RA CP 8 Sept 1747.

*Chapter 15: Negotations*

1. Yorke, *Life and Correspondence of Hardwicke*, Vol. I, 654. Letter dated 11 April 1748 (NS).
2. Conway to Walpole, letter dated 29 April 1748 (NS), Lewis. Vol. 37.
3. Add. MSS 32,714 f.304.
4. Lord John Russell, *Correspondence of 4th Duke of Bedford*, Vol. II. Letter dated 10 October 1748.
5. Ibid. Letter dated 29 April 1748.
6. Cumberland to Newcastle in a private letter from Eindhoven, dated 31 July 1748, in reply to Newcastle's letters of 11, 23 and 24 July. RA CP 38.
7. Fox Correspondence, Roxburgh Club 1915.
8. Add. MSS 32,684 f. 68, September 1748.

*Chapter 16: Army Reform*

1. Chatsworth Papers, Pelham to Hartington, 1 September 1748.
2. Letter to Bland, 7 November 1748, Dorset CRO, D 86/X4.
3. RA CP 40/f. 141-f.259, October 1748.
4. Lord John Russell, *Correspondence of 4th Duke of Bedford*, Vol. II. Cumberland's letter dated 12 November (NS).
5. Dorset CRO, D 86/X4 Fox to Napier, letter dated 1 November (OS).
6. Paget and Whitley (ed.), *Letters of Thomas Gray*.
7. Houlding, *Fit for War: The Training of the British Army*.
8. Cumberland's letter, written on 2 December 1756 at St James's, is quoted in Pargellis, *Military Affairs in North America*, p.254. Based on Cumberland Papers at Windsor.
9. RA CP 43/12, 13.
10. Bodleian Library 23187 C3. See also Journals of House of Commons, 13 Feb-7 March 1749 (NS), Parliamentary History Vol XIV, pp.434-5.
11. RA CP 43/191, 10 April 1749.

*Chapter 17: Windsor*

1. Dorset CRO, D86/X4.
2. RA CP 44/9, 25 January 1750.
3. Letter to General Blakeney, 18 November 1750. Dorset CRO, D86/X4.
4. Letter, Vilworden, 26 Sept 1745. Goodwood Papers, West Sussex Record Office.
5. The man in question was Sgt Stevenson, whom Cumberland had promoted to a commission. Anecdote, one of three about Cumberland, in Colburn H. *George III, His Court and family*, 1820.
6. Cumberland to Loudoun, Pargellis op. cit. p.253.
7. Quoted in Charteris II p. 73.

*Chapter 18: The Regency Crisis*

1. Letter, H. Walpole to Sir Horace Mann, 21 March 1751.
2. Newcastle to Hardwicke, 10 August 1749, Add. MSS 35,410.
3. Sandwich to Newcastle, 29 August 1748, Add. MSS 32,716.
4. Newcastle to Pelham, from The Hague, 20 May 1750; see Coxe, *Administration of Henry Pelham*, Vol. II, pp.336-407.
5. Pelham to Newcastle, Coxe Vol. II.
6. Pelham to Fox, 7 June 1750; Holland House Papers, British Library.
7. Coxe, Vol. II.
8. Quoted in Brooke, *Walpole's Memoirs of George II*, Vol. II, p.103.
9. Yorke, *Life of Hardwicke*, Vol. II, p.46.
10. Quoted in Brooke, op. cit. Vol. I, p.71.
11. Fox's 'Letters' *Roxburgh Club* 1915.
12. Quoted in Charteris II p.76.
13. This comment is recorded in a letter of Lady Fawkener now in the Royal Archives: CP 57/200.
14. Lord John Russell, *Correspondence of 4th Duke of Bedford*.
15. Coxe, Vol. II.
16. Marquis de Matignon to Lady Denbigh. HMC 4 Denbigh.
17. Quoted in Brooke op. cit. Vol. I p.143. See also Add. MSS 9191, f. 110, Fox to H. Williams.

*Chapter 19: New Dimensions*

1. Quoted in Pargellis, *Military Affairs in North America*, pp. 8-9.
2. Fortescue, *History of the Army*, 1899, Book IX, chapter 2, p.264. See also Charteris Vol. II, p.118.
3. National Army Museum 8708-48-1. And see 'Journal of Colonel John Adlercron, 1754-7' RA CP 45 f. 47.
4. RA CP, Inventory 1765.
5. Rathbone (ed.), *Letters of Lady Jane Coke to Mrs Eyre*, 1899.
6. Newmarket Match Book, Jockey Club.
7. Add. MSS 32,736 (Robinson to Newcastle, 15 September 1754).
8. Add. MSS 32,736, f. 591 (Newcastle to Albemarle, 28 September 1754).
9. *Diplomatic Interventions: France*, Camden Society, 3rd series, Vol. XLIX.10. Quoted in Charteris Vol. II, p.126. See also Add. MSS 32,851, f. 564 (Robinson to Newcastle).

11. Add. MSS 32,737 f. 207 (26 october 1754).
12. Cumberland's verbal instruction was confirmed by Napier in writing to Braddock, RA CP 45/103.

*Chapter 20: Universal War*

1. Quoted in Pargellis, *Military Affairs in North America*, p.64.
2. See *Gentleman's Magazine*, April 1755.
3. Add. MSS 32,996, Cabinet Memoranda.
4. Quoted in Pargellis, p.82.
5. Quoted in Charteris Vol. II p.131. See also Beckles Willson, *Life and Letters of James Wolfe*.
6. Quoted in Fortescue, *History of the Army*, Book IX, chapter 2, p.279.
7. Add. MSS 35,393, f.232 (Cumberland to Robinson, 2 August 1755).
8. Add. MSS 32,858, f.291.
9. Add. MSS 32,858.
10. Quoted in Pargellis, p.137.
11. Chatsworth Papers (16 July 1755).
12. Add. MSS 51, 375 (Cumberland to Fox, 25 September 1755).
13. Quoted in Pargellis, p.251 (Cumberland to Loudoun, 2 December 1756).

*Chapter 21: First Blood*

1. B. L. Add MSS 32,858 August 25 meeting at Cumberland's rooms.
2. Add. MSS 51,387 (Fox: letter to Welbore Ellis, 12 June 1756).
3. Add. MSS 51,375 (Cumberland: letter to Fox, 31 May 1756).
4. Taylor and Pringle, *Correspondence of William Pitt*, Vol. IV.
5. Chatsworth papers 230 (Fox to Devonshire, 11 Oct 1756).
6. BL Holland House Papers (Bateman to Fox, 26 Oct 1756).
7. Quoted in Pargellis, p.262.
8. Quoted in Pargellis, p.263.
9. Quoted in Ayling, *Chatham*.
10. Basil Williams, *Pitt*, Vol. I p.305.

*Chapter 22: Sacrifice of Hanover*

1. Add. MSS 51,375.
2. Ibid.
3. RA 52967 (5 May).
4. The King's instructions are fully reproduced in Charteris Vol. II, Appendix II. The instructions were countersigned by the King's Electoral Minister, Munchausen. Although the English ministers paid for the Hessian contingent, they knew nothing of these instructions.
5. BL Holland House Papers, Add. MSS 51,375 (Cumberland to Fox, 2 May 1757).
6. Chatsworth Papers 397/29.
7. Chatsworth Papers 332/5 (Cumberland to Devonshire, 20 June).
8. Chatsworth Papers 332/3 (Cumberland to Devonshire, 23 May).9. Ibid.
10. Brooke, *Walpole's Memoirs of George II*, Vol. II, p.284.
11. Quoted in Coquelle, *L'Alliance Franco-Hollandaise*, pp.80-81.
12. Chatsworth Papers 397.
13. Charteris, Vol. II Appendix II.

*Chapter 23: Kloster Zeven*

1. There is a very full account of the battle in Chatsworth MSS 397/36.
2. Ibid.
3. RA Windsor Georgian 52970.
4. Ibid.
5. Add. MSS 32,872 (Newcastle to Hardwicke, 3 August 1757).
6. Add. MSS 32,997 (Newcastle to Lady Yarmouth, 17 September 1757).
7. Chatsworth MSS 33/25 (Cumberland to Devonshire, 20 June 1757).
8. RA CP 55/108.
9. RA CP 55/110.
10. Fox's 'Letters' *Roxburgh Club*, 1913.
11. Add. MSS 32,874 f.148 (Newcastle to Hardwicke, 18 September 1757).
12. RA CP 56/256.
13. RA CP 56/260.
14. Quoted in Brooke, *Walpole's Memoirs of George II*, Vol. II, p.282.

*Chapter 24: A Private Man*

1. Add. MSS 33,075.
2. Add. MSS 32,874.
3. Add. MSS 32,874 f 163. See also Fox's letter to Bedford, 12 October, in Russell Vol. II.
4. Brooke, *Walpole's Memoirs of George II*, Vol. II, p.284.
5. Lewis, *Letters of Horace Walpole*(to Selwyn, 11 October 1757).
6. Barrington Papers, Suffolk CRO, Ipswich, H4 174.
7. Quoted in Pargellis, op. cit. p.410.
8. Savory, *His Britannic Majesty's Army in Germany*, p.58.
9. Sandwich Papers, Mapperton MSS (16 August 1757).
10. Ibid.
11. Fox's 'Letters' *Roxburgh Club*, 1913 (29 August 1757).
12. Bodleian Library, eighteenth-century pamphlets.

*Chapter 25: Turn of the Tide*

1. Sedgwick, *Letters of George III to Lord Bute*.
2. Mortimer, *The Jockey Club*, p.20 et seq.
3. Walpole's letter (27 April 1758, to Horace Mann) is quoted in Charteris II pp.212-215.
4. Barker, *Walpole's Memoirs of George III*, p.82.
5. Lewis, *Letters of Horace Walpole* (to George Montagu, 13 November 1760).
6. Lucy Sutherland, *Fox as Paymaster*, EHR.7. Lewis, *Letters of Horace Walpole* (to Horace Mann, 10 September 1761).
8. PRO WO 34 (14 February).
9. RA CP 61/A/89 (Coote's diary).
10. RA CP 57/207 (9 November 1761).

*Chapter 26: The Peace of Paris*

1. Chatsworth MSS, fourth Duke of Devonshire's diary.
2. Ibid.
3. Add. MSS 32,937, April 1762.

4. British Museum 1762 – 3843 402/423 Cartoons.
5. RA CP (Windsor, 24 February 1762).
6. Ilchester, *Fox, Lord Holland* (3 August 1762).
7. Albemarle, *Memoirs of the Marquis of Rockingham*, Vol. I, pp.124-3.
8. Ibid.
9. Chatsworth MSS 332/18 (Cumberland to Devonshire, 15 October 1762).
10. Ilchester, op. cit. (2 November 1762).
11. Chatsworth MSS 332/20 (Cumberland to Devonshire, 31 October 1762).
12. Chatsworth MSS 332/19 (24 October).
13. Add. MSS 32,945 (Cumberland to Newcastle, 25 December 1762).
14. Barker, *Walpole's Memoirs of George III*.

*Chapter 27: Return to Duty*

1. Add. MSS 32,945 f.341.
2. Wesley's journal is quoted in Charteris II p.59.
3. Add. Mss 32,949, f.254 (Newcastle to Albemarle, 1 July 1763).
4. Ibid f.256.
5. Ibid.
6. Ibid, f.268 (4 July).
7. Bedford CRO, Robinson Papers L 31/108, September 1763.
8. Chatsworth MSS 332/23 (Newcastle sent a copy of Cumberland's letter to him to Devonshire, 13 September).
9. Add. MSS 32,952 (ff.141, 188 and 241) contains a detailed report of Cumberland's interview with Pitt on the Wilkes affair.
10. Ilchester and Stavordale, *Life and letters of Lady Sarah Lennox*.
11. Lewis, *Letters of Horace Walpole* (to Lord Hertford, 1 November 1764).
12. Add. MSS 32,966.
13. Ibid (Albermarle to Newcastle, 4 March 1765).

*Chapter 28: The Last Act*

1. Add. MSS 32,966 f.110.
2. Grafton MSS 423/248, East Suffolk CRO, Bury St Edmunds.
3. Pitt's letter, dated 18 June 1765, is in Taylor and Pringle, *Correspondence of Pitt, Earl of Chatham*.
4. Albermarle Papers, Suffolk CRO, Ipswich (2 July 1765).
5. Add MSS 32,967 folio 70 19 June.
6. Norton, *Edward Gibbon's Letters* (No.69 to Stanier Porten 1765).
7. Langford, *The First Rockingham Administration*, p.15.
8. Ibid.
9. Bedford Estates MSS 8/L11 (Sandwich to Bedford, 2 July).
10. Albemarle, *Memoirs of Rockingham*, Vol. I pp. 238-9.

*Chapter 29: Death*

1. Add. MSS 32,969 (Faddy to Newcastle, 21 August).
2. Ibid f.376 (13 September).
3. Add. MSS 32,970 (21 October).
4. Add. MSS 32,969 f.257 and 32,950 ff.80, 82. See also Henley MSS, Northampton CRO.
5. Albermarle, *Memoirs of Rockingham*, Vol. I p.243.

6. Add. MSS 32,970 (24 October).
7. Add. MSS 32,971 ff.224, 226. See also Albemarle, *Memoirs of Rockingham*, Vol. I pp.244-5.
8. British Museum No.4123 Cartoons.
9. British Museum No.4124 Cartoons.
10. Quoted in *Journal of Army Historical Research*Vol. XIV p.223.
11. Fitzwiliam MSS WWM R156, Sheffield Library.
12. *Annual Register*, 1765.

*Chapter 30: Epilogue*

1. *Boswell's Life of Johnson*, English Classics, Macmillan 1922, Vol. II p.136.
2. Lord Holland (ed.), *Memoirs of Waldegrave*.
3. Brooke, *Walpole's Memoirs of George II*, Vol. I p.70.
4. Ibid, Vol.III p.2.
5. See, for example, John Brooke, *King George III*, p.123: 'Had the Duke lived even twelve months longer, the political history of George III's reign would have been different.'
    Let Horace Walpole (*Memoirs of George III*, Vol.III, pp.222-227) have the last word: 'He would have made a great King, but probably too great a King for so corrupt a country'!

# Bibliography

Albemarle. *Memoirs of the Marquis of Rockingham*, 2 vols, London 1852
Anson, Sir W. R. *Autobiography and Correspondence of 3rd Duke of Grafton*, 1898
Arkell, R. L. *Caroline of Ansbach*, 1939
Arnett, A. von *Geschichte Maria Theresias*, Vienna 1863-79
Ayling, Stanley. *George III*, Collins 1922
Barker G. F. R. (ed). *Horace Walpole: Memoirs of the Reign of George III*, 4 vols, Yale 1894
Biddulph, J. *Stringer Lawrence*
Bingley, W. (ed). *Correspondence Frances, Countess of Hartford, and Henrietta, Countess of Pomfret*, 3 vols, 1805
Black, Robert *The Jockey Club and its Founders*, 1891
Brooke (ed). *Horace Walpole: Memoirs of the Reign of George II*, 3 vols, Yale 1985
Brooke, John. *King George III*, Constable 1972
Brown, P. D. *William Pitt*, 1978
Browning, Reed. *The Duke of Newcastle*, 1975.
Campbell, Lord John. *Lives of the Chancellors*, London 1857
Charteris, Evan. *William Augustus, Duke of Cumberland, 1721-1757*, 2 vols, 1913 and 1925
Chenevix-Trench, C. *George II*, Allen Lane 1973
Clapham, Sir J. *The Bank of England*, Cambridge University Press 1944
Clark, J. C. D. *The Dynamics of Change*, OUP 1982
Colburn, H. *George III, His Court and Family*, 1820
Colin, J. *Campagnes de Maurice de Saxe*, 1906
------- . *Louis XV et les Jacobites*, Projets de Debarquement
Cook, George. *Eclipse, and O'Kelly*, 1907
Coquelle, P. *L'Alliance France-Hollandaise 1735-88*
Corbett, Julian. *England in the Seven Years' War*, 2 vols, 1907
Coxe, W. *Lord Walpole*, 2 vols, 1798
------- . *Memoirs of Horatio Lord Walpole*, 2 vols, London 1808
Coxe, W. *Memoirs of the Administration of Henry Pelham*, 2 vols, 1829
Croker, J. (ed). *The Letters of Lady Suffolk*, 2 vols, 1824
Cruickshanks, Evelyn. *Political Untouchables*, Duckworth 1979
Davies, J. D. Griffith. *A King in Toils*, London 1938
Dobrée, B. *Letters of Lord Chesterfield*, 6 vols, 1932
Doddington, B. *Diary 1749-61*, London 1828
Doran, J. *Last Journals*, 2 vols, 1859
Dorn, W. L. *Competition for Empire*, New York 1940
Egremont, Lord. *HMC 16th Report*, 3 vols, 1920-23
Findlay, J. T. *Wolfe in Scotland*, Longmans 1928
Forbes. *Culloden Papers 1815*
Forster, Margaret *The Rash Adventurer*, Secker & Warburg 1961
Fortescue, Sir J. W. *Correspondence of George III*, 1927

------- . *History of the British Army*, 1899 Vol II
Hamilton, Sir F. *History of the Grenadier Guards*, 3 vols, 1874
Hare, J. P. *History of the Royal Buckhounds*, 1895
Henderson, A. *Life of the Duke of Cumberland*, London 1766
Holland, Lord (ed). *The Memoirs of Earl Waldegrave, 1757-8*, 1821
------- (ed). *Memoirs of the last Ten Years of George II*, 2 vols, 1822
Horn D. B. *England and Europe in the 18th Century*.
------- . *Sir Charles Hanbury Williams*, London 1930
Houlding, J. A. *Fit for War: The Training of the British Army 1715-1795*, Clarendon Press 1981
Ilchester, Earl of. *Henry Fox, Lord Holland*, 1920
Ilchester, Lady and Lady Stavordale (eds). *Life and Letters of Lady Sarah Lennox, 1745-1826,
with Political Sketch of the Years 1760-1763 by Henry Fox*, 2 vols, 1901-2
Jarvis, Rupert. *Collected Papers of the Jacobite Risings*, 2 vols, Manchester 1971
Jeanroy, Col. *Revue Historique de L'Armée 21946*, Fontenoy
Kriegsarchivs. *Erbfolgegrieg Band IX von le Beau & von Häodl*, Vienna 1914
Langford, P. *The First Rockingham Administration*, OUP 1973
Lanover (ed). *Autobiography and Correspondence of Mrs Delany*, 6 vols, 1861-2
Lehman, Bruce. *The Jacobite Risings*, Eyre Methuen 1980
Leask and McCance. *The Royal Scots*, Thom & Co. Dublin, 1915
Lennox, C. H. Gordon. *A Duke [2nd Duke of Richmond] and His Friends*, 2 vols, 1911
Lewis (Ed). *Letters of Horace Walpole*, Yale 1937 onwards
*Letters from a gentleman in the North of Scotland*, 2 vols, 1754 (5th edition 1815)
Lloyd, E. M. *A Review of the History of Infantry*, London 1908
Lodge, Sir R. *Correspondence of Newcastle and Chesterfield*, London 1930
McLachlan, A. N. Campbell. *A Sketch of Cumberland's Military Life*, 1876
Maclean, Sir John. *Poyntz Family Memoirs*, Exeter 1886
McLynn, F. J. *The Jacobite Army in England*, John Donald 1983
Malmesbury, Earl of. *The Letters of 1st Earl of Melmesbury and His Friends, 1745-1820*, 2 vols,
1870
Manners, W. E. *Marquis of Granby*, London 1899
Marples, M. *Poor Fred and the Butcher*, Michael Joseph 1970
Marshall, D. *Eighteenth Century England*, Longmans 1962
Marshall, John. *The Duke who was Cricket*.
Masson, F. *Bernis Memoirs*, Paris 1828
Menzies, W. *Windsor Park*, 1864
Middleton, R. *Pitt and Newcastle (unpublished thesis), Exeter University 1968*
Miles, H. D. *Pugilistica: A History of Boxing*, 2 vols
Mortimer, Roger. *The Jockey Club*, Cassell 1958
Murray, C. de B. *Forbes of Culloden*, IPC 1936
Namier, L. *Structure of Politics at the Accession of George III*, 1957
Norton, J. E. (ed). *Edward Gibbon's Letters*, 1956
Oliver, J. B. *The Rise of the Pelhams*, Oxford 1956
Onslow, R. *Newmarket and the Heath*, 1971
Paget and Whitley (ed). *Letters of Thomas Gray*, Oxford 1935
Pajol, C. *Les Guerres sous Louis XV*, 3 vols, 1886
Pargellis, S. *Lord Loudoun in North America*, Yale 1933
------- . *Military Affairs in North America, 1748-1765*, Appleton Century, New York 1936
Plumb, J. H. *Sir Robert Walpole*, 2 vols, Chatham 1953
Pond, J. *Racing Calendar from 1751 onwards*
Prebble, John. *Culloden*, Secker & Warburg 1961.
Pringle, Sir J. *Observations on the Nature and Cure of Hospital and Jayl Fevers*, 1750
------- . *Observations on the Diseases of the Army*, 1752
------- . *Discourse on ... Improvement for Preserving Health of Marines*, 1776
Prior, C. H. *History of the Racing Calendar and Stud Book*
Ranby, J. *Treatment of Gunshot Wounds*, 1744
Rathbone (ed). *Letters of Lady Jane Coke to Mrs Eyre, 1747-1758*, 1899
Richmond, H. W. *The Navy in the War of 1739-48*, 3 vols, 1920
Rolt, R. *Memoirs of the Duke of Cumberland*, London 1766

Rude, G. *Hanoverian London*, 1971
Russell, Lord John. *Correspondence of 4th Duke of Bedford*, 3 vols, 1842-6
Sandby, William. *Thomas and Paul Sandby*, London 1892
Savory, Sir R. *His Britannic Majesty's Army in Germany*, Clarendon Press 1966
Saxe, Maréchal de. *Espagnac, Histoire de Saxe*, Paris 1775
------- . *Lettres et Memoires*, Paris 1794
------- . *Mes Reveries*, 2 vols, Amsterdam 1757
Sedgwick, Romney (ed). *Letters of George III to Lord Bute*, 1939
------- . *Lord Hervey: Memoirs of the Reign of George II*, 1931
------- . *Lord Hervey's Memoirs. The Death of the Queen 1737*, Batsford 1963
Shepherd, E. W. *Coote Bahadur*, London 1956
Skrine, E. H. *Fontenoy and the War of Austrian Succession*, 1906
Smith, W. J. (ed). *The Grenville Papers*, 1852-3
Speck, W. A. *The Butcher*, Basil Blackwell 1981
Sutherland, Lucy. *The East India Company in the 18th Century*, 1952
Tayler, H. *History of the Rebellion 1745-6*, Oxford 1944
Taylor and Pringle (eds). *Correspondence of William Pitt, Earl of Chatham*, 4 vols, 1838-40
Terry, Sanford. *The Albemarle Papers*, New Spalding 1902
Thomas, B. D. G. *British Politics and the Stamp Act*, Oxford 1975
Thomasson, K. *The Jacobite General*, 1958
Thomasson, K., and E. Burt. *Battles of the '45*, Batsford 1962
Thompson, Mrs A. (ed). *The Letters of Lady Sundon*, 2 vols, 1847
Tunstall, Brian. *William Pitt*, 1938
Valentine, A. *Lord George Germaine*, Oxford 1962
Voltaire. *Siècle de Louis XV*, Paris 1826
Waddington, R. *La Guerre de Sept Ans*, 1899
Waldegrave, Lord. *Memoirs of the Years 1754 to 1758*, 1821
Ward, Sir A. W. *Great Britain and Hanover*, 1899
Warrant. *More Culloden Papers*, 1929-30
Watson, Steven. *The Reign of George III*, Oxford 1981
Western, J. R. *The Militia in the 18th Century*, Routledge 1965
White, I. Manchip. *Marshal Saxe*, Hamish Hamilton 1962
Whitworth, Rex (ed). *Gunner at Large*, Leo Cooper 1988
------- . *Lord Ligonier*, Oxford University Press 1958
Wilkins, W. H. *Caroline the Illustrious*, 2 vols, 1904
Williams, Basil. *Carteret and Newcastle*, Cambridge University Press 1943
------- . *Pitt*, 2 vols, Longmans 1913
------- . *The Whig Supremacy, 1714-60*, Oxford 1949
Willson, Beckles. *Life and Letters of James Wolfe*, London 1909
Winstanley, D. A. *Personal and Party Government, 1760-66*, 1910
Wyndham, H. A. *A Family History, 1688-1837*, 1950
Wyndham, Maud. *Chronicles of the Eighteenth Century: Correspondence of the Lytteltons*, 2 vols, 1924
Yorke, Philip C. *The Life and Correspondence of Philip, Earl of Hardwicke*, 3 vols, Cambridge 1913

**Manuscript Sources**

Cumberland Papers, Royal Archives, Windsor (in toto: some not on microfilm)
  RA Georgian 53932 etc
  RA Add. 28131

Royal Housearchive, The Hague.
German Archives at Hesse Darmstadt, Hanover, Lower Saxony.

*American collections*: Chesterfield MSS, University of California, Berkeley: Loudoun MSS and Calcraft MSS at Huntington Library, San Marino.

*British Library*: Anson Papers; Carteret papers; Egmont papers; Egerton papers; Hardwicke papers; Studholme Hodgson papers; Holland House papers (Henry Fox); India Office papers (Bengal, Madras, Bombay, etc); Kings MSS; Leeds papers (Holdernesse); Mitchell papers; Newcastle papers; John Norris papers; Stowe MSS; Tyrawley papers; Joseph Yorke papers.

*Family Collections*: Bedford papers, Bedford Estate Office. Bloomsbury, London. Bute papers, Mount Stuart. Chatsworth papers, Chatsworth. Rutland papers, Belvoir. Sandwich papers, Mapperton. Spencer papers, Althorp (Poyntz etc).
*County Record Offices*: Albermarle papers, East Suffolk. Amherst papers, Kent. Anson papers, Bedford. Barrington papers, East Suffolk. Burke papers, Northampton. Bury papers, East Suffolk. Clavering papers, Herfordshire. Dartmouth papers, Stafford. Fitzherbert papers (Gally Knight), Derby. Fitzwilliam papers, Northampton. Ryder Henry Fox letters and books, Dorset. Grafton papers, West Suffolk. Goodwood papers, West Sussex. Marchioness Gray papers, Bedford. Keppel papers, East Suffolk. Lennox papers, West Sussex, Lonsdale papers, Cumbria. Lucas papers, Bedford. Northington (Henley) papers, Northampton. Blackett Ord papers, Northumberland. Pennington papers, Cumbria. Ramsden papers (re 1745), Cumbria. Ridley papers, Northumberland. Robinson papers, Bedford. Sackville papers, Kent. Howard Vyse papers, Buckinghamshire.

*Other museums, libraries, etc*: Jockey Club Match Books and Pond's Calendars, Jockey Club, Newmarket. Lord George Murray papers, Worcester College, Oxford. Brynmaur Jones and Sykes papers (Vol. 13), Hull University. Pelham, Galway and Fawkener papers, Nottingham University. Rockingham papers, Wentworth Woodhouse, Sheffield. Temple, Newsam and Irwin papers, Leeds (Sheepscar). *Journal of Common Council*, Guildhall, London. Cumberland's Order Book, Campbell of Stonefield MS, Agnew of Lochnaw, Seafield, GD24 etc, and R. Napier papers, Scottish Record Office, Edinburgh, Campbell of Mamore, Bland papers and Letter Book of 20th Earl of Crawford, National Library of Scotland, City Council Minute Book, Edinburgh District Council. Studholme Hodgson Order Books, Lancaster City Museum. Regimental Order Books, Major Wood's diary, Mëuller's *Complete Treatise of Artillery 1757 and the RA Diary 1746-58*, at Royal Artillery Woolwich. Connolly papers, Royal Engineers, Chatham. *Order Books for 1745ff and court martial reports*, Grenadier Guards. *New Manual Exercise etc* (3rd ed.), pub. Dublin 1760, at MOD War Office Library. *Order Books for 1748ff*, Coldstream Guards. At the Bodleian, Oxford: MS Eng Hist 231, Townshend, Mason 366 (Culloden); also political pamphlets, *A Soldier's Journal (1770)*, *Quarters of the Army(1749)* and *A Letter to a Gentleman of the Army* (Griffiths, London 1757). A Dury and Townshend papers, National Army Museum.

*Public Record Office*. (PRO): WO 1 in letters. WO 4 out letters. WO 26. WO 30. WO 34 Amherst. WO 71 vol. 39, WO 72 and WO 81 Vol. 4 (courts martial JAG etc). Entry Books SP Dom 41. SO 36 (75-79) Scotland. SP 4113. SP 54 (Foreign Military Expeditions 1745-48, Holland). SP 8715, 16, 17 etc (Foreign Military). TI 38, TI 297 etc (Treasury books, 1735ff). PC 16. PC 3029 Granville papers. PC 3030 Chatham papers. PC 3047 Egremont papers. CREST 246 etc Windsor park etc.

## Specialist publications

*American Historical Review*
*Army Quarterly Magazine esp October 1938. A. G. Burne, Fontenoy*
*Articles of War* 1748, 1749 etc
*Camden Miscellany Series*
*Cavalry Journal* (eg A. G. Burne on Laffeldt, April 1937
*English Historical Review* (esp. XIII, XXX, XLV, LXX, LXXXV, etc)
*History* XXXVI (1957): 'Purchase and Promotion'
*Journal of the Society for Army Historical Research* (passim)
*Journal of the House of Commons*
*The Map Collector* No. 44 1988
*Navy Records Society* (Minorca, Cuba, etc)
*Parliamentary Reports*, 1746 etc
*Proceedings of the English Ceramic Circle*, 18 January 1975, 'Chelsea China and Fawkener'

*Roxburgh Club*
*Scottish Historical Society*, 1928 etc
*Thoroton Society* (Nottingham) 1945
*Transactions Cumberland and Westmorland Archaeological Society*, "Clifton Moor' vol. X p. 186-228

**Newspapers**

*Annual Register, General Evening Post, Gentleman's Magazine, Gloucester Chronicle, London Chronicle, London Evening Post, Reading Mercury, St James' Chronicle, Scots Magazine.*

**Other**

*Burlington Magazine*, August 1970, 'Stubbs and Racehorses'
*Observations upon the Prussian Discipline*, 1754 (RACP67)
*The Soldier's Companion. Exercises for the Foot*, 1757 (RACP62)
*Cavalry Drill*, (BL Royal MSS 239)
political satirical cartoons (see under Cumberland in British Museum Catalogue)
military training manuals of the period (Dalrymple, Bland, Symes, etc)
*Numbers of Men able to bear arms in France*, London 1744
Historical Manuscripts Commission Reports: see indexes for references to Cumberland
Cumberland's Clothing Book 1742
Barclay's Bank (Goslings Branch) − Cumberland account

# INDEX

Army of Observation, his staff, 181-2; views on Newcastle, 189; illness, 189; fights at Hastenbeck, 190-4; signs with Richelieu at Kloster Seven, 197; resigns all appointments, 199; at Proclamation of George III, 208; his jewellery bought by George III, his finances, buys town house, 211; plans conquest of Havana, 215; discusses peace terms with George III, 217; dismayed at Fox, 217; interview with Pitt 218; on Wilkes, 225; health, 209, 229; visits Pitt, 232; tries and fails to replace Grenville Ministry, finally puts together a new administration under Rockingham — health, 236-7; dies, 238; creditors, 239; his achievement, 241-3

Daun, General, 113, 119; at Kolin, 189
Denmark, Princess Louise of, 22, 29; mediation at Kloster Seven, 196-8
Derby, 63-4, 68-9
Désaguliers, Captain, 73
D'Estrées, Maréchal, 185-7, 189; advances in Westphalia, 190; at Hastenbeck, 191-3; sacked by Louis XV, 195
Dettingen, Battle of, 31-3, 37, 73-4
Devonshire, 4th Duke of, as Hartington, 169, 177; as Duke, 178, 187; Lord Chamberlain, 189, 214, 216; resigns, 218, 221, 226; dies, 231
Dodington, George Bubb, Lord Melcomb, 41, 136, 144
Dorset, Duke of, and Bragg's Regiment, 132
Drummond, Lord John, 53, 61, 64, 70
Drury, Sir Thomas, financier, 69
Dupleix, Joseph, 124, 156
Duquesne, see under Forts
Dury, General, 1st Guards at St Cast, 206

East India Company, 123-4, 155, 169, 176
Eclipse, stallion, 207, 227
Edinburgh, 53, 59-60, 70-71, 76, 88, 91, 97, 123
Egmont, Lord, Tory supporter, 19-20; opposes Army Act reforms, 136, 138, 144; and Constitutional Queries, 145-6
Egremont, Earl of, Sec of State, 214, 224
Eton College, 11, 19

Faddy, Peter, Valet, 230, 236-8
Falkirk, Battle of, 71, 74-5, 78, 87

Fawkener, Sir Everard, 44-5, 52, 89; at Aberdeen, 100-1, 108-9, 110; in Holland, 112, 125, 141, 150, 152, 173, 183, 187, 199, 223
Ferdinand, of Brunswick, General, 199, 202, 205, 208
Ferguson, of HMS *Furnace*, 93, 99; finds Lord Lovat, 101
Findlater, James Ogilvy, 6th Earl of, and Seafield, 81-2, 91, 103
Finisterre, 117, 123
Fitzwilliam, Captain, Hon. John, ADC, 73
Fletcher, Andrew, Lord Justice Clerk, 74
Fleury, Cardinal, 18, 37
Flitcroft, Henry, architect, 11, 141, 158
Folliott, General J, 1st Guards, 36
Fontenoy, Battle of, 47-52, 73-4, 83, 90
Forbes, Duncan, Lord President, 73, 76, 79, 83, 91-3, 97, 99, 103
Forts, Augustus, 59, 72, 79, 92-3, 97, 102
   Belvedere (Windsor), 222
   Calcutta, 176
   Crown Point, 155
   Cumberland, 166
   Duquesne (Pitt), 161, 163, 165-7, 208
   George, 72, 79
   Le Boeuf, 156
   Oswego, 176
   St. Philip (Minorca), 174-5, 180
   Sandberg (Hulst), 115
   William, 59, 72, 79
   William Henry, 201
Fountaine, Sir Andrew, 7, 11
Fox, Henry (1st Lord Holland), 2, 42; Sec at War, 94, 103, 108, 124; and army reductions, 129-132; on Army Act, 1749, 136-8, 140, 143, 148; blames Pitt over Regency Bill, 149; and Cumberland's illness, 154; allies with Pitt, 159; at Windsor, 160; enters Cabinet, 164; Sec of State, 170; and Minorca, 175; resigns, 177; offers to serve with Pitt, 178, 182, 188; Paymaster again, 189, 190; welcomes Cumberland home, 199; lends money, 210; at Windsor, 216; joins Bute to obtain vote for peace, 217-219; retires with Peerage, 221; begs for re-employment, 234-5
France, 27-9, 31-3; attempts invasion, 37-40, 42; Fontenoy, 46-49; and Stuarts, 52-3, 80, 106, 110; Laffeldt, 114-5; negotiates for peace, 126-8, 132-3, 156-7; and North

America, 164-7; and Minorca, 173-6;teams up with Austria, 184-6; attacks Hanover, 187; Hastenbeck, 190-1; Convention of Kloster-Seven repudiated, 202; raids on French Coast, 201; Peace of Paris ends war, 216-9, 231

Fraser, Simon, Lord Lovat, 77, 101

Fraser of Achnagairn, Mrs, 99

Frederick, Prince of Wales, 5, 8, 9, 10, 12; marriage, 13, 17, 20; and Pitt, 22, 30, 41, 50, 60; organizes opposition to Cumberland, 121, 138, 144; dies, 146-7

Frederick, William I of Prussia, 10

Frederick II, The Great, of Prussia, 10; invades Silesia, 27, 129, 154, 157; advises France to attack Hanover, 168; signs Convention of Westminster, 174; invades Saxony, 176, 180-1; asks for Cumberland's help, 180-1; defeated at Kolin, 189; calls for more British troops, 190, 198, 202, 205; and peace terms, 215-7, 220

Frederick of Hesse-Cassel, marries Princess Mary, 22-3; 70; in Scotland, 76, 79, 181; in Westphalia, 186

Freind, Dr, Headmaster, 9, 10

Fuller, General, at Hulst, 114-5

Gay, John, Poet, 8

George 1st King and Elector, 5, 6, 8, 9; his Will, 17, 101

George II King and Elector, as Prince of Wales, 5, 6, 8; as King, 9, 10, 12, 13, 17; support for Hanover, 22-3; and Dettingen, 27-30; 50, 53, 55, 57; attitude to '45', 68-9, 71, 76, 88, 91; illness, 107; comments on Laffeldt, 120, 122; goes to Hanover, 127-8; Regency problem, 147-9; humour of, 153; 155, 157, 164, 178; and America, 179; on defence of Hanover, 181-2, 188; on Hastenbeck, 194-5; wants peace for Hanover, 196; changes his mind, 197; demands Cumberland's return 198-9; repudiates Kloster-Zeven, 202; ageing, 204, 207; dies, 209-10

George III, birth, 18; 147, 149, 168; and Hanover, 205, 207; accession of, 209; marriage of, 212; cartoon of, 215; discussions with Cumberland, 216-7; abandoned by Bute, 220; on Wilkes vote, 225; illness and Regency plan, 230-1; at Ascot Races, 232; asks Cumberland's help in forming administration, 231-3; accepts

Rockingham ministry, 234; appoints Albemarle administrator of Cumberland's estate, 238; arranges for Cumberland's funeral as Captain-General, 240

George, Prince (later George IV), Cumberland Godfather to, 216

Gibraltar, 131, 143, 174-5

Gideon, Sir Samson, financier, 69

Glasgow, 70, 91

Gordon, Mrs of Aberdeen, Affair of China, 100-1

Grafton, Charles 2nd, Duke of, 219, 223, 226, 228, 232-3; accepts office, 234; Chief Mourner at Cumberland's funeral, 240

Granby, Marquess of, 98-9

Gray, Thomas, poet, 104, 134, 209

Greening R, gardener, 140-1, 219

Grenville, George, politician, 221, 226-7, 231-2; rude to King, 232-3; dismissed in favour of Rockingham, 234; and Stamp Act, 236

Guards, 1st, 2nd and 3rd Regiments, Foot Guards: see under Regiments

The Hague, 13, 45, 104, 109, 124-5, 127, 129, 184

Handasyde, General, 62, 71

Handel, 12, 88, 98, 135

Hanover, 5, 8, 9, 13-4, 17-8, 23, 27-8, 30, 37, 76, 127-8, 164, 170, 174, 177-8; Army of Observation to protect, 180, 181, 184-7, 190, 202-3, 208

Hanoverian troops, 37, 44, 59, 70-1, 75, 77, 79, 85, 99, 104, 109, 110, 113

Hardwicke, Philip, 1st Earl of, see under Yorke

Harrington, William 1st Earl of, 16, 41, 107, 124

Harwich, 45, 125, 183

Hastenbeck, Battle of, 190-3, 203

Hawke, Admiral, 123, 168, 173, 175, 208

Hawley, J. General, 'Hangman', 68, 70-1, 74, 84-5, 90, 100-11

Hay, John, 83

Herring, Thomas, Archbishop, 71, 97, 98

Hervey, Lord, 13, 15, 19

Hessian Troops, 28; in Scotland, 70, 73, 76, 97, 104, 109-10; at Laffeldt, 119; in UK, 169-70, 174, 177-8

Hodgson, Studholme, Captain, ADC, 73, 95-6, 112, 115; Stud Manager, 151; Major General, Belle Ile, 211-2, 238